AF469059

TREVOR FELCEY

NATURE'S INSTANTANEOUS TEXT

Oak Reflection, 1998
Mixed media on paper, 26x26cms

TREVOR FELCEY

NATURE'S INSTANTANEOUS TEXT

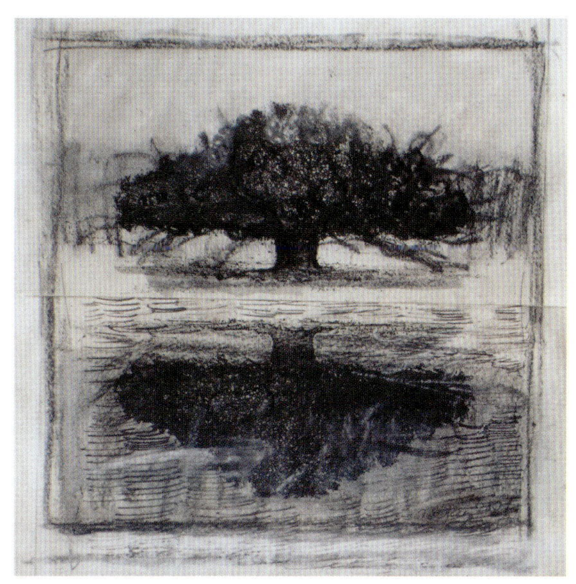

ANDREW LAMBIRTH

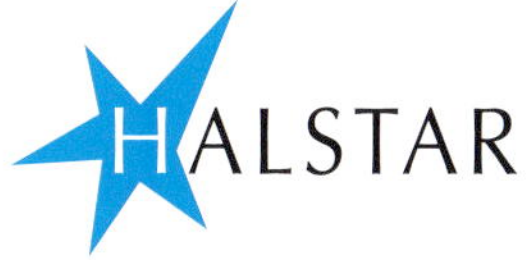

First published in Great Britain in 2009
Revised and updated edition 2016

British Library Cataloguing-in-Publication Data
A CIP record for this title is available from the British Library

ISBN 978 1 906690 17 5

HALSTAR
Halsgrove House,
Ryelands Business Park,
Bagley Road, Wellington, Somerset TA21 9PZ
Tel: 01823 653777 Fax: 01823 216796
email: sales@halsgrove.com

An imprint of Halstar Ltd, part of the halsgrove group of companies
Information on all Halsgrove titles is available at: www.halsgrove.com

Printed and bound in China by Everbest Printing Investment Ltd

INTRODUCTION

'We want to describe the indescribable:
nature's instantaneous text.'

Osip Mandelstam

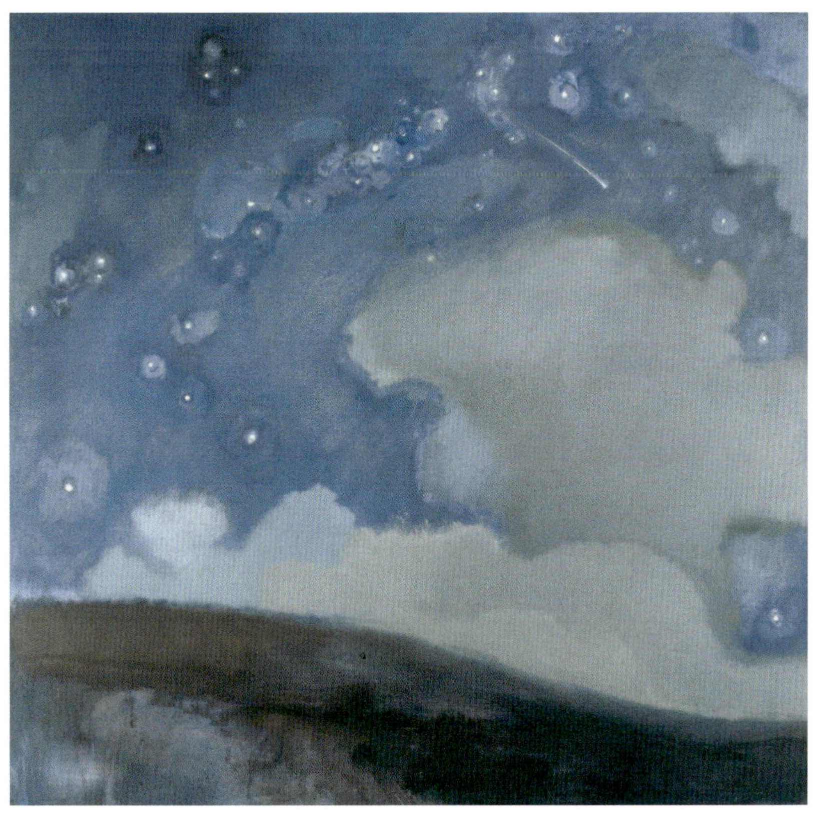

Night Sky, 1993
Oil on canvas, 91.5x91.5cms

TREVOR FELCEY is a realist painter of large integrity. His paintings are not dull transcriptions of appearances, but are deeply-felt statements about the world we live in, matchless evocations of things, people and places he finds beautiful. His paintings are about ideas, but not the literary or cod-philosophical ideas behind so many so-called conceptual art works. Felcey's ideas are to do with visualizing – about ways of seeing. If they could be written, he'd be a writer. As it is, he's one of our finest painters in the great tradition of Western art: conveying real emotion about visual events that stir him.

Felcey paints landscapes, still lifes and portraits. He draws and paints constantly, very often the two activities working in tandem. He makes exquisitely beautiful pencil studies of trees, and substantial paintings of individual trees which are more like portraits than landscapes. His still lifes have the true vibration of the real, while his pictures of people include nudes and figure paintings as well as straightforward portraits. He is a versatile artist utterly dedicated to the pursuit of reality as envisioned in two-dimensions and translated into paint, ink, charcoal or graphite. He also makes prints, being an occasional but highly effective etcher. But his main activity is with the pencil and the brush.

PREFACE

TREVOR FELCEY is one of the English art world's best-kept secrets. His work is not known and admired by a large public – though it could and indeed should be – and if he has a substantial reputation among fellow-painters, that doesn't mean that the word is out on the street. Felcey is such a good artist that he deserves to be more widely known. The aim of this book is to remedy that situation by providing a general introduction to his work and career, and some sort of context within which to view a selection of reproductions of his paintings, drawings and prints. It is profoundly to be hoped that a favourable public response to his work will coax Felcey into exhibiting it more often. Our present society is not so full of beauty that we can afford to ignore any longer such an expert of aesthetic uplift. Felcey's work must be seen.

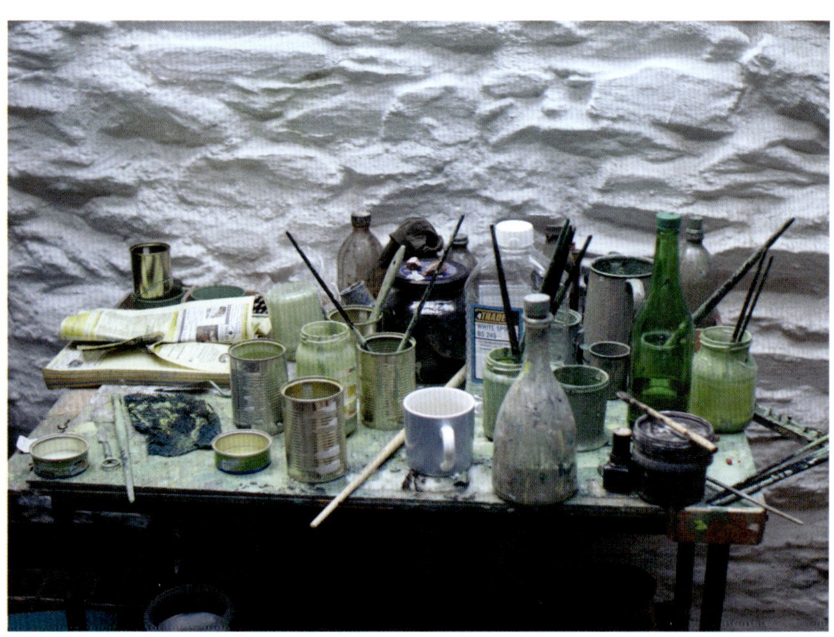

FOREWORD

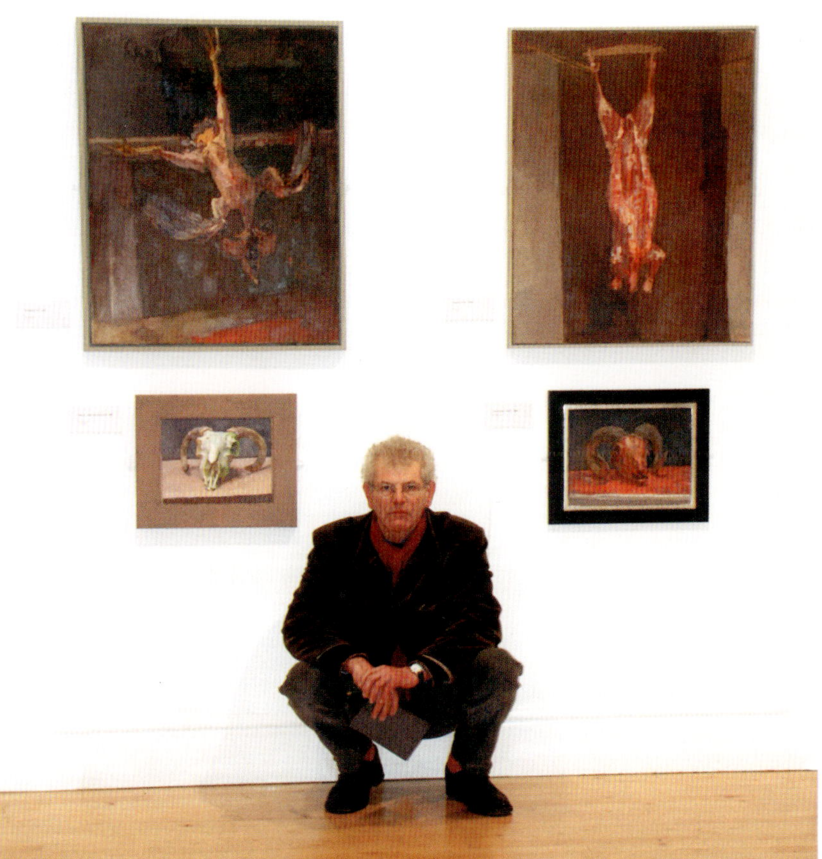

THIS PHOTOGRAPH was taken at Trevor's successful one-man show held at the Royal Albert Memorial Museum & Art Gallery in Exeter in 2005. It was at that exhibition that Trevor and I first met in the context of artist and publisher, and it was from this meeting that this book was eventually to come about.

In recent years I have been able to indulge my interest in painting through the publication of a number of art-related books under the Halsgrove and Halstar imprints. It is a rare privilege to work with a painter in the creation of a book for it provides one with a unique insight into their art, their inspiration and method of working. Also, because of the short but intense working relationship during the book's gestation, it provides an opportunity to get to know the artist personally. I have no idea what this means to them for I have never dared to ask, but for me it is always a great pleasure, not least in being able to observe at close hand the 'scene of creation'.

In working with Trevor this experience has been truly revelatory for his artist's eye is trained to see the simple things in nature that an untrained eye often fails to notice. On more than one occasion a discussion has been interrupted by Trevor lightly remarking on the shape of a tree, the movement of grass before the wind, the shadows at a particular time of day; ordinary things which the artist reminds us are extraordinary.

This book, now newly revised and updated, offers the reader an opportunity to be similarly delighted and enlightened.

Simon Butler FRSA
Associate Publisher, Halsgrove

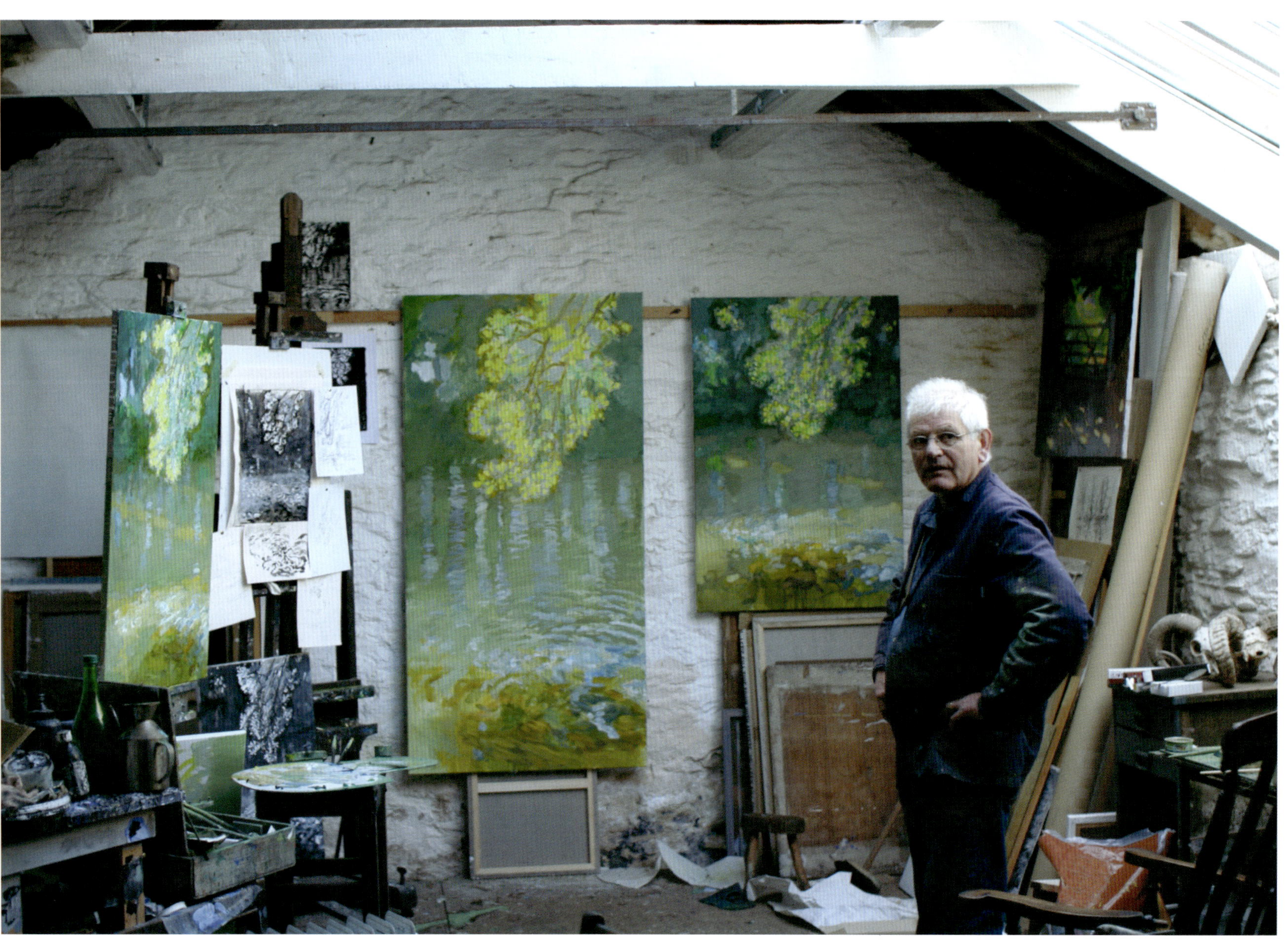

TREVOR FELCEY

Groundings

Felcey is an unusual name, and the artist is convinced that his ancestors were Jews from eastern Europe. In fact he believes he's of Czechoslovakian descent, hence his liking for rollmops for breakfast and heavily seasoned meat, and such un-English delights as sourdough bread. 'We're obviously immigrants – we're the only Felceys in the country', he says. He can trace his family back to the 1880s, to a tailor born under the sound of Bow bells, Samuel Felcey. 'And my uncle was also a tailor, Reuben Felcey.' Trevor Felcey was born at Ferring, on the West Sussex coast, on 25 August 1945. He remembers very little about it as the family moved when he was four or five up to Cleethorpes, another coastal town, this time next to Grimsby. He lived there until he was eighteen, and it was Cleethorpes that made a formative impression on him. 'Gritty' is the adjective Felcey uses to describe the place, with the redeeming quality of 'a very good art school'. He remembers the town as: 'empty wide beaches, big skies, a thriving fishing port, loads and loads of fishing boats'. The young Felcey spent hours watching them. 'Going to the docks was like going to a different world. It was a self-contained place, completely mysterious to me – a town within a town.'

His father was in the navy and away at sea all the time. His upbringing was 'not at all arty'. He had two elder brothers and one sister. 'My eldest brother was eleven years older than me and he went to sea in the Merchant Navy when he was 16.' There was no pressure on him to go to sea but there was evidently a certain family expectation. Did Trevor feel this? Certainly he was not encouraged to be an artist. As he says: 'I was quite good academically, but I was most interested in art. I'd always drawn and painted. It was the thing I liked best. The revelation in my life was when I'd just turned 14 and my middle brother had gone to university – Imperial College in London to do chemistry – and he had a friend in Grimsby, called George Rowlett. And I met George through my brother and that was the first time I'd heard there was such a thing as an art school. I couldn't believe it – that that was what you could do: you could actually go to an art school!' Prior to this, the young Felcey had not really been aware of artists. The discovery was indeed a revelation. 'I just felt my life was sorted then, and that's what I wanted to do.'

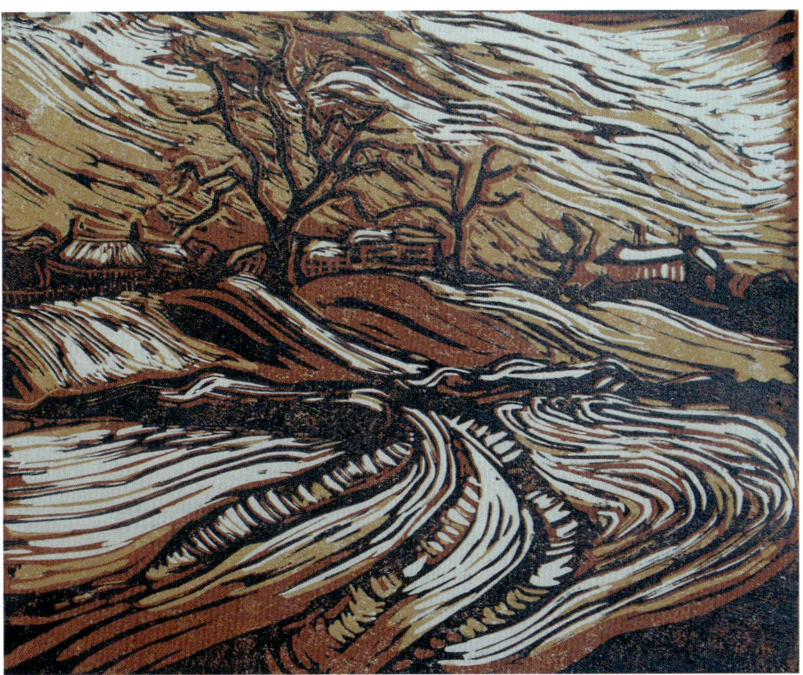

Lincolnshire Landscape, 1960
Linocut, 17x21cms

George Rowlett takes up the story: 'I first met Trev when I was at Grimsby Art School and a drinking chum of his older brother Phil. I had a small attic studio in a house where I lodged and Trevor, madly keen on painting, used to visit every week or so, show what he was doing and see mine. He was as passionate about painting as I was, extremely intelligent and precociously talented. Brain like a sponge, he absorbed all he needed at that time from me in six months or a year. We looked a lot and talked a lot, not just about painting but politics of a leftist sort, nuclear disarmament etc. I was reading Camus, Sartre and Marx with that marvellous juvenile enthusiasm. We were both active, Aldermaston Marches, sit-downs. We enjoyed going to clubs and concerts with others. I may have been useful by showing that things could be done, as my older friends showed me.'

Felcey comments: 'I used to go painting with George when I was 15, and stay in his mother's house. He was making kind of Bratby pictures then. I was painting semi-expressionistic like Soutine.' It was evident that all Felcey wanted to do was follow Rowlett to Grimsby art school, which he soon did. He says: 'Most of the people teaching there – I went part-time from 1960 when I was fifteen – had arrived in the area because they were conscientious objectors during the war and they were working on the land. So the department had a strong ethical feel to it – they were all very committed people. Very interesting. Peter Todd was the chap running it, he was the lynchpin.

'I went to a secondary modern school, but in those days to go to an art school you needed some GCEs so I went to a college of further education for a year and carried on going to the art school part-time. Then I went full-time and did a Foundation Course for a year. I was so keen to go to London I applied for all the London schools – Slade, Chelsea (when Lawrence Gowing was there) – because they were the best art schools with the best painters. I finished the Foundation in Grimsby when I was 18 in the August and came to London that September.'

It was due to Rowlett's example that Felcey prepared to follow his older friend to London and applied for Camberwell School of Art in 1963. Since there was four years age difference between them, it was inevitable that as students they would gravitate more towards their own age groups. In fact, Rowlett remembers spending more time with Felcey at Grimsby than he did at Camberwell. 'He attended Camberwell a year after I had started and I think was in the second intake of the new degree course while I was in the last NDD year, so we moved in slightly different circles of friends. He was always extremely likeable and sociable.' Maggi Hambling, a student at Camberwell from 1964 to 1967 and thus junior to Felcey, saw him in a different, more exalted, light: 'He had the air of a young god: beautiful and serious, he was very much a star.'

It must have been an enormous upheaval for the enthusiastic young student who'd never left home before. Even now he admits: 'It was tough'. But it was something he very much wanted to do. Felcey remembers: 'In *The Sunday Times* there was a great article about Robert Medley and Camberwell [Medley was the inspired and inspiring principal who employed so many good young artists to teach at the school]. Auerbach was teaching there, Kitaj, Uglow. I saw a show of Uglow's at Helen Lessore's [the Beaux Arts Gallery] in 1961. I didn't really cotton on to what Euan was doing then. I was more interested in Soutine.'

Felcey rented a room when he started at Camberwell, but it was very hard; he didn't enjoy the first term at all. 'I was absolutely focused on becoming a painter but I was terribly young and very shy. I suppose I felt that most of the people who were teaching weren't real painters. Robert was great, but he stepped down after the first year and Philip Matthews took over. There was Dick Lee, Chamberlain, Henry Inlander. But it was a very good time, there were some very good students – George was around, Roger Leworthy, Tony Farrell, Maggi Hambling was in the year below, Marc Chaimowicz.'

The two great influences at Camberwell, the twin poles of the teaching, were Frank Auerbach and Euan Uglow. Auerbach embodied the expressionist approach, the direct line from Bomberg's famous search for 'the spirit in the mass', and was an advocate of worked and re-worked charcoal and heavily trowelled paint. Uglow was the high priest of analytical research from appearances: pencil drawing, monocular measurement and the gradual build-up of information on the canvas, rendered in thin paint. Students tended to gravitate to one or the other approach. Rowlett: 'I can't recall Trevor being part of the small group of students, Roger Leworthy, Tony Farrell and perhaps Barry Paine and myself who gathered at Frank's life classes, absenting ourselves from lithography etc. Although we admired many of the same artists I think Trevor was more attracted to the more measured and measuring approach while I was pulled to the more expressive. Not that Trevor didn't feel these things, they were just less obvious.'

Tony Farrell remembers: 'I met Trevor at Camberwell in 1964 and even at that early stage thought he was an accomplished draughtsman. He stood out from his contemporaries as did Rowlett and [John] Kiki. Trevor seemed to steer an independent course between the two powerful influences of Auerbach and Uglow.' Felcey himself identifies the chief early influences on his work as Auerbach, Kossoff and Bomberg. 'At Camberwell when I got there Frank was only doing an evening class. Every Wednesday it would be life drawing all day and various people came in to teach. Kossoff came in, Timothy Behrens. Tony Fry was around, Tony Eyton, Patrick Procktor. Kitaj was good, though I wasn't very keen on his paintings.' In that mêlée of conflicting personalities and styles, Felcey kept his head down and worked as concentratedly as he could.

'I spent seven years at art schools and though I worked terrifically hard I don't think I was a good student', recalls Felcey. 'I was so blinkered about what I was doing, I couldn't really take on information.' Why was this? 'Insecurity?' he hazards. He certainly had various preconceptions of what it was going to be like, romantic notions which were far from the reality. He took refuge in work, and waited for these chrysalis days to pass.

Living in London, were his subjects primarily urban? 'I was doing landscapes as well. There are some big pictures of the cliff at Cleethorpes. There's also an etching of it. One is in a photo of my MA show at the College [Felcey studied at the Royal College from 1966–69]. There were others also : a very yellow painting of a bridge in Paris and also some Welsh landscapes [Felcey went to Wales on a painting trip in the second year]. All the paintings that I can see in that photo from the MA show were done outside the College, although I spent all my time painting in the Life Room.' He remembers there being no teaching for the postgraduates, although Carel Weight, Ruskin Spear and Robert Buhler were all on the teaching staff. Felcey thinks they'd been there so long they just got on with what they wanted to do, though he recalls Weight being very supportive.

'I remember Carel Weight saying to me that he thought I was a landscape painter and I felt very put out by that. Maybe he was right.' Yet Felcey continued to paint the figure with industry and passion (a practice he continues to this day), and to set up the still life subjects he also likes to paint. In those years of Pop and Abstraction, figure painting was seen as anachronistic, definitely un-cool. Felcey recalls: 'By the third year, I think I was the only person working from the model. I used to work in the boiler room and I had a model to myself.'

What other art was he looking at in these years? 'There was a very good Bonnard show at the RA in 1966 that was important. By the end of Camberwell I'd started to look around a bit more. That was the time when the Americans were being shown solo at the Whitechapel – Johns, Rauschenberg. That seemed so different, there was something exciting about them, and there was a brief period when I was influenced by Abstract Expressionism.' What did he think of Pop art? 'I found that much more difficult.' In truth, Felcey found it empty, vacuous and is rather dismissive of it. As he says of this period: 'The overriding thing I'd been interested in was really organizing a concrete space.' It was perhaps time to spread his wings.

Felcey went to Paris while he was still at the Royal College. 'The College had just acquired a studio in Paris. I think it was Malraux's idea to bring art back to Paris, to make it an artistic centre again. So they built this great building on the Seine near Hotel de Ville opposite Ile St Louis, and it was just studios for musicians, painters and sculptors. There were ten sculptors' studios at the back of the building, high with a mezzanine floor, beautiful, and the Royal College got one of these. When I was at the College in my second year they started to send students to work there for three months. I was the second student to go, in the spring of 1968, after Ben Johnson.'

While he was in Paris, Felcey met a beautiful girl of Algerian Jewish descent, who was briefly to be his wife. 'It was my first real time abroad. I'd started to learn French and suddenly was thrown into this exotic other world.' He was taken over by it. 'I left in July. She came over to England in September.' They had two daughters together but the marriage broke down in 1971 and Felcey's wife and children went back to France. 'I'm very close to my daughters and we get on very well but it certainly made me for the next 10 to 12 years after that just completely focus on my painting. The divorce was quite difficult and I couldn't cope with any real relationship at all. It had a strong knock-on effect.' Looking back on it, Felcey sees this – although painful – as forcing an even stronger focus on painting.

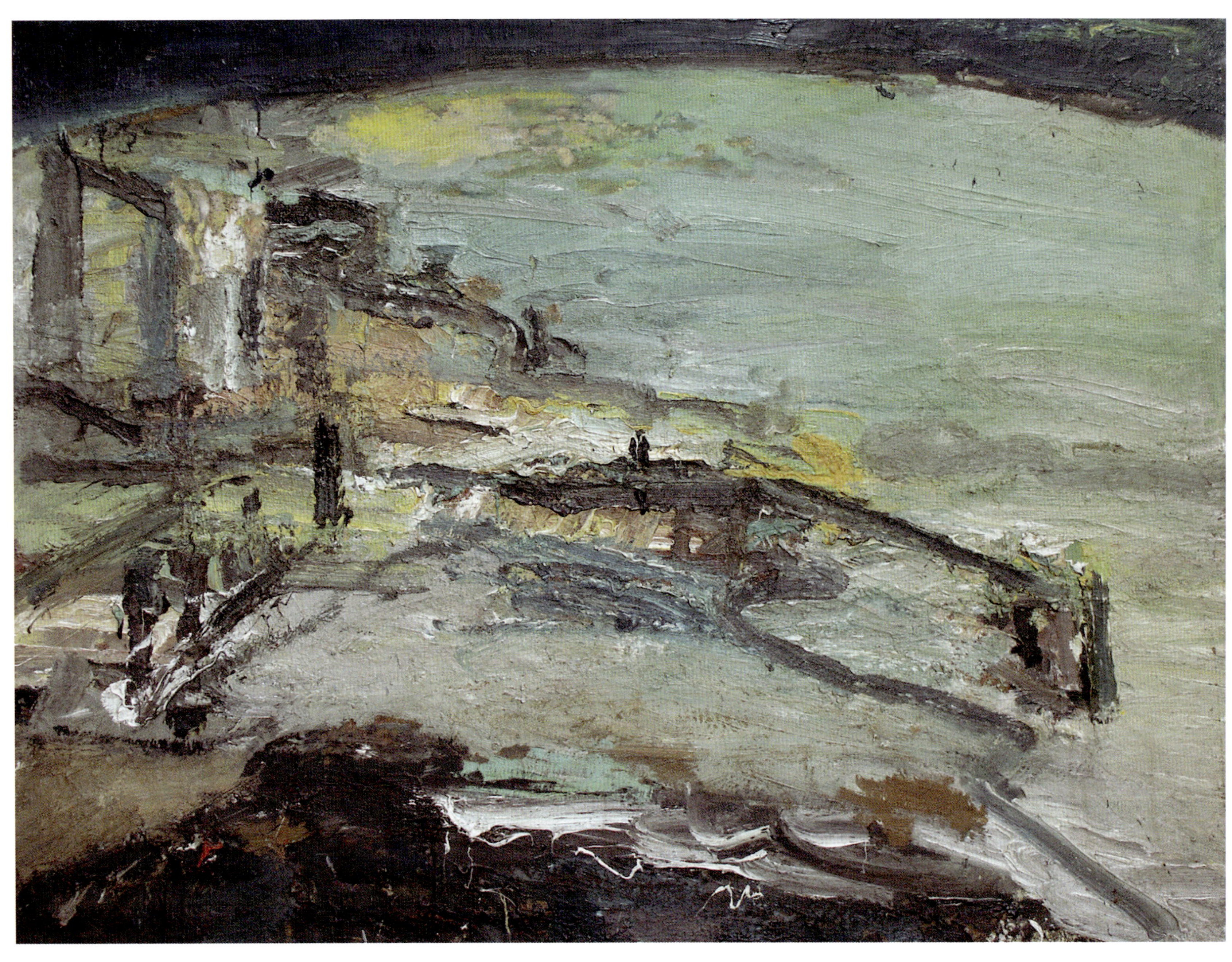

Under Putney bridge, 1969
Oil on canvas, 102x127 cms

It seems that in these early years, Felcey was more attracted to an overtly expressive interpretation. As he says: 'I did my thesis at the Royal College on Bomberg. Peter de Francia helped me quite a lot with that. I got an introduction to Lilian Bomberg and went up to the house. That was quite an eye-opener. She was so bitter.' Bomberg had died in obscurity and poverty in 1957, a great unrecognised prophet. Even so perceptive a critic as David Sylvester had failed to appreciate his worth. Lilian Bomberg felt – with some justification – that everyone had dumped her husband, even the Borough Group, his students. Felcey comments: 'It was an immense shock for me to meet somebody so bitter.'

He was young and impressionable and still (despite his student years) romantic about being an artist. 'I was aspiring and hopeful. And then I found de Francia a bit difficult. In my last year he said: "Well, you can't stay in London. You're never going to be a successful painter with what you're interested in, unless you call somebody like Dorothy Mead successful."' [Mead was a founder member of the Borough Group and a great advocate of Bomberg. Although an influential teacher, in her lifetime she never had a solo exhibition of her own work, and it remains largely unknown to this day]. Felcey was shocked by such bluntness. 'I just found that so kind of cynical, I didn't want to know really.'

Life after Art School

But he stayed in London, got some part-time teaching to enable him to survive, and painted. It was Euan Uglow who threw him a lifeline. 'I found it hard to connect with Uglow when I was at Camberwell. I still knew him when I went to the Royal College and I was still in contact when I left the College. I was only 23 or 24 then and I saw a lot of him and he was immensely supportive. Euan had got me a bit of teaching with Patrick Symons. Patrick came to see me when I was in my last term at the College and gave me an evening class teaching life drawing at Chelsea. The next year I was doing a day a week. I was teaching with Patrick, Norman Norris, Ken Kiff, Simon Willis, and I got so much from that. That was a good period.' Felcey maintains that he learnt more then than he ever did as a student, and he was now in a better position to understand what Uglow was about.

Uglow's message was really quite complex and sophisticated. Why should a young man or woman, a student fresh out of the egg, have the equipment or experience to understand it? Of course most don't, which is why they simply tended to copy Uglow's ideas without understanding them, and parrot his opinions. The fact that Felcey delayed his approach to Uglow's ideas until he was mature enough to understand them made them of more lasting importance and significance to him.

At this point, the two key inspirations in Felcey's life were Uglow and Patrick Symons. Was Symons even more crucial than Uglow? 'No, I think Euan was more important. What I responded to in Euan's pictures was this pared-down spatial idea, absolutely to the point, nothing kind of descriptive to it.' Yet it does describe the thing seen, it is a form of realist painting, surely? 'Nothing literal. Patrick was a very literal painter, he liked being literal.' And that approach wasn't of such interest to Felcey. 'I was terribly close to Patrick. On some levels he was an influence on me – in the whole idea of the geometry, the totality of a painting. In that he was also an influence on Uglow – the geometry really came from Patrick, I think.'

Symons was obsessed with geometry, and knew a great deal about it. Uglow took enough of that obsession to feed his own interests and to structure his pictures, but his particular obsessions lay elsewhere. (Felcey's own attitude to geometry – in that he can take it or leave it – is much more healthy and pragmatic). It is nigh impossible to sum up Uglow's philosophy in a few words, but he was principally concerned with making something new: with giving 'an image to an idea'. Each picture was a process of distillation – of concentrated scrutiny of a subject bound up with the resolution of a particular set of problems, to be solved formally, aesthetically, emotionally and intellectually. Uglow used a radical form of realist depiction to do this. 'I think painting should be extreme', he said.

'Uglow was a terrific example', says Felcey. 'I went to his studio a lot. Looking at the book of Uglow's complete paintings is like the story of my life. I remember most of the paintings being painted.' Felcey saw the pictures in progress but admits that Uglow didn't say much about them. He was rather in awe of him. 'Nobody asked him questions really. I remember asking Patrick George something about a Uglow picture and whether he'd asked him, and he said "Ooh no, I would never ask Euan anything like that". It was like the whole thing's taboo, really. We'd talk about pictures by other people.'

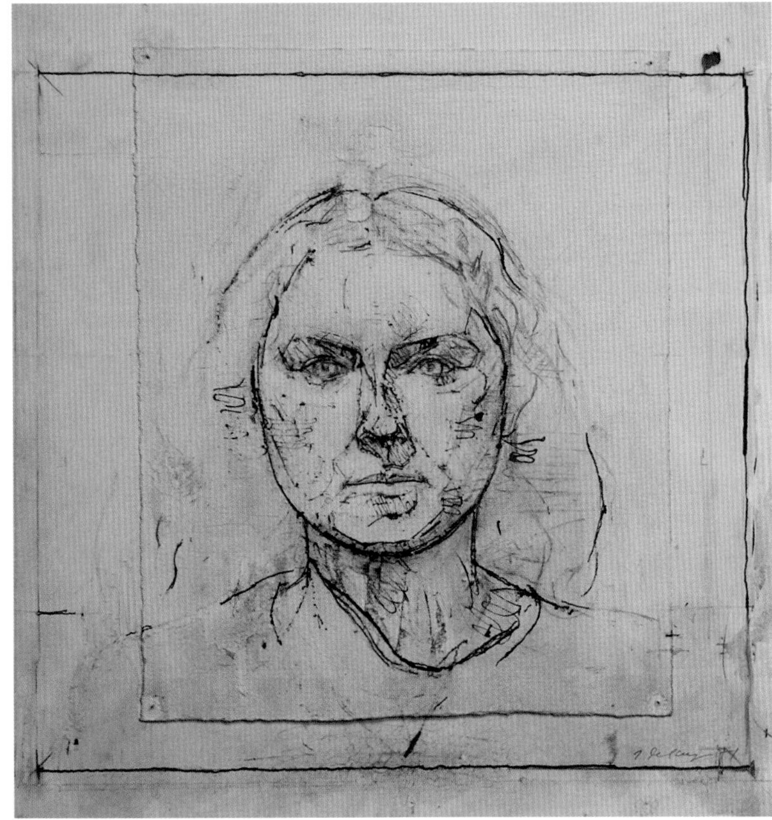

Head of Mary, 1971
Pencil, ink on paper, 33x33.5cms

Felcey learnt a lot from visiting this network of artists – mostly friends and associates of Uglow – in their studios. Symons gave him the entry to many, such as Patrick George and Anthony Eyton. 'I used to go and see Tony Eyton in his studio in Hanbury Street. It was important to see what people were doing.' What about other artists coming to see his work? 'Euan used to come. He'd say things. He helped me terrifically.' Amongst Felcey's fellow-teachers at Chelsea, Norman Norris was particularly important to him. 'Norman's got such a mind – the ramifications when he's talking about one of your paintings – you can see endless possibilities of how this thing might develop. He was very inspiring. Talking about other paintings in relation to yours.'

Piero della Francesca was still very much a benchmark for those artists. 'Not so much for me at that time', insists Felcey. 'It took me a long while to come to Piero in a really strong way. He was terrifically important to Uglow, but for Symons it was Cima.' Giovanni Battista Cima da Conegliano, c1459/60–1517/18, was a Venetian painter mainly influenced by Antonello da Messina and Giovanni Bellini. There are several paintings by him in the National Gallery, including three Madonnas and *The Incredulity of St Thomas*. If Cima was important to Symons, then we can be sure that Felcey became very familiar with his work, for the two were much in each other's company.

Going West

'Patrick brought me down to the Westcountry for the first time', says Felcey. 'I'd never seen a landscape like it. I knew London to Lincolnshire, but nothing much else. That was in 1969–70. The other thing Patrick reintroduced into my life was botany. When I was a young boy I was terrifically interested in plants, but it had such little street cred in the school I was in (basically the opposite), that I dropped it.' George Rowlett was also deeply interested in nature and would botanise with Symons. It was Symons who legitimised botany again for Felcey. 'That was terrifically important. After six or seven years at art schools in a London environment it was a fantastic reintroduction to the landscape.' Felcey would come down to Dorset and stay for a couple of weeks in the summer, to paint and talk.

'Very early on, we also started painting on Wimbledon Common with the students from Chelsea. Near the end of the year on the Foundation Course we used to take them all out on to the Common painting for a month. I would be painting a picture, Patrick would be painting, and we'd carry on after the end of term. Some of the students would stay on too. They could paint absolutely what they wanted. As it progressed – we did it for several years – students would come back from previous years, so it became a very rich environment. They'd be coming from all schools – from Wimbledon, the Slade – because they'd gone on from Chelsea to other places, and it became a very intense, productive time. That lasted 10 or even 15 years, after I left. I was 10 years teaching with Patrick at Chelsea, 1970–80.'

That was the period when Felcey painted the first of the oaks. 'There's one of an arch of oaks [*Oak Arch*, (49)].* It was a marvellous subject – an arch of oaks with a little oak tree standing in the middle, centre stage.' Tony Farrell remembers seeing those first oak tree pictures, and being

*Numbers given in round brackets throughout refer to the page number in the book on which the painting appears.

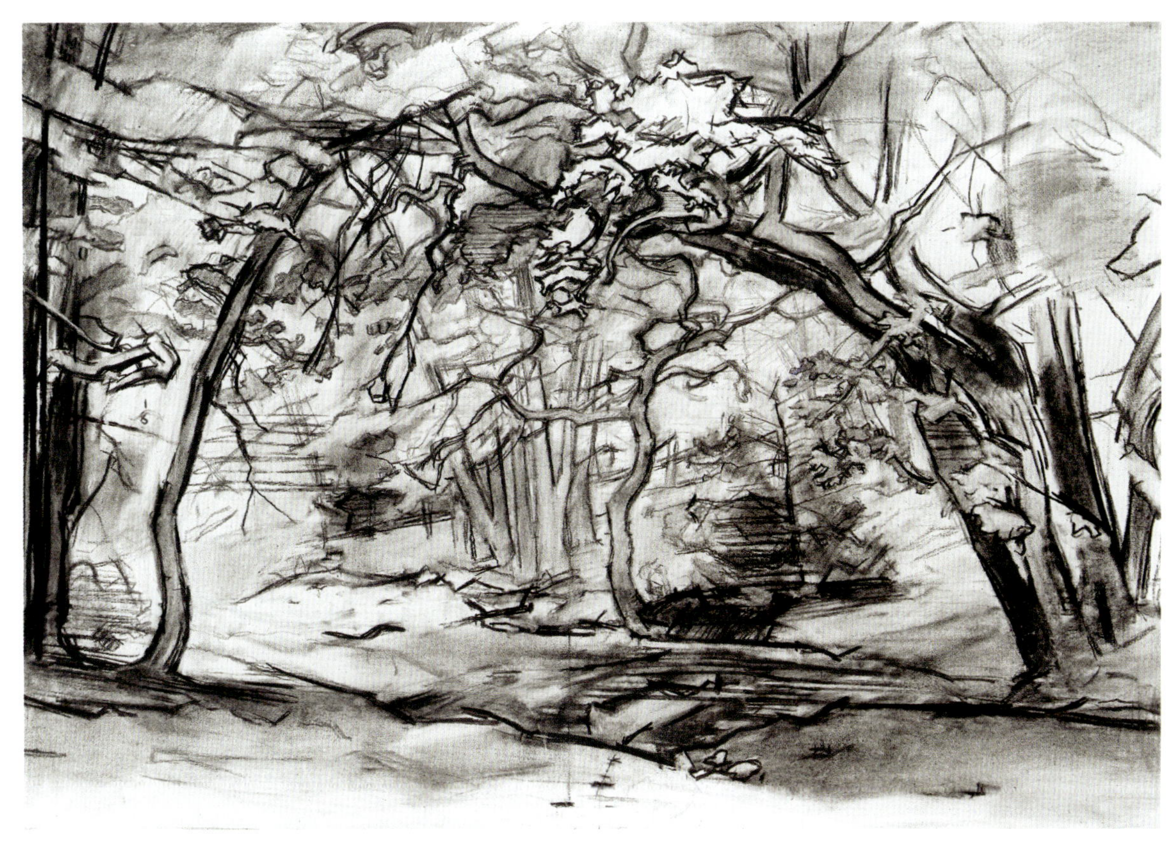

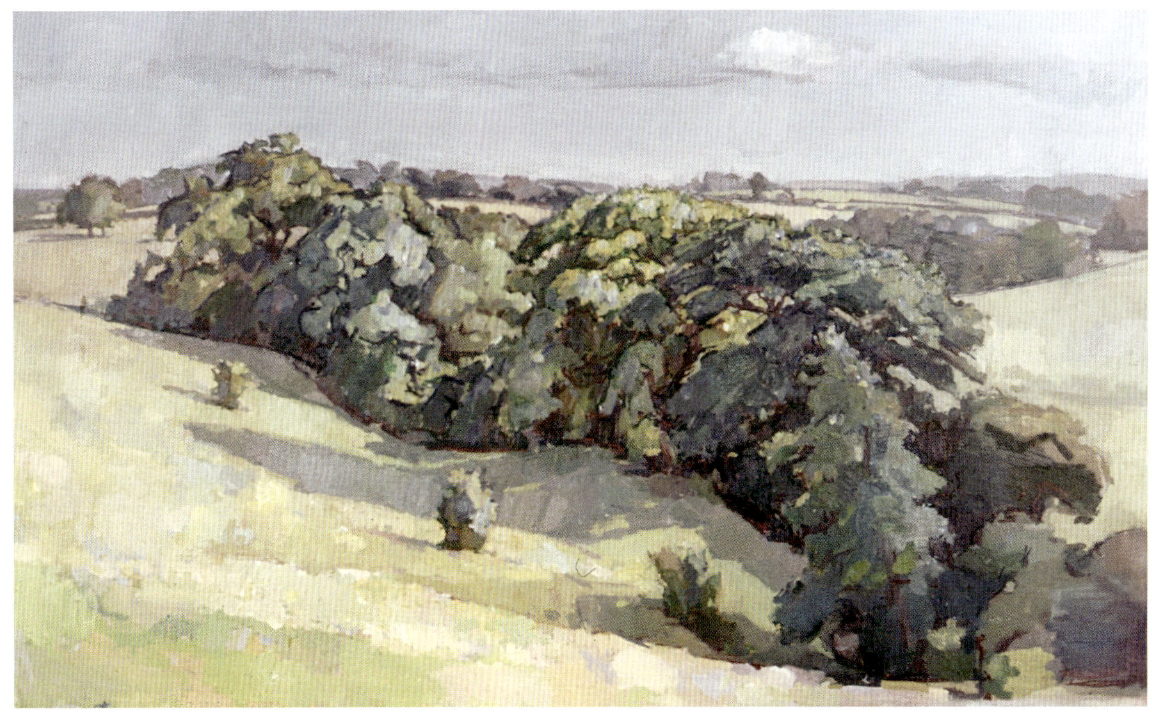

Top

Oak Arch drawing 1977

Charcoal on paper, 65x96cms

Bottom

Hanger Ryme, 1981

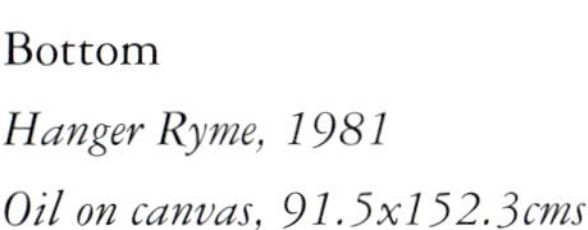

Oil on canvas, 91.5x152.3cms

impressed by them. Then came the Richmond Oak in 1979 (44) and 1980 (45), after the Wimbledon oaks. Then shortly after that Felcey partly moved to Devon. In 1974 he worked in Greece (a country he has periodically returned to, with enjoyment), and two years later for a spell in France. That year, 1976, he had a one-man show at Brunel University, where he had taught part-time since 1970. His exhibiting career has always been erratic, with occasional solo shows every now and again, but not more than half-a-dozen in thirty years. Group exhibitions are obviously less demanding, and Felcey tends to look upon them with more favour. He began showing at the Royal Academy Summer Exhibition in 1970, and showed regularly between 1975 and 1999. In 1980 he showed at the National Portrait Gallery and in 1982 in the survey 'British Drawing' at the Hayward Gallery.

In 1981–82, Felcey was living for the best part of a year in Dorset. Patrick Symons had bought the little house next to his own schoolhouse at Ryme Intrinseca, and Felcey rented it from him. As a long-term arrangement it didn't work, as Felcey couldn't really afford it, and his life became too split between there and London. However, it did give him the chance to do some landscape painting. Some of the work he produced then was shown in a rare one-man exhibition in 1982 at the Ian Birkstead Gallery in Great Russell Street, London, including the major painting now in America called *Hanger Ryme* (15). Also shown was a beautiful reclining nude, *Katy* (46). The paint in these pictures is not smoothly applied, but slabby, rough, vigorous, with every inch of the canvas activated and alive.

A substantially-documented group show entitled 'The Making of Five Paintings', and curated by David Shutt at the London College of Printing in 1984, featured work by Felcey in addition to Shutt himself, Kapil Jariwala, Paul Knight and Cherry Pickles. It was an exhibition intriguingly about process. As David Shutt wrote in the catalogue's foreword: 'These pictures are made from the continuous pre-occupations of the painters: they are not "projects"... The purpose is to exhibit the manner of arriving at the painting: the first pictorial thoughts and, where they are still evident, the subsequent building of ideas towards the final image.' Commenting about Felcey's work in particular, Shutt wrote: 'Felcey delights in reciprocity; the spiral of a candlestick, rediscovered in the figure; the saraband of a fabric design and the rococo twist of a branch in a tree, all potent convolutions of nervous energy in his work: but above all, discovered without exaggeration, essentially as they *are*.'

The exhibition was not a manifesto. There was no shared aesthetic, no common procedure, though Felcey, Jariwala and Shutt were all interested in the geometry of the rectangle – 'the square of the rectangle, the reciprocal shapes within it and some of those ideas associated with "dynamic symmetry"'. Shutt goes on: 'Felcey is strongly aware of significant focuses on the surface, and avoids placing a special event in the motif on them, since to do so would, in his view, arrest the eye in the restless search for visual unity.'

Later he writes: 'Drawing is vital to Felcey's picture-making in two ways. First, as preliminary investigation to find some edges from the motif, and discover the rectangle which is specific to it, but this role is constantly re-questioned through the painting, and there is frequent evidence of new thought around the edges of the picture. The second may also be continuous through the development of the painting: an attempt to re-imagine an aspect of what he sees, in a shift of language back to drawing media. In this role, the drawings acquire taut, nervous knots as the artist tries to grasp and extend possibilities, and the more protracted studies acquire great density of thought. The radiance of light from each particular facet of surface is (as in the paintings) the real subject of these studies. The earlier ideas about shape often recur in these drawings, in an attempt to push them, and the imagined surface articulation, into a homogeneous pictorial unity.'

Each contributing artist was asked to say something about their first ideas for the painting. Felcey's statement in the catalogue is as follows:

'For quite a few years all my work has been done directly from the model. However – I decided to paint a picture solely from drawings. I thought there would be less chance of just chatting about appearances, and, through the drawings, less likelihood of using undigested material.

'I didn't make any colour notes, and, although I painted the picture in the same room as the set up, I didn't find it any use in referring directly to it, when painting. The whole idea seemed to highlight the very pertinent problems between appearances and invention.'

Reproduced in the catalogue were photographs of the painting in progress, the main working drawing (47) and three smaller drawings, all in pencil, and a charcoal study. The development of ideas is evident in these preliminary works, and it is revealing that the charcoal study is by far the most sensuous of the group, dealing more emphatically with the weight and mass of the body. All the drawings are good on movement through posture and the way form is articulated by light. The main working drawing with its geometrical divisions and substructure (the rectangle and its various diagonals) is both a fascinating blueprint for the painting and a superb and satisfying piece of drawing in its own right. In it can be seen those correspondences to which David Shutt alluded: the spiral in the candlestick echoed in the stem of the table, triumphantly echoed in the disposition of the figure itself. An excellent and rewarding theme for an exhibition, it tells us a lot about Felcey's methods and practice in the mid-1980s.

In 1986, Felcey suffered a major accident whilst renovating his studio in Wandsworth. Falling off a stool, he put his arm through a cracked glass pane and badly injured his left arm, severing the artery, nerve and tendons. He received generous support from the Artists' Benevolent Fund, which enabled him to live during the enforced six-month convalescence. Teaching was still his regular source of income, and when he'd recuperated he took over as Head of Foundation Studies at the Byam Shaw School of Art in London (1987–91). He would have carried on living in London, but the joint-owner of the house wanted to sell up, and Felcey had long wanted to live in the country, so he grasped the opportunity. In 1987, he moved to Devon and settled in that part of the country he has made his home ever since. When he first moved to the Westcountry he painted a number of austere and gloomy pictures of stones and dead animals. Some of those rock pictures have now been painted over, usefully re-cycled as they did not come up to Felcey's high standards.

Although he welcomed the peace and seclusion of the countryside in which to paint, he was still travelling up to London to teach and earn a living. Felcey enjoys the dialogue of teaching, but grew to resent the amount of time it required and the consequent interruption to his painting schedule. In 1991 he was the recipient of a Lorne Award which enabled him to give up teaching for a year. It was a taste of freedom he found immensely seductive. On his return to the Byam Shaw he was appointed Head of Studies, but his impatience with the demands of teaching could not be curbed for much longer. In 1992 he returned to part-time teaching and finally gave up completely in 1995 in order to paint full-time. Since then, there have been occasional lapses, as when he was invited in 2000 to be a visiting professor at the New York Studio School, but for the most part, teaching is now a thing of the past.

One of the ways in which the trip to America was celebrated and memorialised was in a painting entitled *New York Window* (18). This is one of a group of window paintings all produced in 2001, which was something of a year of travel for Felcey. As a consequence, he painted different windows in the different cities in which he stayed. Berlin – to which Felcey briefly moved – received the most extended treatment, with four variants on the theme. The first *Berlin Window* (18) is really quite austere, while *Berlin Window with Chair, Sunny* (18), captures a completely different, lighter mood, almost as if opening a window onto the Mediterranean (the sub-theme might be construed as shedding new light). Another version portrays the same sunny conditions, without the chair, whilst a fourth depicts the window open, in a plainly and simply constructed rendition which is nevertheless full of colour. *Paris Window* (18), with its wrought iron and inward-opening full-length casements, is almost baroque in comparison to the austerities of the first Berlin version, while *New York Window* is all to do with space and how light both creates and dissolves form. Altogether, a rich and intriguing series of paintings.

Unfortunately, Felcey does not relish the prospect of exhibiting his work, or rather, the distraction and pressure which a deadline imposes on him. He prefers to build up his paintings gradually, explore his ideas and pursue the routines of the studio and country life untroubled by events in the wider world. This does not mean he leads a blinkered existence, for he has an enquiring mind and a keen interest in other people. He just knows how time in the studio can be dissipated if he is not extremely disciplined about putting in the hours. In addition, he doesn't find that the threat (or promise) of an exhibition focuses his mind and helps him to finish work. On the contrary, it sends him all over the place.

In the late 1990s there was however another spurt of activity on the exhibiting front, with work being included in 'The Importance of

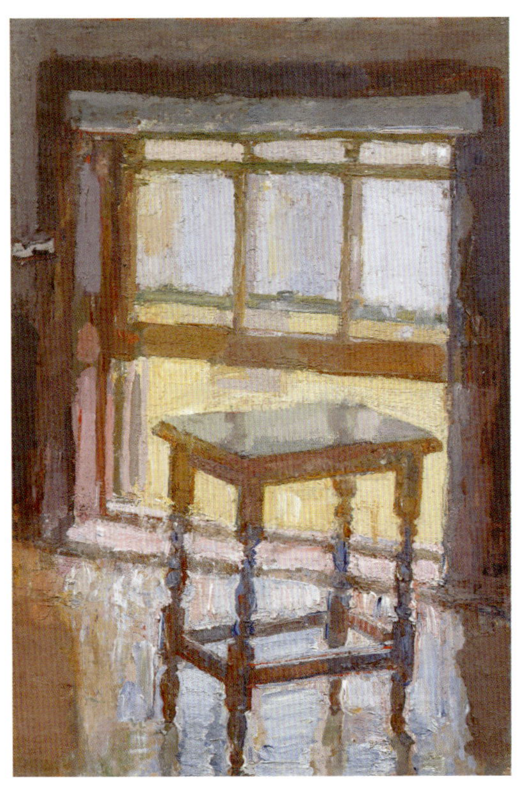

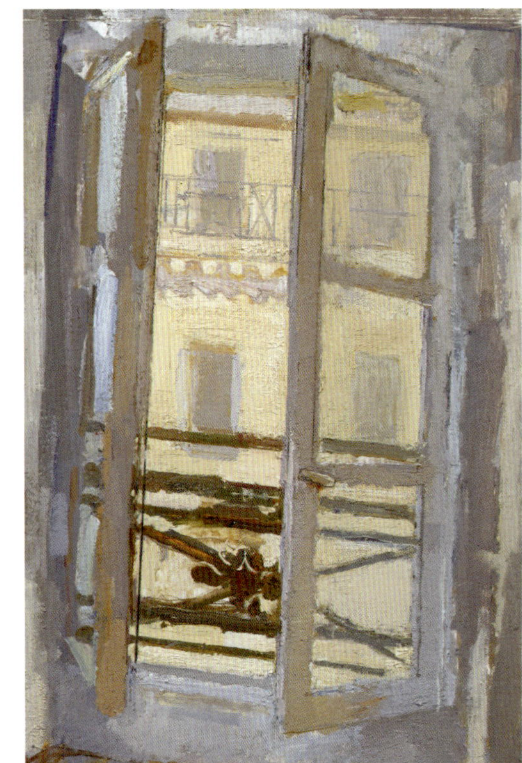

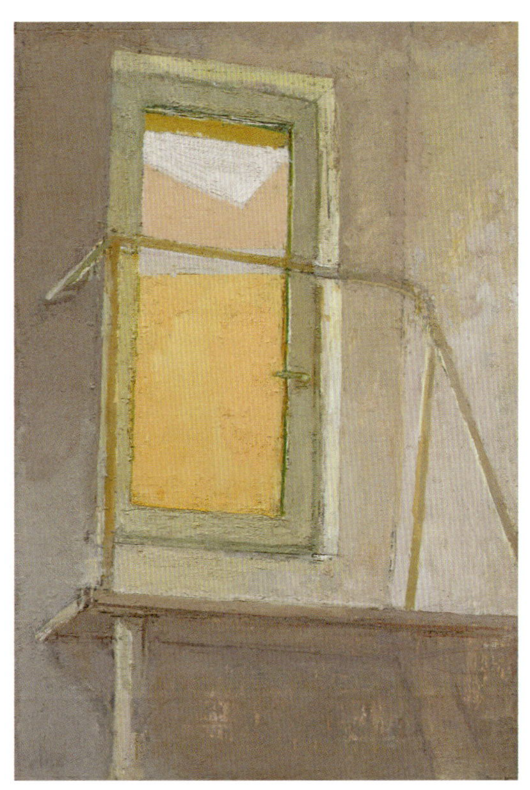

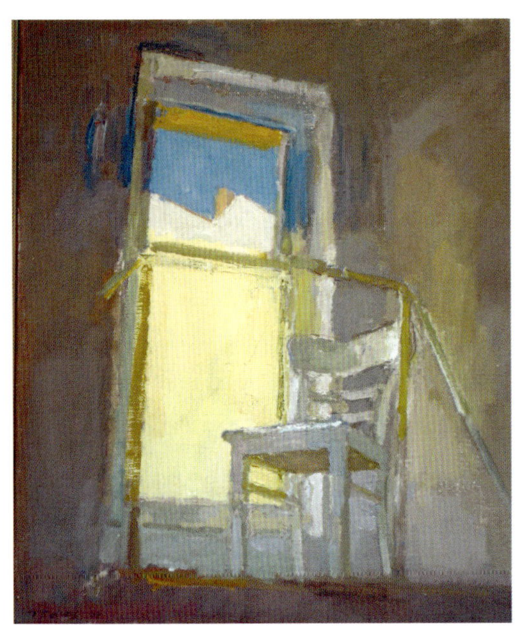

Clockwise from top left

New York Window, 2001
Oil on canvas, 35.6x22.9cms

Paris Window, 2001
Oil on canvas, 35.6x22.9cms

Berlin Window, 2001
Oil on canvas, 35.6x22.9cms

Berlin Window with Chair, Sunny, 2001
Oil on canvas, 50x40cms

Drawing' at Canterbury Museum and Art Gallery in 1998, and in mixed exhibitions at the Stephen Lacey Gallery in London. There was even a solo exhibition at the Plough Arts Centre in Torrington, Devon (1999), followed by a group show at Valentine Evans Fine Art in Hertfordshire (2001). This in turn was succeeded by Felcey's most prestigious one-man show to date, at the Galerie Hofmann + Kyrath in Berlin, also in 2001. This exhibition was called 'Constellations', featured the tree and wave paintings, and was accompanied by a substantial catalogue containing an essay by the present writer. Since then, Felcey has shown regularly with Chris Insoll at The New Gallery, in Portscatho, Cornwall, and in 2005 at the Royal Albert Memorial Museum & Art Gallery in Exeter, a smaller version of that substantial show travelling to Brunel University in Middlesex.

In a statement written in December 2004 for the Exeter exhibition, Felcey identifies a 'core of energy' in all his subjects, 'emanating from an innermost point, radiating out to the extremities of the form. This is visible in the radiance of an apple, the bulge and glow of a cheek, the tip of a branch. They are a kind of blossoming and culmination of this energy.

'The space around the forms also has energy. There is a tension between things, in their dialogues and interactions that they have with each other (and particularly with oneself).

'When I consider these two energies together – this outer and inner – the forms seem precariously suspended between these forces, almost as if they might dissolve (or explode) under these pressures, and I am very aware of the fragility of everything and how elusive it all is.

'Perhaps that's why good paintings sometimes seem like apparitions. Anyway, it's this kind of tension, of the outer and the inner, that I would like to have in my paintings.'

In an introductory note for that Exeter exhibition (which ran January –March 2005), the artist Susan Derges elaborated on this inner/outer theme. She writes perceptively of Felcey's deep involvement with 'the landscape, seasons, people, animals and history of Dartmoor and the South West', and the gradual dissolution of the boundaries between them and him. 'The distinction between inside and outside seems almost irrelevant or inappropriate when what has been created out of this daily endeavour [the artist's commitment to painting and drawing] is more like a process of unfolding states, the one mirroring the other: nature reflecting the person back to himself and the person echoing the processes of nature in his inner life.'

Derges continues: 'Whether the subject is still life or landscape, the images in these paintings suggest an experience so newly encountered that naming things has not yet happened. The painting is a response that is triggered by the subject because it is personally significant and meaningful.' I think that image – of 'an experience so newly encountered that naming things has not yet happened' – goes straight to the heart of what Felcey is about. He captures that directness of vision so well, and manages to pass it on undiluted to us.

The paintings and drawings of trees represent how Felcey encounters a tree in different circumstances at different times through a year and 'represent', according to Derges, 'an experience of being that is not purely emotional in a personal sense but deeper and closer to states that exist in nature also. Being of an archetypal nature these states and images resonate with our own feelings, memories and sense of the natural world, generating powerful metaphors, rather than merely objects that exist quite separately from ourselves.

'However romantic this approach may seem, there is nothing fanciful or purely imaginary in Trevor Felcey's relationship to his local environment. His knowledge of the way it works is achieved through an active engagement with the land, the animals that graze it, what is grown on it and the symbiotic relationships of all these parts to the whole.

'It is the whole, including the person, that is represented in these works. Some are closer to the inner world of his imagination while others are fastidiously and almost obsessively observed over long periods of time and the forms become almost crystallized in comparison to the fluidity of the memory paintings. Both approaches carry a trace of the tension or difficulty involved in getting the language of painting to meet the complexity and energy of the subject encountered. But the resolutions arrived at through this struggle achieve images that communicate all the freshness of the first experience.'

As has already been noted, Patrick Symons was a great supporter and friend of Felcey who supplied not just constant encouragement but an example of high standards in life and art. When Symons was killed in a tragic street accident in Paris in 1993, his large circle of friends and acquaintances was devastated. In the foreword to the catalogue for the Symons Memorial exhibition at Browse & Darby in London, in the spring of 1994, Felcey recalled Patrick's particular gifts and achievements. He wrote:

'One of the highlights for students (and it was practically written into the course) was the yearly invitation to his house and studio in Camberwell to see his collection of works by artists he admired, and his own work in progress. The house was crammed full of paintings and drawings, as well as a myriad of other things that had special interest for him, dried plants, shells, mathematical constructions, sculptures – a kind of artists' Aladdin's cave, and yet there was something spartan and basic about it all. Everything had a purpose, and contained ideas which could be related back to his thoughts on painting. For the students it was an inspiration, and a lasting experience.'

Felcey could be describing his own home in the stout-walled medieval house in a village on the edge of Dartmoor. Paintings and drawings, photographs and reproductions of Old Masters, plaster casts and smaller objects collected over the years adorn it. A vast low table in the sitting room is of Felcey's own design and make. On it stands a clockwork spit jack, that can be wound up to rotate the meat that would be hung from it over an open fire. (This ancient kitchen implement reminds me of Euan Uglow's similar liking for culinary equipment. He was the only person I've ever met to own a duck press.) There is a wealth of usage and history here, a context that is both personal and impersonal. Many hands have wound the spit jack, many eyes have gazed upon the Pollaiuolo cast of a young man's head, or the green granite Egyptian head from Berlin. A full-length cast of Santa Giustina by Gregorio Allegretto (1442–76) reclines along one wall, taken from the side of a sarcophagus in the V&A. This could only be an artist's room, and there is a working aspect to it. There is, to borrow Felcey's own words, something spartan and basic about it.

There's obviously something essential for this artist to be had from living on his own, in relative isolation, on Dartmoor. The relationship

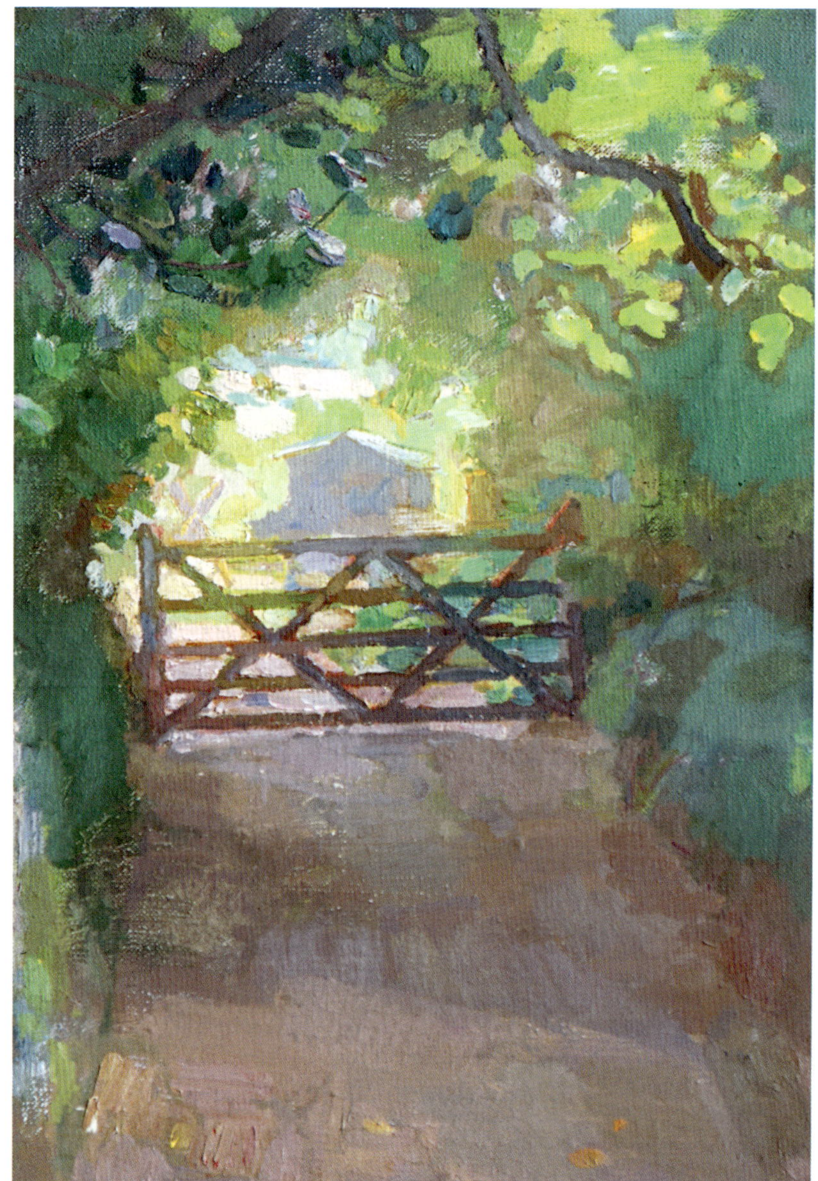

The Gate to the Studio, 2001
Oil on canvas, 60x40 cms

with the land he has nurtured (Felcey has a smallholding, and keeps sheep and chickens) and with the wider context of the surrounding landscape, is very important to him. Nevertheless, he doesn't want to be entirely isolated. He paints portraits partly to keep in touch with people, and to give himself a social life through contact with models. But for long stretches of time, he paints and reads and thinks about what he is trying to achieve with his art. He is, for example, a great admirer of van Gogh and enjoys re-reading his letters. In 1882, van Gogh wrote: 'I have had very little contact with painters lately. I have not been the worse for it. It is not the language of painters but the language of nature to which one ought to listen.'

Painting from nature was really a 19th century invention. Traditionally, in the 17th and 18th centuries, oil painting was an elaborate technique reserved for the studio, and drawing was what you did in front of nature. Few artists painted in the open air. As Lawrence Gowing put it: 'it was in fact an unusual painter who trusted the oleous paste in its sticky inconvenience to record the hazards of the open air. We have come to trust it, rather against reason, because something ungovernable about it seems to agree with transitory subjects and momentary responses.' In the 19th century, *plein air* painting became an artistic creed, not just because paint tubes made the stuff more portable, but because painting in front of the landscape was taken to embody a new kind of truthfulness. Painting from nature was also considered to be an effective remedy for depression, as an activity which serves to take us completely out of ourselves. Both Constable and Cézanne discovered the truth of this. There was evidently something healing in the process of discovering a unity within a subject, the relationships within the wholeness of the landscape.

For Trevor Felcey, painting in front of the motif has from student years been a central tenet of his artistic practice. He makes pencil drawings from nature, but he also paints in oil. Lawrence Gowing, in a further quotation from his thoughtful essay in *Painting from Nature*, the catalogue for a 1980–81 Arts Council touring exhibition, describes the making of a *plein air* oil study: 'A sketch that is evidently made with oil paint at a certain moment in an actual place registers the experience against our sense of an irrefutably existent physical stuff, hurriedly handled with inevitable self-revelation.' The key phrases are 'irrefutably existent physical stuff' – taken to mean both the paint and the things seen – and 'inevitable self-revelation', meaning the element of the artist's personality, or personal response, which appears in the picture. These are crucial aspects of Felcey's work: the physicality of the subject and his response to it, and the self-revelation entailed in the process of making. Both inform and enrich the pictures under discussion in this book. And in Felcey's case, the pictures made *en plein air* are not just studies, but full-size finished paintings.

Dartmoor is the last wilderness of southern Britain. Much of it is barren moorland, a landscape of tors and granite outcrops. It is also one of the best-preserved prehistoric landscapes in Europe, consisting of hut circles, cairns, stone circles or rows, interspersed with boundary banks. Alongside these remnants of an earlier civilization are such oddities as Wistman's Wood, near Two Bridges, full of stunted oaks. It was once perhaps part of a larger forest now retreated to a single valley, a strange and cheerless place. Geoffrey Grigson wrote that in Wistman's Wood 'oak trees hung with fern and felted with moss scramble over granite blocks in a green light of their own'.

It has long caught the eye of writers, as a scene of unrivalled desolation. Wordsworth wrote:

> *'I looked upon the scene both far and near,*
> *More doleful place did never eye survey,*
> *It seemed as if the spring time came not here,*
> *Or nature here was willing to decay.'*

Felcey was moved enough by the strange shapes, right-angled branches and truncated forms, to want to paint there. 'It is an extraordinary place, Wistman's Wood, it's the highest oak wood in England. These trees are several hundred years old and none of them are above 15 feet high. So miniature and weird.' In response, Felcey made a somewhat weird but beautiful painting, *Two Oaks in Wistman's Wood* (77), altogether more cheerful than Wordsworth's response but no less individual.

In 1996 he discovered the Whiddon Oak. He also paints other striking examples, such as a procumbent oak and the tree outside his studio, but the Whiddon tree has proved a lasting favourite. Medieval pollarding led to the distinctive umbrella shape of Whiddon Oak. Felcey's paintings of this tree are records of his dialogue with his idea of it. Each painting for Felcey should be a journey. The painting is the discovery and final form of the idea. It is the fruit of Felcey's long meditation and emotional response to a corner of nature, as seen through a temperament.

This great oak is situated in Whiddon Deer Park, the rocky slopes and lichen-clad woods opposite Castle Drogo near Chagford on the edge of Dartmoor. The first painting of it was *Whiddon Oak - Summer* (87)

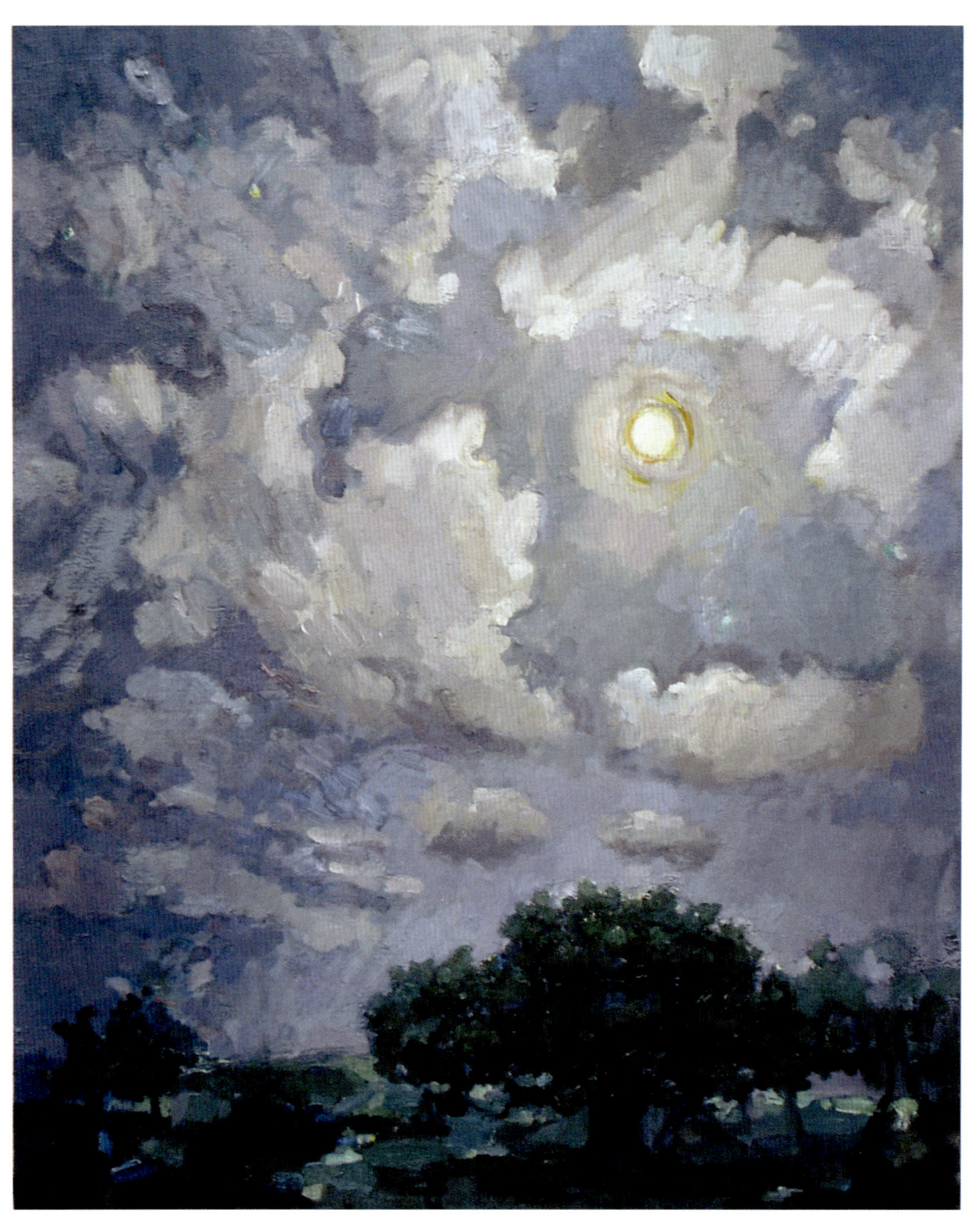

Full Moon, Cloud and Whiddon Oak, 2007
Oil on canvas, 90x71cms

which was painted *in situ*, Felcey wrapping the canvas overnight in polythene to protect it from animals and the elements. It evolved over a three-month period and depicts the tree in full foliage, over-arched and framed by a tree on the left nearer to us. During its evolution, the painting needed to overleap its original bounds, and Felcey had to unroll the canvas an inch or so on the right and adjust the stretcher. The original rectangle of the painting was thus significantly altered, but that didn't worry Felcey, who is more interested in making a good picture than in adhering to geometric rules of proportion. The most important thing was that the idea behind the painting – the tree lighting up the space like a giant candelabra – was not affected in the slightest by this change.

Trees have stimulated and provoked some of Felcey's best and most searching paintings of recent years, but he has not neglected other features of the local landscape. He has painted the un-picturesque moorland, tracing in several works the source of the Teign. Another theme to appeal to him has been the moor at night. Not an easy subject of course, but Felcey likes to set himself a challenge. One of the earliest paintings of it is the deliciously washy oil on canvas, *Night Sky* (5). Pondering the difficulties of night paintings, Kenneth Clark has written: 'A large area of dark paint cannot be made to look convincing by optical processes alone; it must have been transmuted into the medium of the poetic imagination.' This is precisely what Felcey achieves.

In 2007, he embarked on a new series of night paintings. *Full Moon, Cloud and Whiddon Oak* (22) was painted from memory and imagination, much more from the imagination than usual, which generated the movement right through this great sky, sucking back into a deep space. 'It seems to me the tension is about the top of the oak tree which slices back with the light of the moon hitting it,' comments Felcey about the enhaloed effect of the painting. He used no drawings for that, it was a matter of re-creating it. The result is that in the shapes of the cloud around the moon, you can feel the energy moving there like a turbine, or a propeller. It is a kind of sky dance, and reflects the way the paint was put on. Felcey worked on the painting, on and off, over a couple of months. He only paints in monochrome by artificial light, reserving his full palette for the subtle light of day. So he would have painted this one during the day. There are only four or five stars here (there were more, but Felcey took them out), just enough to remind us that it's a clear night. Not a star-scape like some of his paintings.

That same year, 2007, Felcey discovered a new subject for his night pictures: fire. The subject of gorse-burning quickly inspired four paintings. 'They happened in a very silly way. My daughter was here staying and she said "what I'd really like to see would be a really dark night painting without any light, just darkness." That sounded kind of interesting and I started a small picture which I tried to make as dark as possible but it was painted over a picture of a side of beef. Every time I scratched something out I'd get down to this red, and the painting seemed so much better with a bit of light in it – it seemed so much darker. That's how that painting happened, serendipity really.' Is the subject of a fire at night more or less difficult to paint than, say, an oak tree? 'I find them all impossible – I'm just trying to find a way to do it.'

Felcey doesn't generally paint over unsuccessful pictures but sometimes it happens (for instance, the rock paintings he did on first moving to Devon). 'Sometimes I like painting over old pictures. You've actually got to put something so strong down to read with all these other things happening. It's quite nice to have something to kick against.' Does that suggest, I wonder, that the prospect of a blank canvas is more of a threat than an excitement? 'It is a bit terrifying. That's why you take a great big brush and get something on to it.' Chance can play an important role. 'You just have to follow it if it feels right.' Does that mean he feels he has to forego rational control sometimes? 'Yes, absolutely. Sometimes it's very very abandoned. It's amazing how abandoned you can be if you're not thinking at all – it just comes out right.'

For the obvious reason that there's no light to see by, there are no night drawings done on site. This means that the night paintings either rely on daytime drawings or on Felcey's memory and imagination. This tends to confer on them a freedom of expression – or perhaps one should say a leeway – that the paintings done strictly from appearances don't have. Whatever the case, the night paintings – which include *Starshine, Moonshine, Earthshine* (105) and *Night Moor* (107), as well as the fire paintings - have proved to be one of the most spectacular groups of work within Felcey's recent output. Interestingly, there is a mixed media study, or drawing, for *Night Moor* (108), monochromatic and exciting in loosely applied browny-greys and whites, but this must have been done from memory, and is correspondingly atmospheric rather than packed with information.

Another difficult subject to appeal to him is the breaking wave. Not just a simple seascape, but the moment of impact and complex movement when wave hits shore. Felcey was moved, like Seurat in his sea paintings, by the immense whiteness of water and sky, by the proportions and distances of sea and firmament, brought into focus by the shoreline. Above all, by the movement inherent in the subject and the challenge that provoked. When painting a tree, Felcey has to locate a stillness at the heart of it, amid the actual movement of leaves and branches. But these visual disturbances (sometimes distractions) are minimal in comparison to the perpetual movement of the restless sea. Its whole cycle of advance, collapse and retreat is only relaxed when the tide goes out, and even then the sea is never still. How to convey that perpetual motion in a settled image? As early as 1993 he made an exquisite Japanese ink drawing of a wave (99), almost incised into the hand-made paper on which it's drawn. This preceded the main group of wave paintings by several years, an intriguing pointer of interest in the subject.

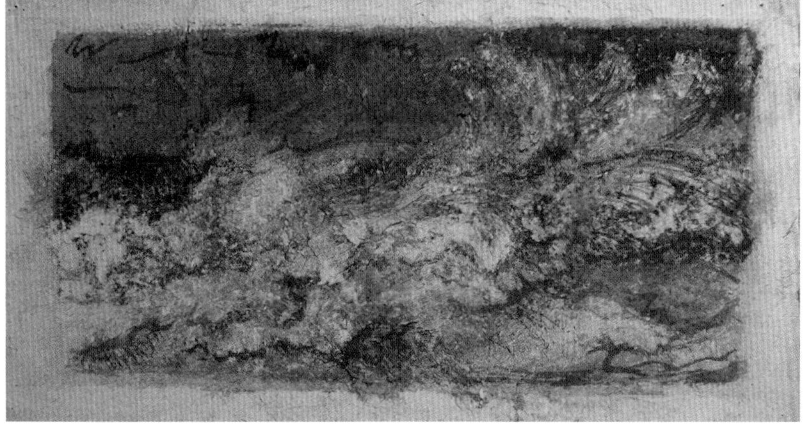

Wave, 1993
Japanese ink on paper, 29x56cms

Felcey started painting waves seriously at Widemouth Bay near Bude in North Cornwall in December 2000, having made a group of small paintings of the sea the previous October. His first studies of waves were made in grey acrylic, a deliberate restriction of the palette to concentrate on movement, with the acrylic used a little like watercolour for its fluidity. These images capture the boiling mass of the edge of the sea where it meets the shore, like engulfing mouths with monstrous tongues. How to record on paper the swiftness of the incoming surge of the tide, the crashing of a wave, and the grating withdrawal? The patterns of the water and spume, hurled skywards, occasionally suggest more formalized water-courses such as fountains, and from time to time even the dynamic wildness of fireworks.

I asked Felcey whether it struck him as a fairly impossible thing to paint? 'Yes it did. I didn't feel I had any models, any paintings of waves in my head. Obviously there are quite a few Courbet waves, but I certainly didn't want my pictures to be anything like that.' Was it an easy subject to draw? 'I found it impossible initially. The first drawings I did were just terrible scribbles. Then I did some good drawings on that day, and it was a great date – 01.01.01.' These are all to do with catching the energy on the wing, and a little bit like water coming down a mountain – a waterfall. There's a different kind of solidity to those drawings. Felcey occasionally makes little colour notes on them. 'They do seem very random marks, but they're all about something, and I suppose making all these drawings is about imprinting the memory of the wave in your mind as much as anything. Rather than just the information that's in the drawing. The sharpness of the front of the wave as it's coming over the still water is so particular there's no real way of drawing it. It's extraordinary.'

The paintings are equally remarkable. Look at the puddling at the front of *Wave No I* (95), and then the way it goes off in spray. 'That happens particularly on the north coast [of Cornwall] because you get a wind going into the sea, against the waves.' The paint also seems to describe cliffs, eroded cliffs in a sense (remember Felcey painted cliffs in Wales and Cleethorpes when he was at the Royal College.) *Wave No II* (101) is an altogether gentler image, like a green and pleasant landscape. 'I did have great clouds in it at one point but I took them out. It was an interesting project because the criteria are crazy really.' How on earth do you paint a wave? Is it memory – a mental snapshot, or simply weeks and months of experience? 'My approach was to go back time and time again, making drawings, little paintings until I'd got the idea of the movements absolutely in my head. The kind of cup of the inside of the wave.'

I asked Felcey if he used photographs at all? 'No, not really. I did do one thing from a photograph. It wasn't using the photograph as information, it was just because I loved the photograph. The photograph was the subject. As a way of gathering information, a drawing for me is much more useful than an edited version of what's out there in front of you.'

As John Berger has observed, the act of drawing 'is a way of learning to leave the present, or rather, of gathering the past, the future and the present into one.' This is not something that can be done by the camera.

Felcey's point is that you should do the editing yourself, not leave it to a machine. 'A photograph removes you from the thing. It's never really of the present, it's always past.' And his paintings very much occupy the present. 'One wants them to be absolutely present.' In the sense of both being there and in the present tense – the wave is crashing as you look at it. 'One is trying to do something about that moment, that presence, that eventuality.' What remains especially striking about these interpretations of waves is their abstract quality. Horizontal bands of colour meet and mingle, ranged relatively flatly down the picture plane, with a variety of vivid brushmarks and gestures to convey movement. Without their titles, these paintings could easily be taken for particularly expressive abstracts.

Felcey also worked at Strangles Beach, near Crackington Haven (you couldn't invent better names), where the undertow is so strong it hurls rocks around. Felcey, who has swum there when the weather has begun to turn rough, comments that it can be 'really ferocious'. First-hand experience of the sea mingles with the artistic heritage of wave paintings: Turner, Hokusai and Courbet are the leading exemplars and inspirations, but only in a general and unspecific way. Not Constable? No. Felcey loves his drawings and the big full-scale painted studies for the later paintings. Also the direct sketches of clouds and other observed details, but for him Constable's sea pictures do not stand out. He declares: 'I'm not trying to imitate water, but to find a form which embodies a wave.' That desire to give body to his subjects reinforces the very personal and intense identification the artist makes with his motifs. They are all *portraits*, whether people, trees or waves.

A Note on Materials

Felcey is devoted to oil paint and admits that acrylic is really a dead substance. 'Oil paint is the most marvellous thing because visually it never dries, it's always liquid. The only time I use acrylic is when it's monochrome. I don't use colour as the colour changes. They're drawings really. When I was doing those big tree drawings in acrylic, I always wet the whole surface as I was working on them because the surface changes tonally. There are a couple of wave studies in acrylic that have ended up quite thick, but I don't really like using it like that.' More often, Felcey will use acrylic as if it were watercolour, or as a wash with ink. He likes using both Japanese and Indian inks, sometimes with a reed pen. 'I like Japanese inks because of the great tonal range. Then when it gets too dense, you can start using Indian ink as a kind of new range on the top which extends it.'

He makes oil studies on board but not on paper. Charcoal he uses quite a lot, sometimes with ink or pastel, or black crayon, but not coloured crayons. Pencil is his great standby, and only very occasionally will he use watercolour. The single example reproduced here, a study for *The Source of the Teign* (71), is delicate and beautiful, and makes one wish he made more. When he's using oils, Felcey sometimes prefers a panel support to canvas. 'I like fairly coarse canvas. What I do a lot is paint on canvas stretched over board, so it's got some absolute resilience. It doesn't give. You can scrape off without digging great holes in the canvas. Scraping back is very much a part of the process.'

Felcey is very particular about the preparation of his supports. 'As a primer I tend to use a half-chalk ground which gives you a semi-absorbent surface so the paint initially goes right into the ground and dries quite quickly so you can build up on top of it. That surface gives you the chance to re-paint easily. That half-chalk is the most fabulous ground because it's glue-size based with chalk and titanium and some oil. Two coats of size which go into the canvas, then the half-chalk ground on top which kind of melts the size and goes into that. Then the paint goes into that. So it's all clearly keyed together as one sandwich.'

His palette now consists of about 14 colours: 'cadmium lemon, cadmium yellow, Indian yellow, cadmium orange, cadmium scarlet, cadmium red, permanent rose, permanent alizarin crimson, monestial green, emerald green, cadmium green, French ultramarine, cobalt, and then different blues for different paintings: cerulean blue, Prussian blue, monestial blue. I don't use earth colours very much. Sometimes burnt sienna – that's the only transparent earth colour.'

Generally he puts paint on quite fast, but a lot of the process is thinking about it. 'I've painted a lot of paintings very quickly but they can just go on and on and on.' There's no rule – some can flow, others can procrastinate – it just happens. The long gestation of some pictures has as much to do with thinking about their possibilities, and how they might be realized, as with solving formal problems. Felcey spends a lot of time in the studio just looking – particularly in the evenings. Mulling, rather than consciously analysing.

Drawing and Painting

In conversation about his early years as a painter, I asked Felcey whether he was then doing more painting than drawing? 'No. I've always drawn a great deal. Landscape, model, interior, still lifes – the lot.' In those days, he carried a sketchbook with him to be able to draw anything anywhere. Now he has folders for small pieces of paper but he doesn't actually use a book because, as he says, 'the drawings I do are usually about paintings and I stick them on the wall.' And nowadays he prefers to use a drawing board. 'I don't like the idea of making a book, I'm focused on the drawing I'm doing.'

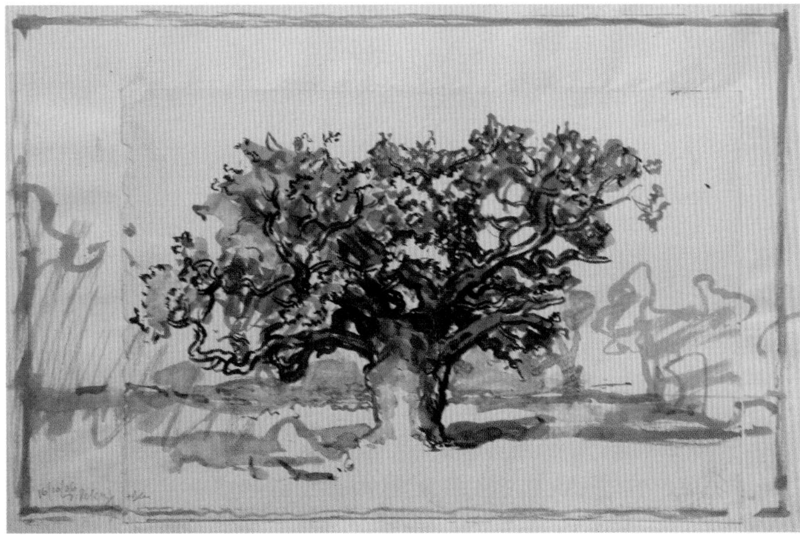

The Richmond Oak, 2006
Ink on paper, 24x36cms

Asked whether it's a typical strategy to start on one piece of paper and then add others to it, Felcey replied disarmingly, 'No, it's ineptitude, I think. I can't believe that three drawings of the same tree should all grow off the page.' (this actually did happen). How does he decide on the size of a piece of paper he's going to work on? 'You try to get it right. Recently I've started paintings where I haven't wanted to draw beforehand to discover the shape and I've taken a canvas which I felt would be far too big so that I could discover the edges as I went along, and I actually haven't gone off the edge. Then I can cut the canvas down and re-stretch it. As soon as I've decided on the shape I'll cut it down and carry on working on it.'

Felcey is emphatic: 'I would never make a drawing and then paint a picture from that drawing.' He generally draws and paints concurrently. 'You can't really start a painting unless you have a particular idea about the light. The light is synonymous with the subject – that's the idea of the painting.' So he starts with an idea. 'Several subjects are done from drawings, but if the subject is ephemeral, you have to hold it in your head. I'll start the painting if I've got a strong enough idea, though not necessarily all the information I might need, before I've decided on the shape. So it's not like I complete a drawing and then paint a picture from it, the drawing goes hand-in-hand with making the painting.' The drawing is a kind of research or gathering of information for the painting. 'A summing up – an edited version of what one's thinking about, and that's terrifically important really.'

The painting might end up as a summary of the summaries. 'The drawing is about the idea that's in the painting, so the discoveries have got to go straight into the painting.' It's in the studio that drawings play such an important part in his practice. He might do some drawing and then put paint on the canvas. If he's working outdoors, he tends just to paint. To start with, he draws very fluidly with a big brush in paint – red or yellow or blue – in a colour that seems appropriate to the picture, rather than in charcoal or pencil. He doesn't need to do drawings if he's painting in front of the motif because he's actually there, on site, gathering the information directly.

'I might do a lot of small paintings if the light's not quite right for the big one. There are a number of Whiddon Oak paintings like that, done early in the morning.' A painting is about a particular time of day

– a particular light. Usually he can paint for about four hours while that light lasts. But the light is not the entirety of the subject. 'One isn't just painting about the moment, it's a duration of time, and as you're there with the subject, the idea of the picture distils.'

The idea is not therefore written in stone from the outset. 'I think it's a kind of feeling. You've got an idea for a picture and the actual making of the picture is a discovery of that idea. It's a kind of unearthing. I think one's got an immense capacity to understand something in a kind of gut way – the totality of something – and then the painting is another kind of process of actually trying to understand what that is. One might not have a specific vision of it, it's a kind of discovery.'

The shape of the painting, the rectangle, comes from the subject – 'I don't try and make something fit in to a shape.' It's not as if he wanted to use a double-square or some other geometric shape that might be a favourite and impose that on a subject. So how important is geometry to him? It seems that he uses it when it suits him and not when it doesn't. 'I'm always trying to draw about the whole shape. I'm aware of the edges. One's intuitively aware of the diagonals, middles, relationships within it, whether one actually uses it in a measured way or not. Sometimes I do, sometimes I don't.'

He might draw in the diagonals or square up a canvas. 'You can see on some of the pictures where some of the geometry is drawn. The beautiful thing about a root 2 rectangle which is A4, the half of it is the same shape as the whole so it makes a very powerful thing – the diagonal of the half to the diagonal of the whole meets at 90 degrees so it's a very strong physical thing on that shape. One might draw that in, not actually to place things on it but to feel the energy of its relationship to them. It's a bit like Matisse saying he used a plumb line so that he could feel the arabesque more. Obviously the geometry is the energy to the whole shape.'

Both Uglow and Symons relied very heavily on a system of monocular measurements taken in relation to fixed points and a plumb line to trap appearances. What is Felcey's attitude to measuring? 'I don't measure any longer, other than by eye. I don't find it at all useful because I draw from the centre of things not the edges and you can't measure a centre. The edges have got to come together to feel that the centre's right, so pinning down an edge doesn't help me at all. A fixed edge can be death in my paintings, because I really am drawing from the centre of things which is why it's so hard to bring things together, to get them to meet.'

Is that the biggest struggle in the work? 'Yes.' In a sense, it must be like trying to put the explosion back in a box and make some sort of order out of it. But a painting must not be too ordered or you are in danger of losing its vitality. 'One wants the response to be as direct and as fresh as possible. In a way, at any point in the picture, I feel I've got to let go of everything to do something fresh and new on the picture. The ideal is that the last mark on the last day is absolutely painted with the same spirit as the first one. The problem is how one can carry on in that way and accrue something – for something to snowball. Most of the time one feels one's just undoing the whole thing. I think one's just got to trust.'

It sounds a bit like a leap of faith, and perhaps painting belongs to a similar order of experience. There is a mystery at the heart of art, making it impossible ultimately to explain why paintings have the effect they do. It's not just skill and hard work. It's a collaboration with powers outside the artist's rational control. Thus his reply is not entirely a surprise when I ask Felcey whether he finds it easy to know when he has finished something. 'No, I find it terribly difficult. I'm never warming up for something, I'm doing it – this is it. Sometimes I think I go on with paintings far too long – is this something to do with my ego? If you've got a vision of something, what it might be like, you've just got to carry on until you take it as far as you possibly can and come out the other side.'

Trees

Painting trees can solve the problem of formal balance in landscape painting, which needs to achieve a harmony between horizontal and vertical emphases. Most landscape is naturally horizontal, but trees are formidable vertical accents, and Felcey makes the greatest use of them. Yet he does not rely on trees to articulate more general landscape paintings; rather, he takes the focus in closer, and concentrates on trees almost to the exclusion of other aspects of the countryside. He makes detailed, in-depth studies of particular trees, but in doing so, he makes larger points about the tree's role in nature, and our own relationship to our environment.

Auden wrote: 'A culture is no better than its woods', and Roger Deakin in *Wildwood*, his glorious journey through trees, has this to say: 'Woods, like water, have been suppressed by motorways and the modern world, and have come to look like the subconscious of the landscape. They have become the guardians of our dreams of greenwood liberty, of our wildwood, feral, childhood selves, of Richmal Crompton's *Just William* and his outlaws. They hold the merriness of Merry England, of yew longbows, of Robin Hood and his outlaw band. But they are also repositories of the ancient stories, of the Icelandic myths of Ygdrasil the Tree of Life, Robert Graves' 'The Battle of the Trees' and the myths of Sir James Frazer's *Golden Bough*. The enemies of woods are always the enemies of culture and humanity.' Felcey's paintings bear witness to the continuing importance of trees, to the crucial role they play in our real and imaginative lives.

Felcey has been painting oak trees for 30 years. The oak is his favourite tree. 'Staggering aren't they, and pretty important in England.' Is he much moved by the 'hearts of oak' symbolism? 'It's got everything about it.' He wouldn't have been so tempted to paint the beech, for instance? 'No. The beech is like flames. There's something about a fist of oak leaves – that's what they're like, those contained clusters, under pressure somehow – which is also like the whole tree in miniature. The clump to the whole thing is fantastically interrelated. I love the way that oak branches make 90 degree turns that are immensely unexpected. And then stag-headed oaks, which is when the tree is growing and growing and growing and suddenly realizes that it's grown too much for its roots. It has to pull back a bit, so it just cuts off a limb and dies back, in balance again with its roots. Obviously it may do this several times in its hundreds of years of life, just to keep itself in balance.'

The Whiddon Oak is about 400 to 500 years old and represents much history as well as its own particular essence and identity. 'A lot of those paintings are of such archetypal trees – I wanted them to be archetypal but also particular. Portraits of trees. Emblematic and particular.' Revealingly, Felcey has always thought of the oak tree as a wave. Wood also looks like flesh. He paints waves like undergrowth, or mouths. He relishes the evident reciprocity of growing things, how the embodiment and form of one can summon up another. In 1979 he made his first charcoal drawing of an oak in Richmond Park in Surrey (44). It was a single tree, drawn like an explosion.

If you look at any form you have a sense of the energy coming from the core of the form to the outside in a kind of explosion. That's its volumetric presence – its three-dimensionality. It's like a drawing of an oak tree. You have the sense of this thing growing out of the ground, out of its centre and spreading out in this kind of umbrella to all its points. But at the end of the branch it's a spatial position and a culmination of the whole energy coming out of the tree, so it is like an explosion.'

Felcey goes on: 'The reason that great oak outside the studio [the one that features in *The Bole of the Oak* (52)] has four or five great limbs is that it must have been pollarded several times. And the reason that it's got that fantastic root is that it would have been on a substantial bank, and the bank has been taken away. That's why the roots are out of the ground, as if it's standing on tiptoes. One has a sense of what trees have lived through and how we've managed them or reacted to them. They are mirrors to us really, our dialogue with the landscape. One feels immensely connected to them.

'You might meet someone with a wonderful head that you'd like to paint but then you'd have to find the whole idea for a picture which would be about the light, the rectangle, you'd have to find a whole situation that sums up the subject. It's the same with a tree. The first time I saw the Whiddon Oak I thought what a fantastic tree. Then I started moving round it, changing my relationship to the tree and then suddenly something felt right – a particular kind of light – and I had the whole idea for a painting. It's multi-faceted. One is trying to get a particular light, but it's only part of the idea for the picture.'

Fruit trees are not on the same level of grandeur as the oaks and other woodland trees. They are there to yield an annual crop, to be domesticated and grafted specifically for our use, and they do not live to the same great age, passing their prime all too soon. But they have other, very particular and equally lovable qualities. That great prose-poet of the English countryside, Adrian Bell, observed in his delightful book *Apple Acre* (1942): 'While the apple hangs there, it is inviolate; however near you come, it is perfectly to itself, its life the life of the wind.' It

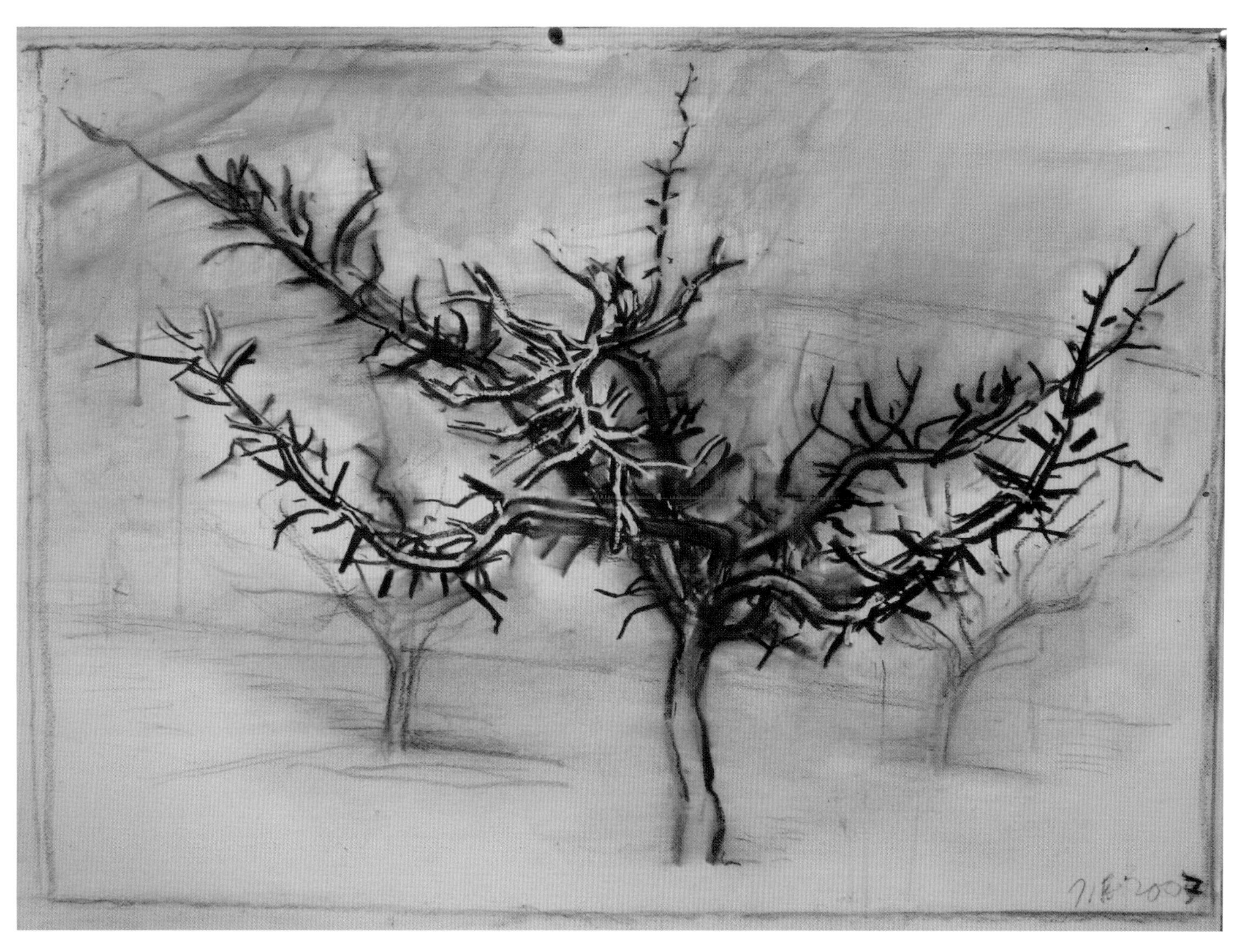

Winter Apple, 2007
Charcoal and acrylic on paper, 54x70cms

is that life of the wind that Felcey captures so brilliantly in his paintings of loaded boughs.

He's also perspicacious when it comes to the bare bones of the tree. There's an apple in his garden which he has pruned to resemble uncannily a tree in Patrick Symons' orchard at Ryme Intrinseca – a drawing of which by Symons is owned by Felcey's friend Chris Insoll. Felcey's own *Winter Apple* (29) is done in charcoal with some acrylic and a slight ink wash. It was the second drawing of that subject, and not a typical one. Felcey comments: 'The differentiations between the marks along the branches are very varied where I'm almost trying to get the charcoal to *be* the branch. It's almost like pushing a piece of paint around.' The various ways of depicting – drawing, painting, etching – have so much in common yet retain their own very distinct qualities which Felcey exploits to telling effect.

What is it about trees? To quote John Berger again: 'Throughout history and prehistory forests have offered shelter, a hiding-place, whilst also being places in which a wanderer can ultimately be lost. They oblige us to recognize how much is hidden.' Certainly if we look at Felcey's ancient time-scarred trunks we are confronted with a different sense of time, a different awareness – the kind of comparison so useful for giving us a sense of proportion about ourselves. Nothing is more necessary today than a global realization of the relative insignificance of man. We are not the lords of all we survey, merely collaborators in a present which through our misdeeds may have no future. Time to learn wisdom from the trees and recognize how much we don't know.

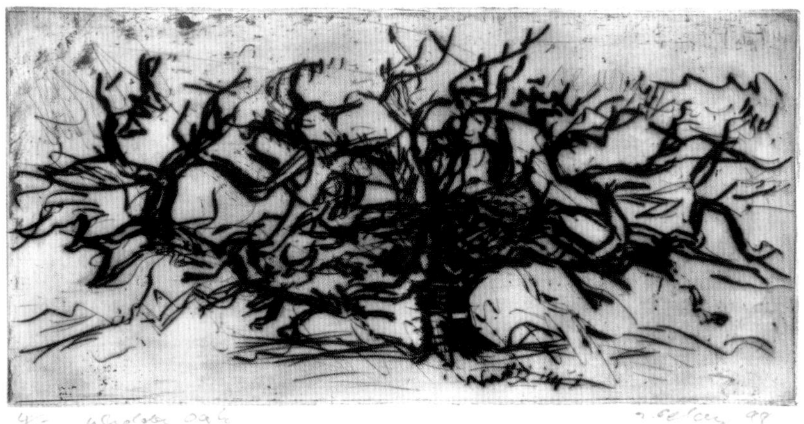

Whiddon Oak, 1998
Drypoint, 10.5x21.8cms

Prints

Felcey is a painter who is also an occasional printmaker. His preferred medium is etching and he has his own press in a groundfloor studio. One of his best and most direct prints is a drypoint *Whiddon Oak* (65) which was done on site out in the deer park in 20 minutes or so, scratched directly on to the plate. As Felcey points out, the technique of drypoint is more about picking up the burr of the metal plate (in this case copper) than about penetrating into it.

Remembered Oak (80) is an etching which developed through a much more prolonged and complex process, and was worked on, on and off, over three years. The plate went several times into the acid, with different methods used – aquatint, burnishing, engraving – all methods of making a mark on a copper plate. 'I like the physicality, the sculptural quality of an etching plate and it is a wonderful way of developing an idea. You change it so much, you can move things about, scrape the plate back down, and yet you can keep all the stages as well, the different printings – it's a terrific way of developing an idea. I like the sculptural element but also the chance element with the acid. You're never quite sure what it's going to do, it's a great kind of alchemy and juggling act.'

He's made a couple of etchings of waves in which an enjoyable scribbly element works with and against the volumetric aspect. 'I suppose that epitomizes what I try to do in some of those pictures of the wave, not trying to imitate water in any way but finding a form which embodies a wave and its different movements: the coming forward, the lip of the wave as it's running fast towards you, then where it's crashed down there's an upward boil as well from the wave, or the spray being taken off by the wind at the top – it's just an extraordinary kind of dynamic movement.'

With the etching of *Procumbent Oak* (83), the painting came first. 'I wanted to make an etching of the subject and I didn't want it to come out the wrong way – the printing process of course reverses the image you etch – and so it was just a nightmare to draw it. I was drawing it in

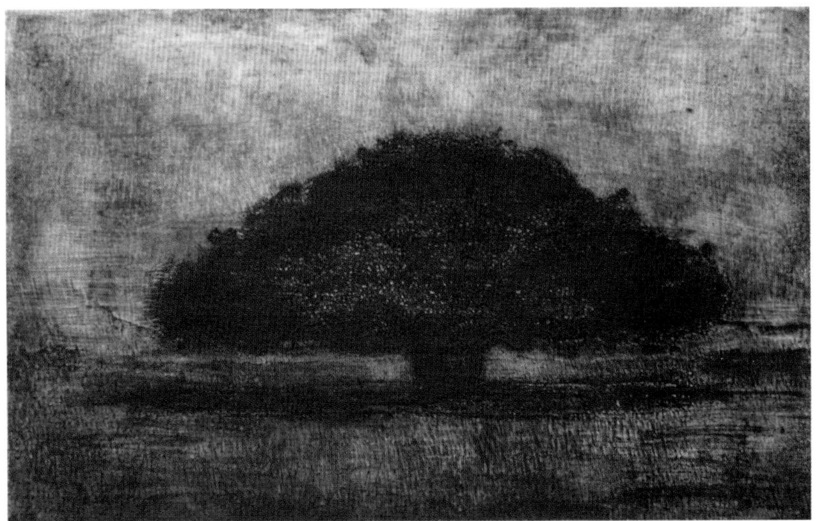

Remembered Oak, 1998
Etching, 17x26cms

reverse from a drawing through the mirror, but I found it so tedious it took me months and months. I kept on abandoning it. Once you've got an idea of the image then you're making marks on the plate about the image, and it was all right. It was changing what was on the paper, mapping out the reverse of a drawing, that was so tedious. It took me about three years to do it in the end. I'd like to have simplified it.'

Included in the selection of work here is an early linocut *Lincolnshire Landscape* (9) from 1960, all force-fields of wild energy, to show that Felcey has not only used other printmaking techniques and methods, but has made memorable images with them. But etching remains his preferred process. Other subjects he has etched include wild angelica, a pine cone, Venice (a drypoint), the head of a girl, *Battersea Bridge* (36) and an aquatint of a standing stone.

Lasting Influences

'The September I came down to London [1962] it was the Soutine exhibition at the Tate.' That was a key early inspiration and influence. There was a Modigliani exhibition on at the same time, but Felcey was not so interested. Soutine has not exactly been a constant influence since then, but recently he has returned to take up an important place in Felcey's life. In this Soutine is perhaps a bit like van Gogh: you like them when you're young but then have to be quite a bit older to fully appreciate him. Their appeal to youth is strong. As Felcey points out: 'They are very approachable painters – you can imagine doing that sort of thing yourself.' Both George Rowlett and Felcey went through passionate Soutine phases as students. And they were not the only ones to feel the Russian-born French painter's power.

As Frank Auerbach has said: 'I can't deny that Soutine had a very great effect on me, especially the Céret pictures. I can't think of him as an expressionist artist, but as a great draughtsman, who follows the form around the back and out the other side. He was a better draughtsman than either Braque or Gris, neither of whom drew very well. There is absolutely *nothing* pedantic about Soutine's drawing; on the other hand, he didn't just make up shapes for the pleasure of making them up. One always feels a correspondence with the motif, at every point.'

De Kooning said: 'I've always been crazy about Soutine... Maybe it's the lushness of the paint. He builds up a surface that looks like a material, like a substance. There's a kind of transfiguration, a certain fleshiness, in his work...' De Kooning perceived the potential for enlarging the concentrated energy found in Soutine's mainly small canvases, painted in front of the motif. Soutine's refusal to invent or to work away from the motif meant that he never painted from memory and always took the canvas to the subject. This had the direct consequence of limiting him in terms of size, a restriction that his modern followers have tried to circumvent. De Kooning used Soutine's example to make bigger paintings in the studio. Felcey has done this too, principally by working in the studio, but also by transporting large canvases to the motif.

Certain artists are present touchstones for Felcey: Courbet, van Gogh, Soutine. He is constantly thinking about them, reading about them, studying their work. Courbet the pure painter (Josef Herman called him 'the first modern poet of painterly matter') is a constant inspiration. As Robert Hughes has written so perceptively about Courbet: 'What the vibration of light would be to Monet, the force of gravity was to Courbet. It is the physical law that insinuates itself into almost every one of his images, confirming their materiality and stressing their essential subject matter – the weighty body of the world.' And again:

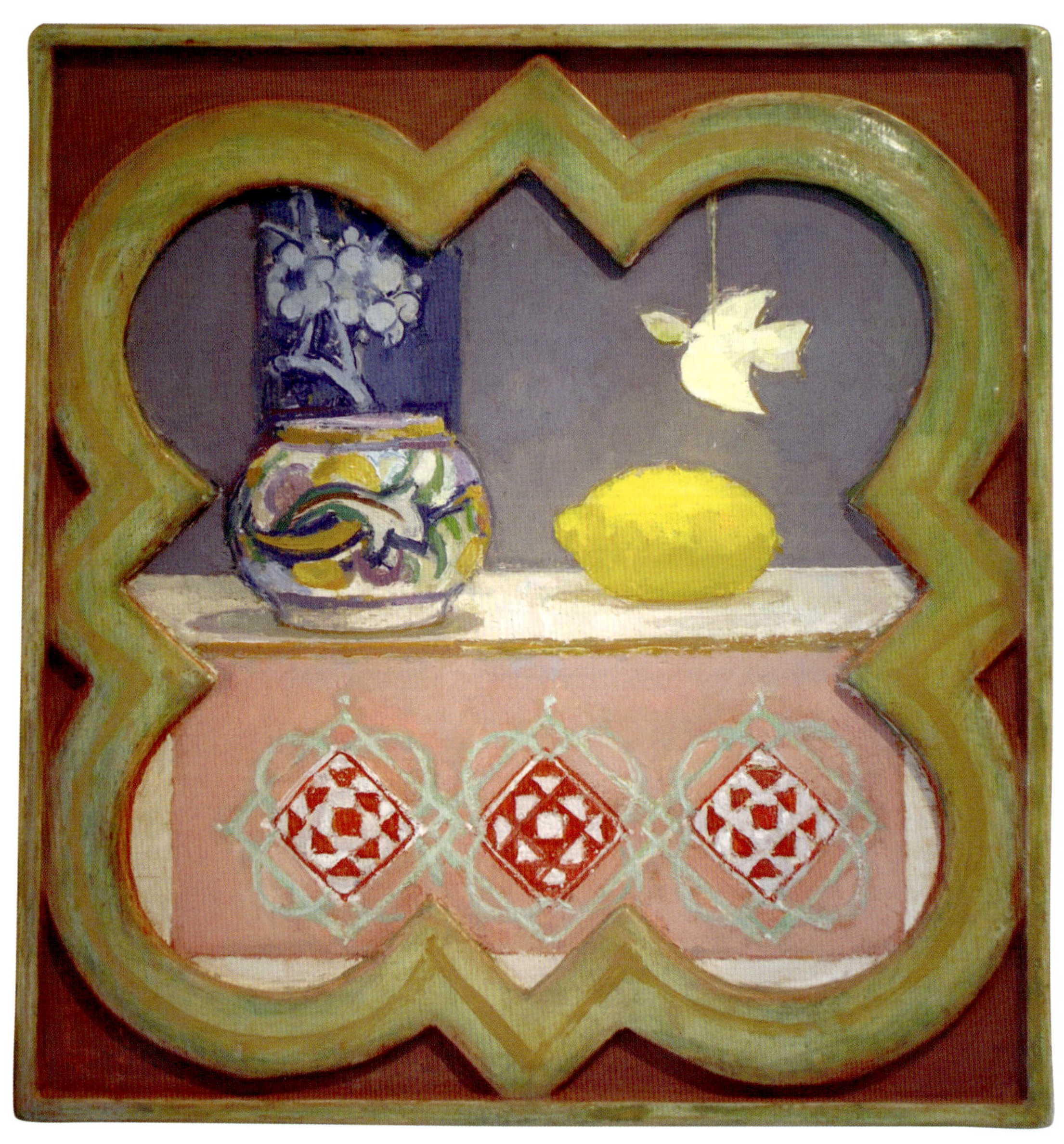

Transcription Still Life, 2003
Oil on gesso board, 39x36cms

'The objectivity of Courbet's work connotes a deep and sensuous love of whatever he painted.' Cézanne emulated the solidity of his landscapes, 'the limestone crags and ledges of the valleys... capped with dense dark green and anchored by thick clefts of shadow... along with the pasty, almost mortared paint that evokes their surfaces'. Both artists, Courbet and Cézanne, play a large part in Felcey's thinking.

From time to time, he also enjoys making transcriptions from Old Masters, whether a painting or a drawing. It is a regular informal activity (as he says 'one's always drawing from other pictures') which occasionally burgeons into a more extended enterprise. Two examples here are *After Rembrandt* (51), an oil on board version painted in 1981 of that master's *Return of the Prodigal Son*, in St Petersburg, and *Transcription Still Life* (32), oil on gesso board (2003). The latter is based on a Pentecost panel by Taddeo Gaddi in Berlin. This is inventively interpreted as a rather strange conjunction of altarpiece, lemon, cut-out suspended bird (like something out of Matisse or Braque) and pot, all presented in a carved wooden surround, painted Lincoln green and pink. In the Rembrandt, Felcey has obviously been fascinated by the intensity of gesture and grouping, in the Gaddi by the importance of still life in sacred pictures.

In January 2008 Felcey saw a big Courbet show in Paris and then in the summer a huge Hokusai exhibition at the Musée des Arts Asiatiques. This retrospective included not only the more famous prints but also some of Hokusai's impressive drawings, which Felcey has described as 'absolutely staggering'. The effect of seeing work of this quality is always the same: to send Felcey back to the studio with fresh enthusiasm to make something of his own.

In May, he began to paint a big fish, *Sea Bass* (135), as a kind of homage to Courbet, whose Paris exhibition he'd just seen and been fabulously impressed by. The main problem was decomposition. When the fish was not posing, Felcey kept it well-watered and covered with a damp cloth. After a couple of days it stopped smelling, but worse things began to happen. First of all it turned a beautiful yellowy-orange, golden really. Then maggots appeared, and when the body of the fish started to change shape, he could bear it no longer. The painting had come to an end. The story is reminiscent of the Soutine legend and one episode in particular when he was painting an ox carcass in honour of Rembrandt.

The beef began to decay as Soutine struggled to complete four or more large canvases paraphrasing Rembrandt. The neighbours complained at the stench, as pails of blood were poured over the meat to keep it fresh-looking and a model was hired to fan away the flies. Soutine's rapture at the colours that emerged as the meat decomposed was only matched by the desperation of the neighbours. Eventually the police were called in, much to Soutine's rage and incomprehension. What had he done wrong? He was only working.

The other two abiding influences on Felcey are of course Auerbach and Uglow. It has been Felcey's achievement to absorb the teaching of both without being dominated by either, and to make a new thing that is very much his own from the inspirations he has imbibed. Felcey's mature work is close to neither mentor, though there remain close parallels to be identified. For instance, consider Auerbach's statement: 'My vision of painting, the picture I had in my head, was of some clearly formal statement; an explosion.' Doesn't this sound rather like Felcey talking about the energy coming out of the canopy of an oak tree? And here is Uglow: 'Painting's too serious to take flippantly. I think one should behave morally with paint, though that doesn't stop one taking risks.' I can imagine Felcey concurring with that.

As for the still life models who have been a constant inspiration to Felcey – Chardin and Zurbaran – it can be seen from his recent work that he's gone beyond them now. He has developed his own style, his own way of doing it, and has created in the process a series of tense, compact and beautiful images. His handling of colour is inventive and personal, and his control of surface is outstanding. The way he can scrape down and have impasto in the same passage is remarkable. And, despite all the work, his surfaces are always fresh. This is no mean achievement. And what he can command on a small scale he is also able to orchestrate on larger paintings. The oak portraits and the night paintings in particular are demonstrations of singular skill and versatility.

Conclusion

Landscape is a means of poetical expression, a search in today's largely aimless world for direction and harmony. We look to landscape as a source of consolation and joy. But as Simon Schama has observed: 'Before it can ever be a repose for the senses, landscape is the work of the mind. Its scenery is built up as much from strata of memory as from layers of rock.' We need to determine and reaffirm our relationship with our surroundings, and landscape painting can help us do that in a way that satisfies the modern mind. Partly this is achieved by giving landscape an air of classical order and permanence, partly by maintaining the immediacy of the sketch. Simon Schama again: 'it is our shaping perception that makes the difference between raw matter and landscape.'

The potentially infinite visual data available in any landscape must be subordinated to a single unifying pictorial idea, or there is no chance of making a successful painting. As a nation, if one may make a sweeping generalization, we are drawn to the romantic interpretation rather than the classical. As Kenneth Clark rather gloomily observed: 'The idea that an appreciation of nature can be combined with a desire for intellectual order has never been acceptable in England.' But the pursuit of order need not be so intrusive that it is off-putting.

Despite his own interest in geometry, and the enthusiasm of his teachers, Felcey is looking for a natural order in things, one that doesn't have to be tied to a rigid geometrical structure. The outmoded belief that form is to do with the intellect, colour with the senses, is too restricted. We need a new unity. Felcey offers this, though quite how he achieves it remains something of a mystery. As he says: 'There are no rules – one is constantly working in a state of terrible uncertainty, which at times can seem to be crippling.' The force of his sensations in front of nature, delivered through a harmonious painted, drawn or etched image, is what he wants to convey undiminished to us, his audience.

Felcey's landscapes are at their most successful when the waves look like trees, the land like waves, when that formal inter-penetration is most in evidence. The flames in the gorse-burning pictures can look like trees, or the mouths of flame look like waves of the sea. This is metaphor at its most visible and powerful – everything stands for something else. 'Like Matisse saying when you're trying to draw a leg you've got to think of something it's like, an amphora or something. You've got to have something in your mind which is a metaphor for this thing in order to get close to it.'

There are no people on Felcey's beaches, watching the incoming tide. Nor are there spectators attendant on his oaks. His wave and tree paintings are to some extent self-portraits: images of the artist solitary in his studio, linking up with the world through the concentrated and devoted activity of making art. People enter the paintings not incidentally but deliberately when they become the subjects of nudes or portraits. However, I think that Felcey's most original paintings are currently his landscapes, though such still lifes as *Plate of Plums* (132) or *Gyroscopic Still-Life* (133), with their singing chromatic intensities, are fierce competitors for pride of place.

'The prolonged, repeated visits to the painting site built up not only relationships within the painting, but also that vital intimacy and sense of belonging to the subject. In this, I think, lies the final celebration.' Felcey is here writing about the art of Patrick Symons, but the words could be applied to his own work with equal accuracy and aptness. He belongs to those subjects he has chosen (or which have chosen him): the night paintings, the regal oaks, the resplendent apple trees and those visions of movement, the waves. All these, and more, Felcey celebrates with a robust and beguiling mixture of care and abandon, most certainly with passion. His paintings are sustained moments of glory and praise.

Felcey deals in visual facts. As Kenneth Clark has so perceptively written: 'Facts become art through love, which unifies them and lifts them to a higher plane of reality; and, in landscape, this all-embracing love is expressed by light.' As he rightly insists, Felcey's paintings are very much about light. The quality of light and time of day are for him events, recorded with the passionate precision which is a form of love. As John Berger wrote recently: 'reality is all we have to love. There's nothing else.' Trevor Felcey knows how to show it.

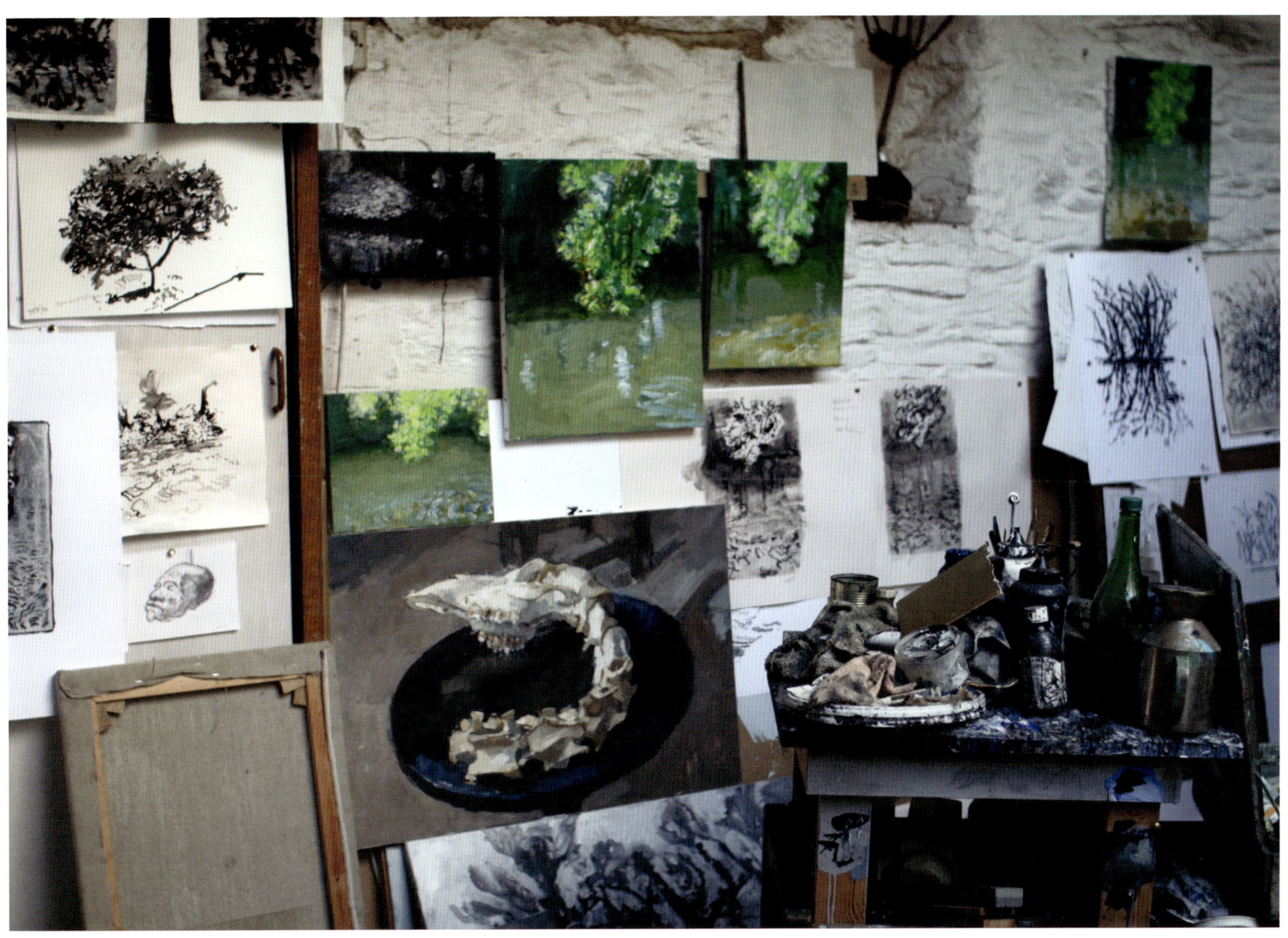

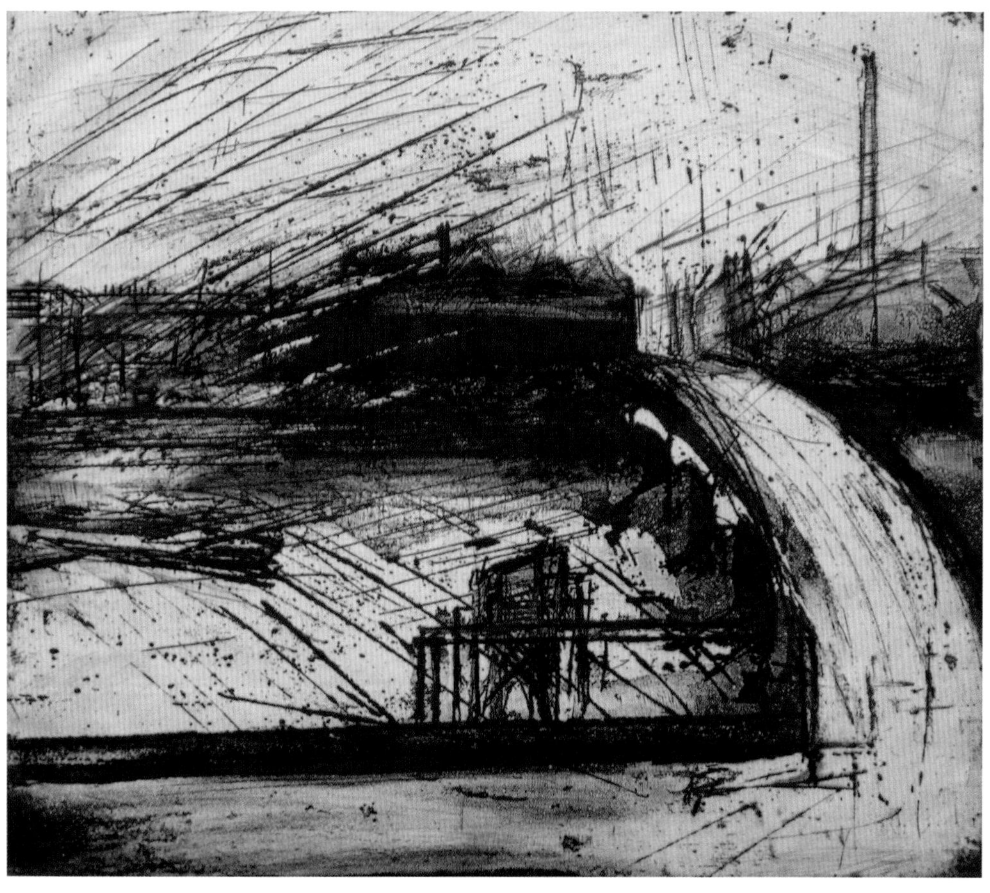

36
Battersea Bridge, 1968
Etching, drypoint 22.5x25cms

37
Summer Garden, 1969
Oil on canvas, 137x127cms

Summer Garden (1969), was exhibited in the 1970 Royal Academy summer exhibition. It depicts an apple tree in a Wandsworth garden, a fine large student work on canvas, as board would have been too unwieldy. Of the paintings here, this and Battersea Bridge (1968) {which won the David Murray prize for landscape} are the ones closest to the Bomberg/Auerbach axis. Note the diagonal vectors of energy criss-crossing through the thickly-impasted creamy paint. In its pale blue, green and yellow livery it looks remarkably fresh after 40 years. It took Felcey a couple of months and most of the summer working outside to paint. 'It's all about the lean of that tree and how it's stuck into the ground', he comments. There are rose bushes either side and a cypress-type tree in the next door garden. The tree behind makes the movement – another cypress tree articulated in darker Prussian blue. The lawn down the front looks a bit like a swimming pool, or a reflection of the sky, the space rather dropping away. Felcey recalls: 'Auerbach liked that painting, so Roger Leeworthy told me; he thought the trunk of the tree had a really great twist in it.'

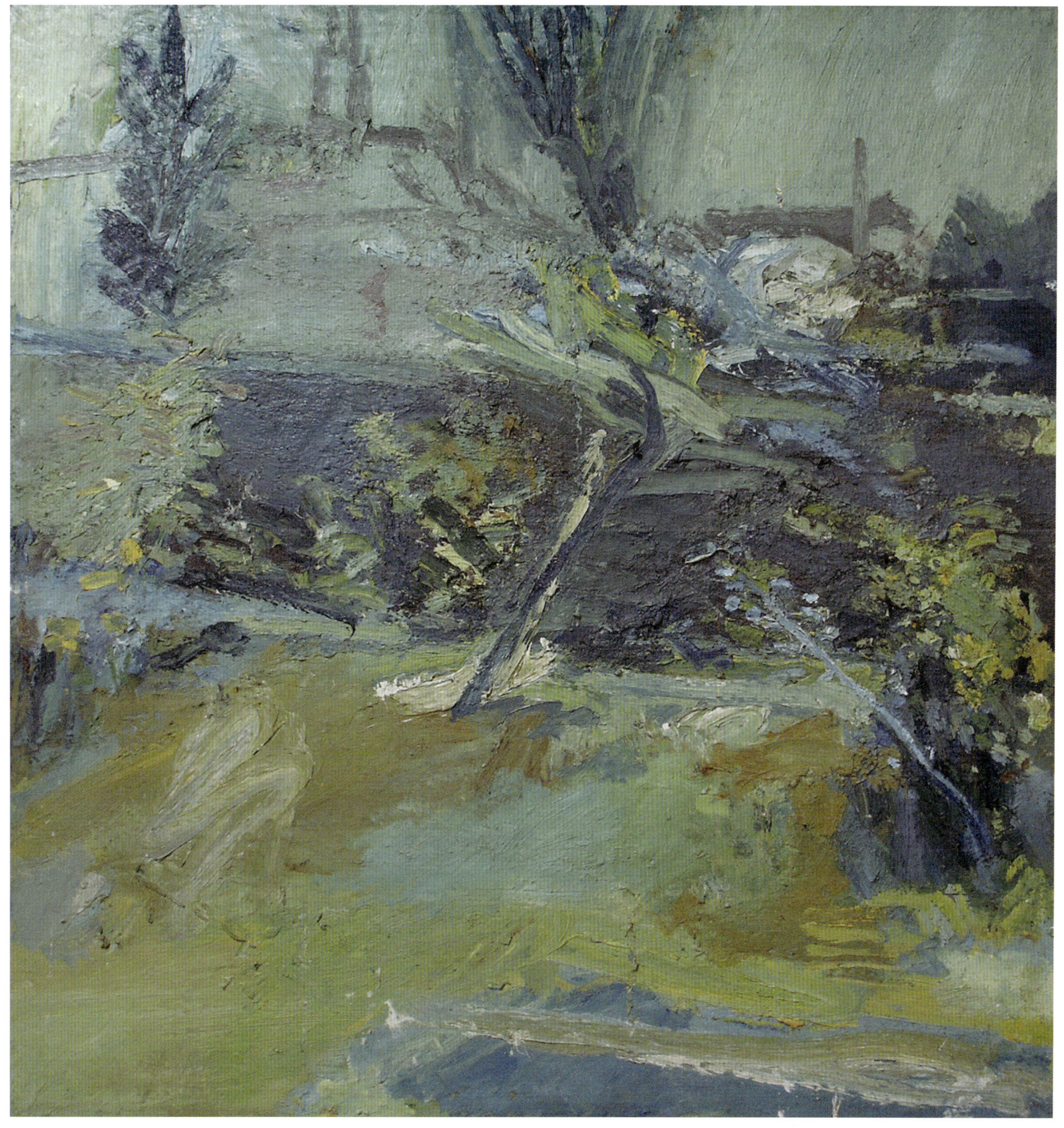

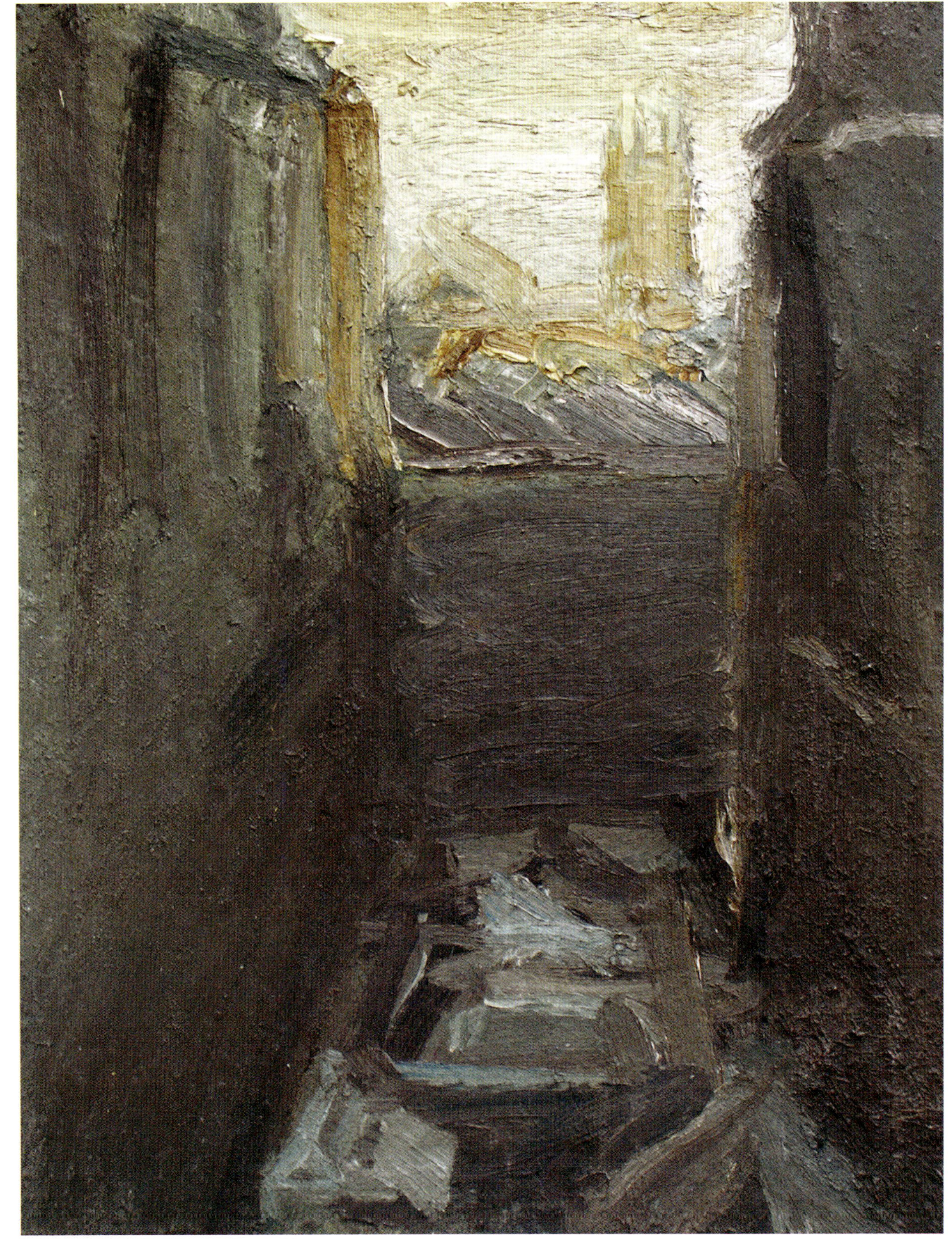

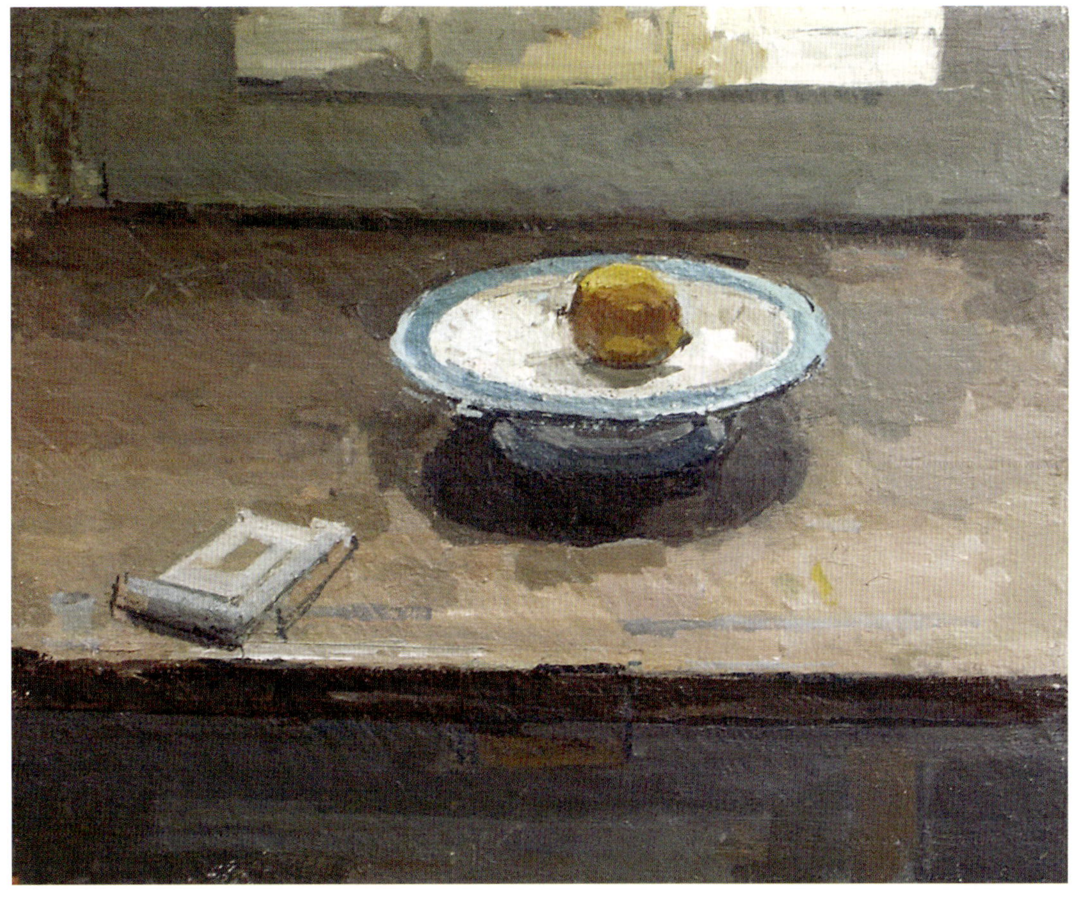

39
Compotiere and Lemon, 1970
Oil on board, 41x51cms

38
Between the RCA and the V&A, 1969
Oil on board, 102x76.5cms

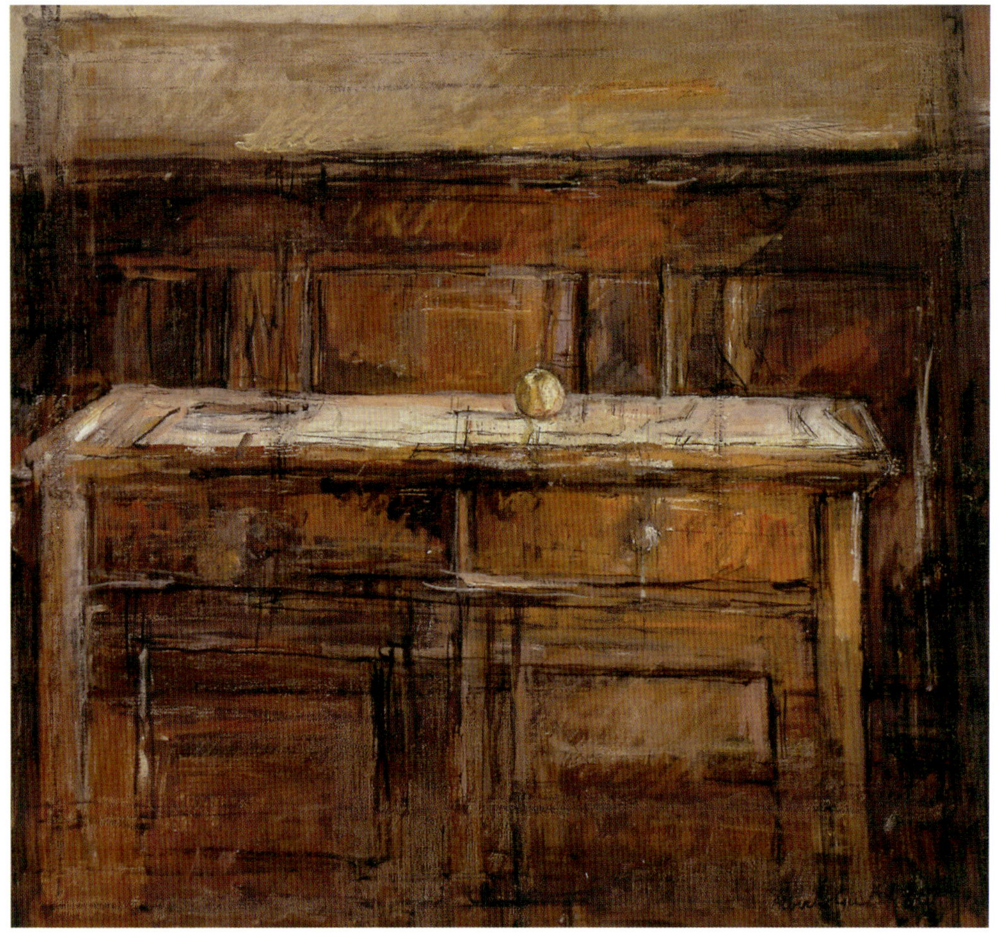

40
Apple on a Sideboard, 1937
Alberto Giacometti 72x75.5cms

41
Studio Table and Window, Putney, 1969
Oil on board, 40.5x49cms

Studio Table and Window, Putney (1969) Although painted around the same time as Summer Garden, this painting records the fact that Felcey had moved to a studio in Werter Road with a north-facing light. It is painted with a more restricted palette of black, yellow ochre and another brighter yellow. 'I found it very difficult to deal with colour. Most of those early paintings are monochromatic, they're tinted drawings in a way. Shortly after that I started to use colour.' Quite a dour picture of the painting table with paint pots and windows behind, it's actually quite light and employs rather effective shapes. Felcey was thinking of Giacometti – who'd had a big show at the Tate in 1966, just before he died – whom he admires a great deal. Of all Giacometti's work, the paintings speak most directly to him. Apple on a Sideboard (1937), for instance, was an inspiration to Felcey, particularly at this time. He says: 'I did a picture of three lemons on a table really thinking about that Giacometti and the trouble he took to locate things in space. One has the feeling that when Giacometti is painting or drawing he's actually trying to describe the space off his eyeball to the subject and you really feel that these things are pressed into a palpable atmosphere. That is such a fantastic quality and I think that was the quality I was after.'

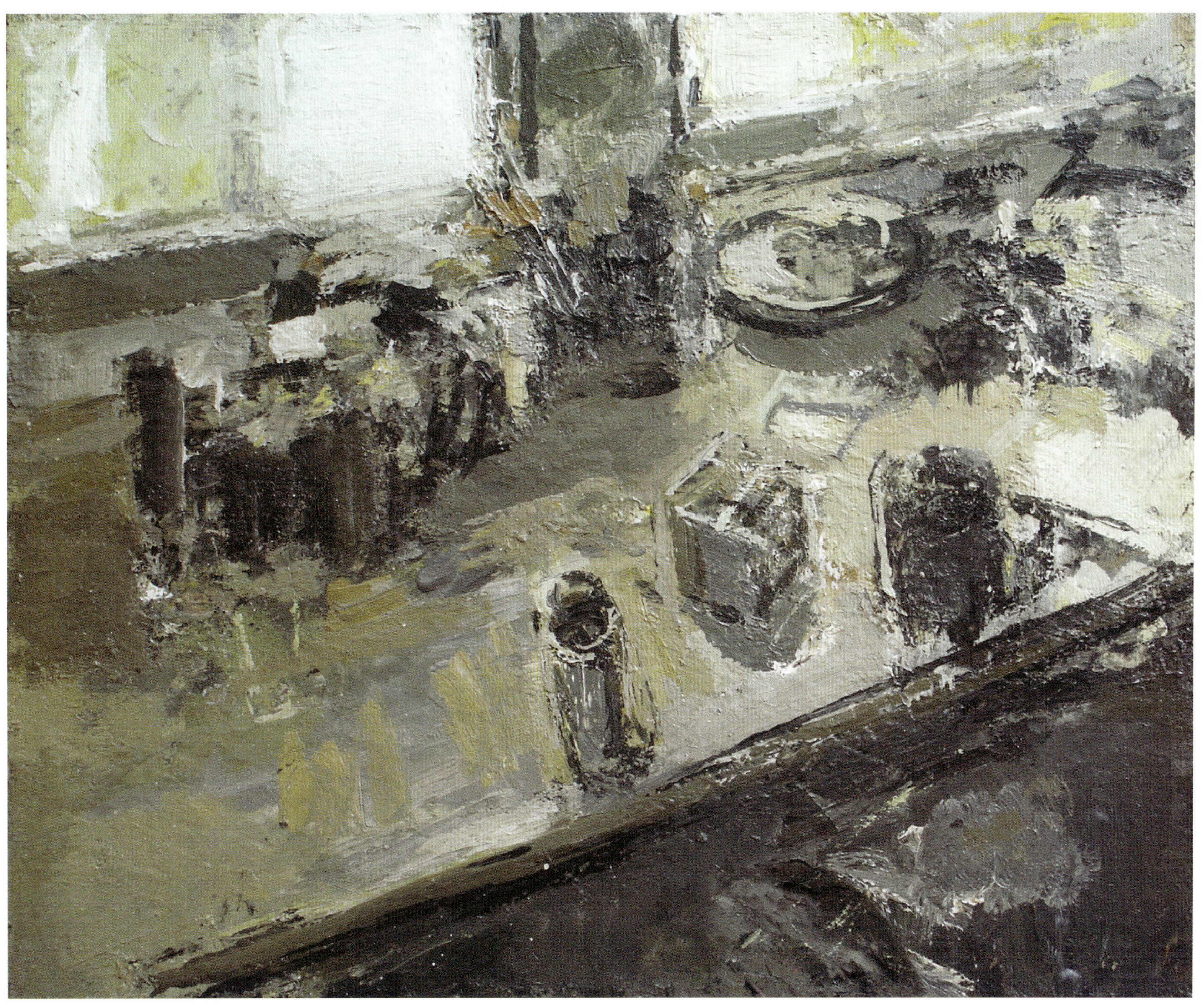

43

Carline Thistle, 1981

Oil on canvas, 59x46.2cms

Carline Thistle (1981) superficially resembles a Uglow painting, and his influence is, as Felcey admits, 'still visible' in it. It depicts the big head of a dried thistle he brought back from Switzerland – 'really beautiful' – and represents at least a month's work. 'In a way I think it was a bit of a breakthrough, this picture. I was using thicker paint than I'd used for a long time – it's much more physical – and also this idea of composite mixtures. It's important that the colours are not well-mixed and that you have the composition visible, the fact that it's made up. It gives it a kind of sparkle, laying out the palette on the painting. Years later, looking at Chardin, I realized that he actually does that. (Like his paintings of plums, which are all red and green, and then on the table are these two marks – a red mark and a green mark. They don't actually denote anything, just the palette.)' The shape behind is not a window but a stretcher leaning against the wall, making a narrow space. The lovely blue is a little reminiscent of the Reckitts Blue Uglow used. Notice how the contours are breaking down more, and the centre starts to be more important.

44

Richmond Oak, 1979

Charcoal on paper

71x91.5cms

45

Richmond Oak, Winter, 1980

Charcoal on paper

53.5x79cms

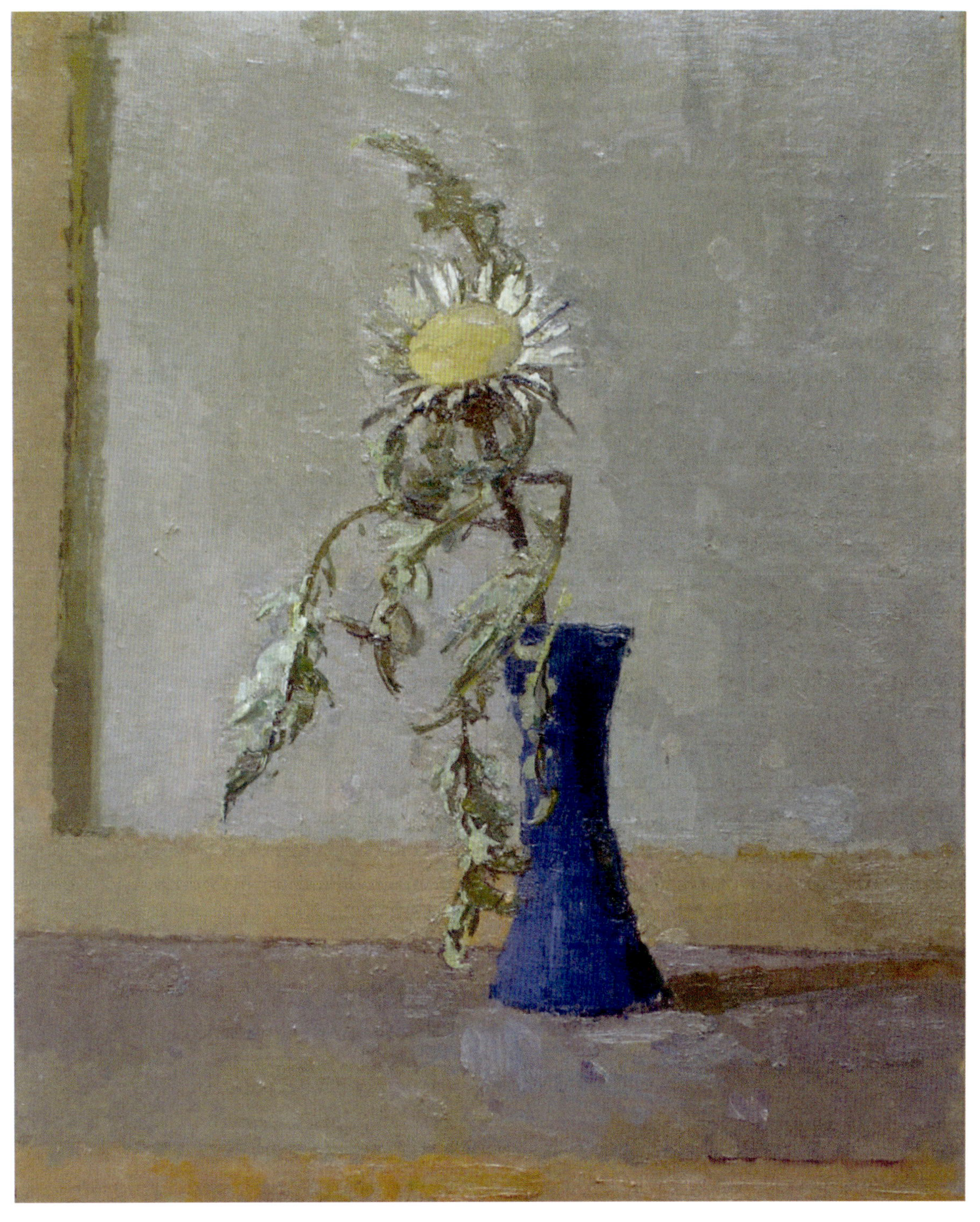

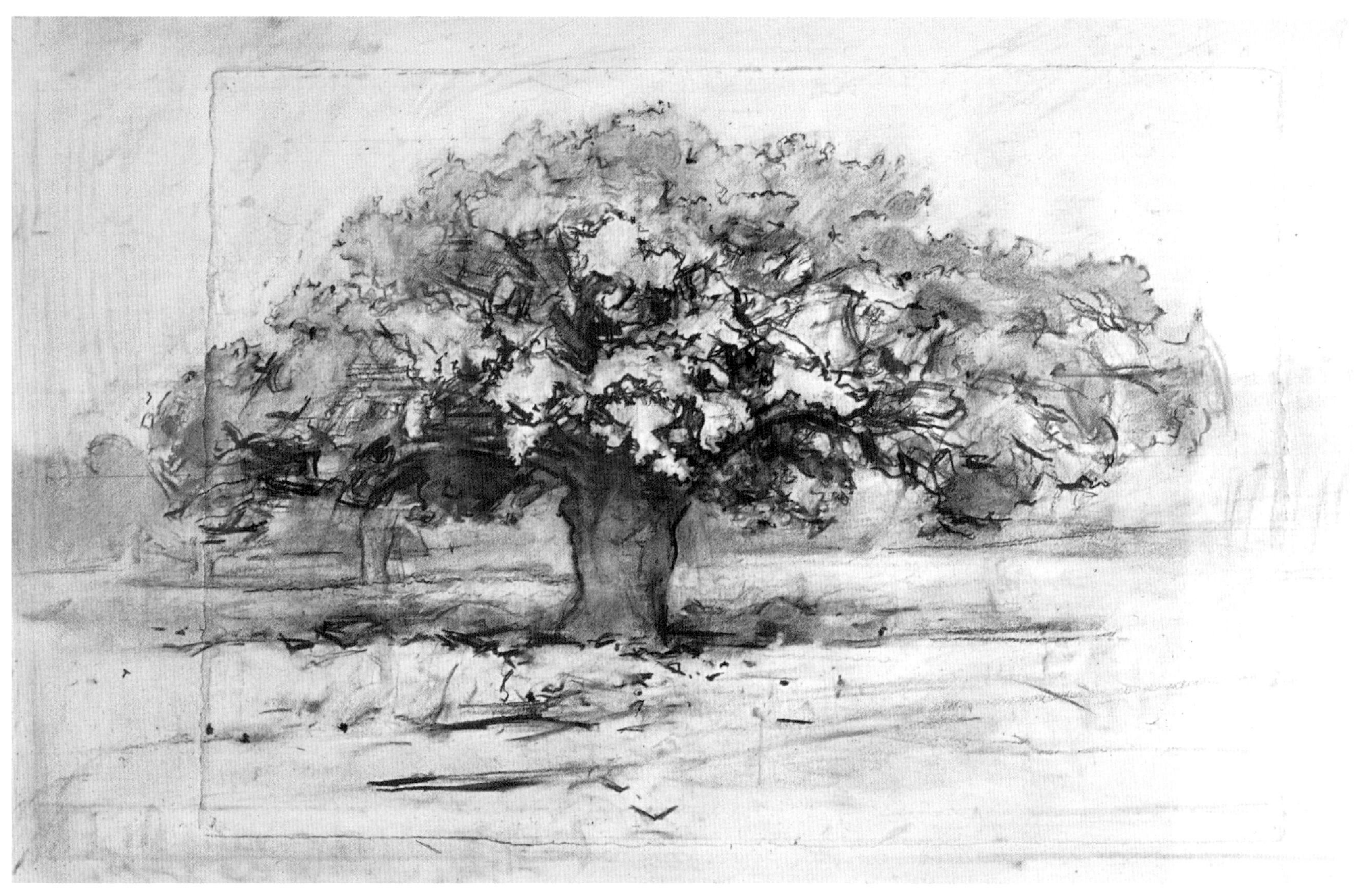

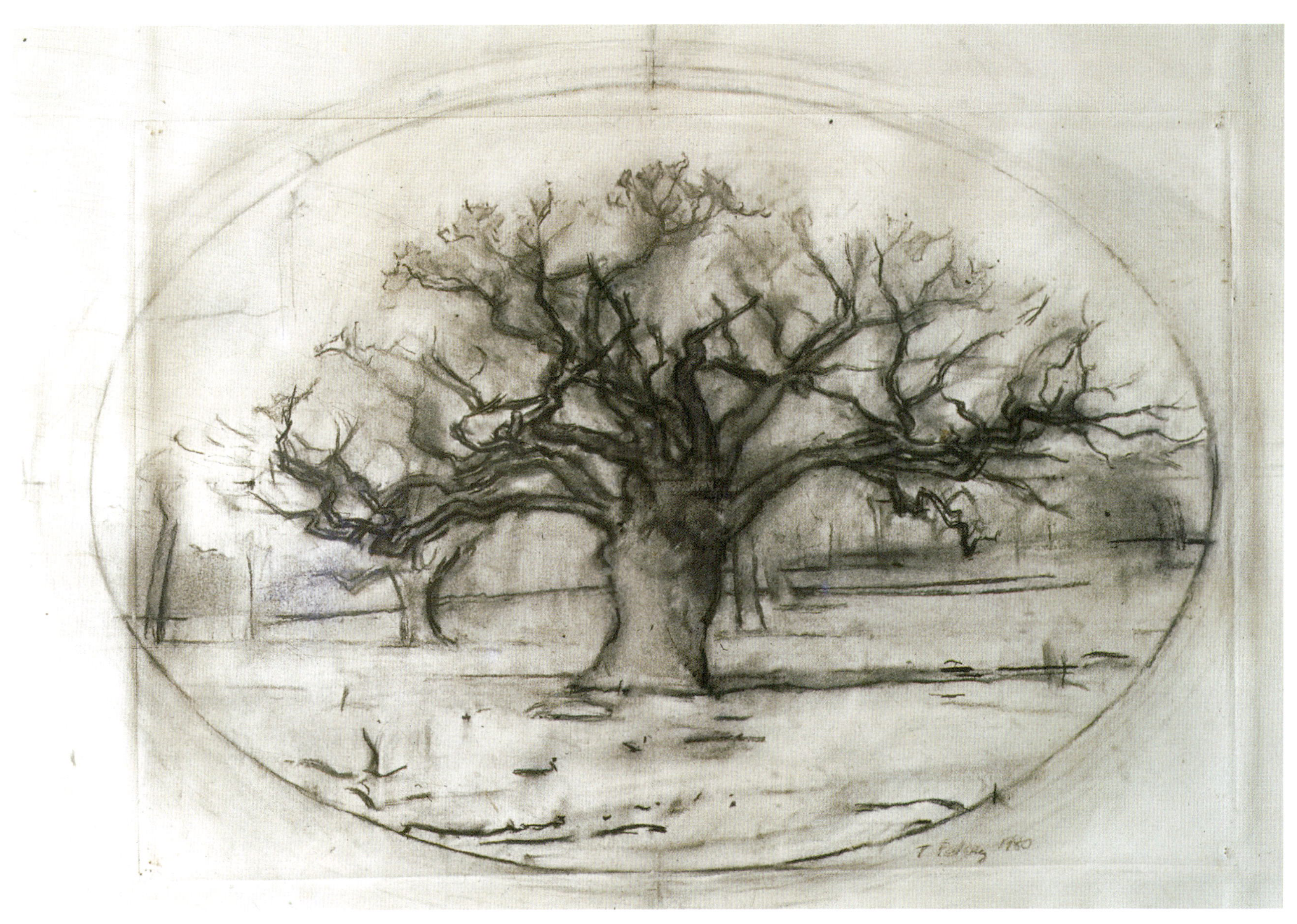

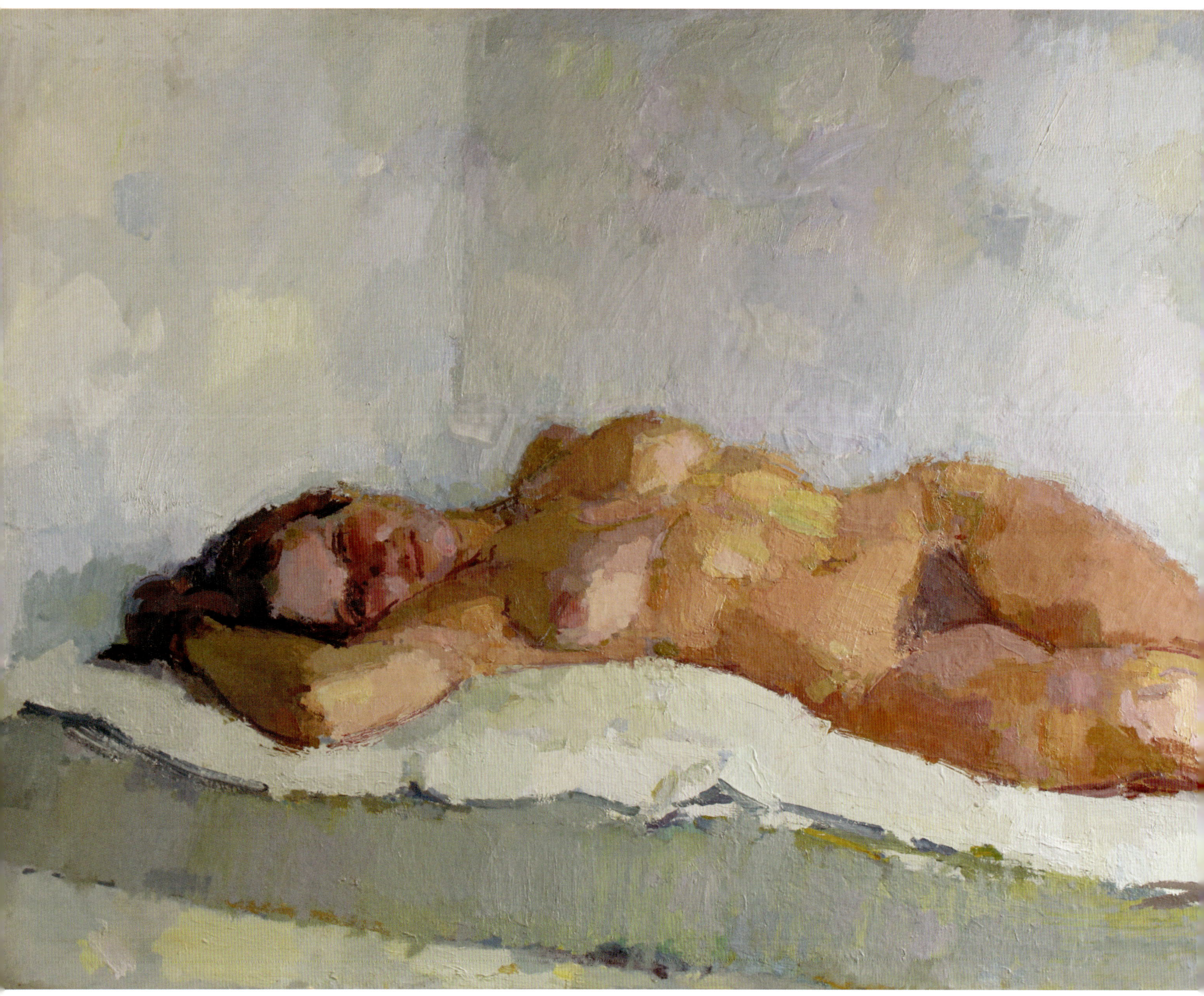

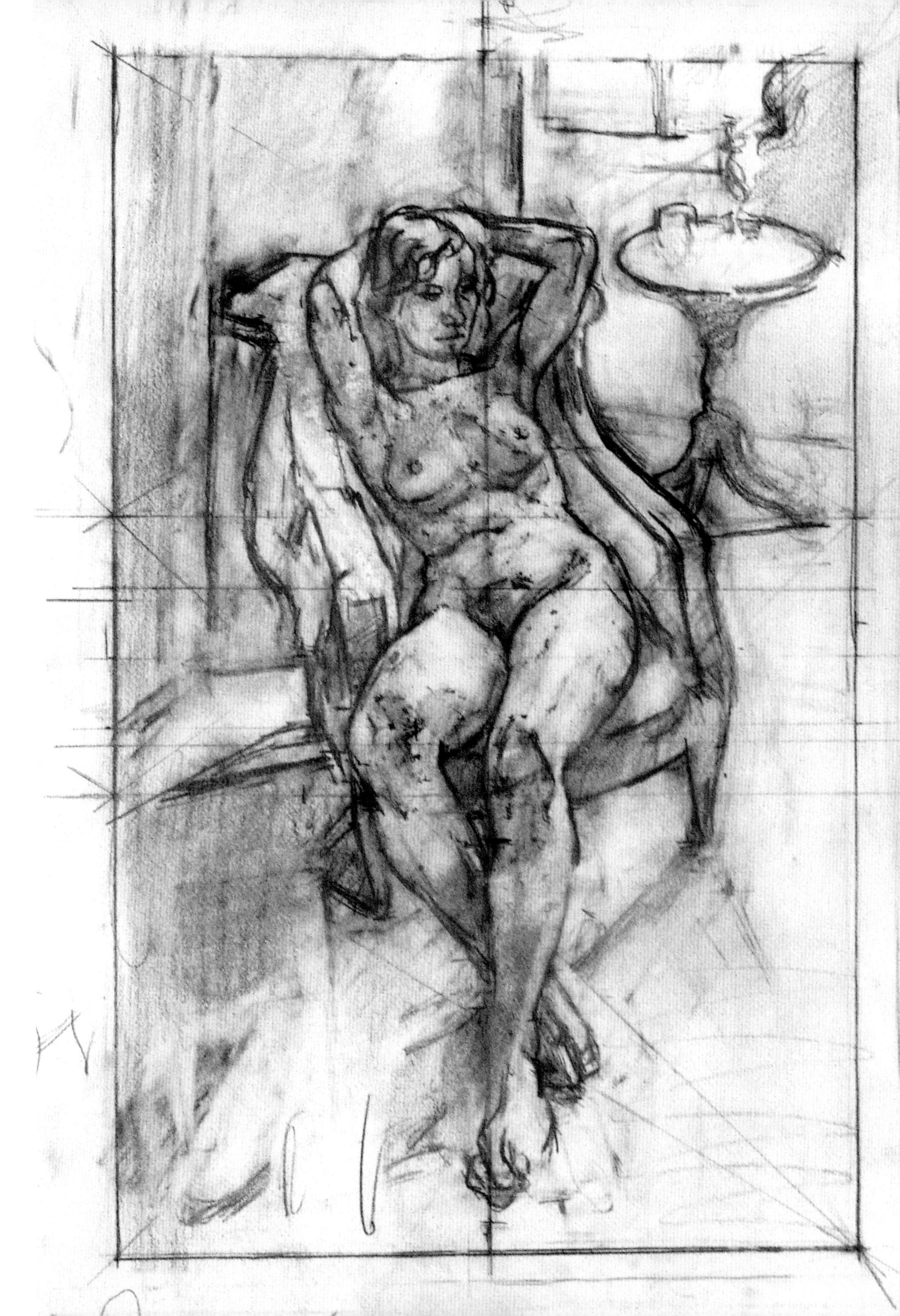

47
Working drawing, 1984
Pencil on paper, 41x25.5cms

46
Katy 1980
Oil on canvas, 95x122cms

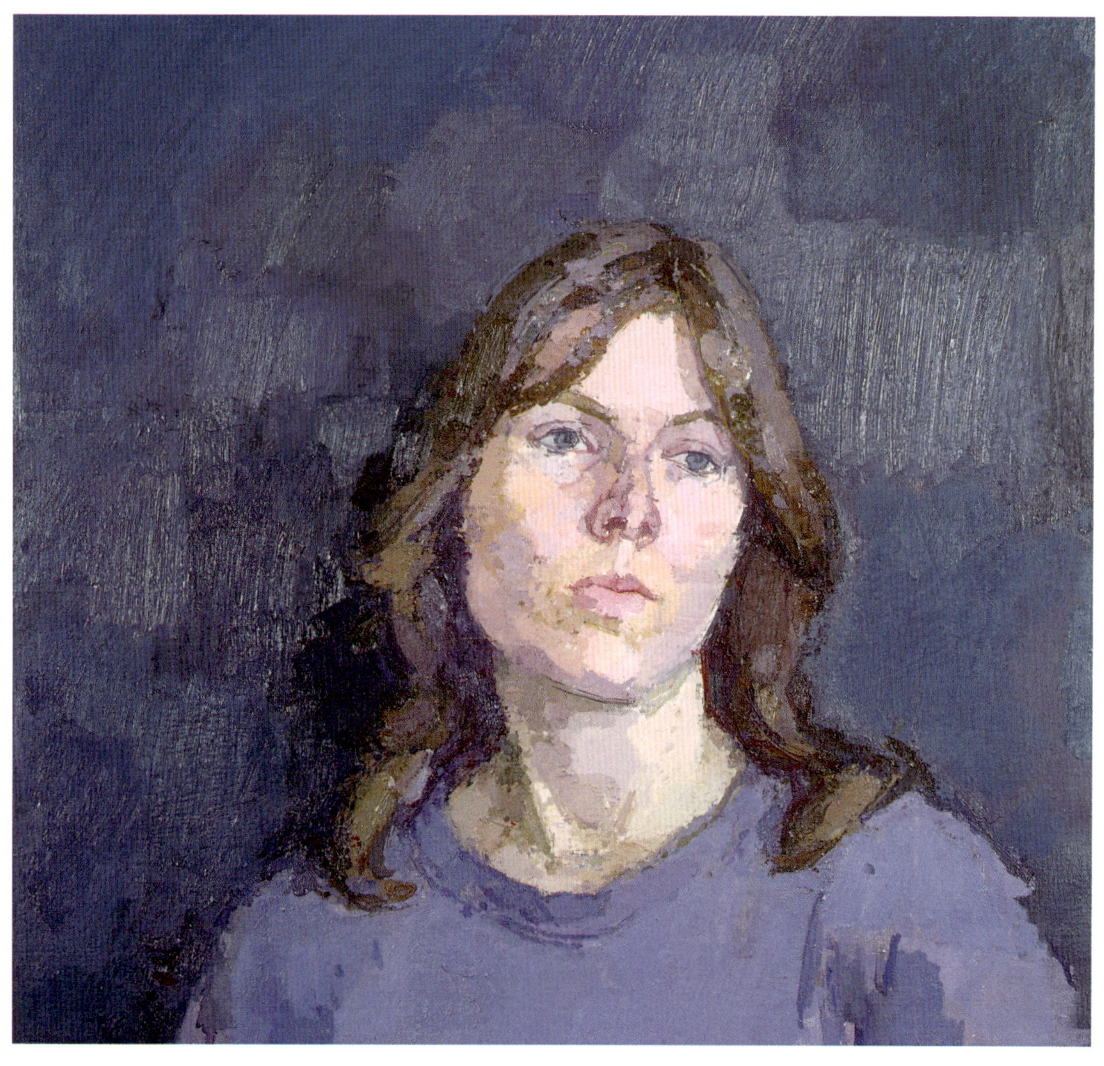

48
Portrait of Sarah, 1982
Oil on canvas, 51.5x56cms

49, left
Wimbledon Arch II, 1982
Oil on canvas, 76.3x45.7cms

49, right
Oak Arch, 1979
Oil on canvas, 71x91.5cms

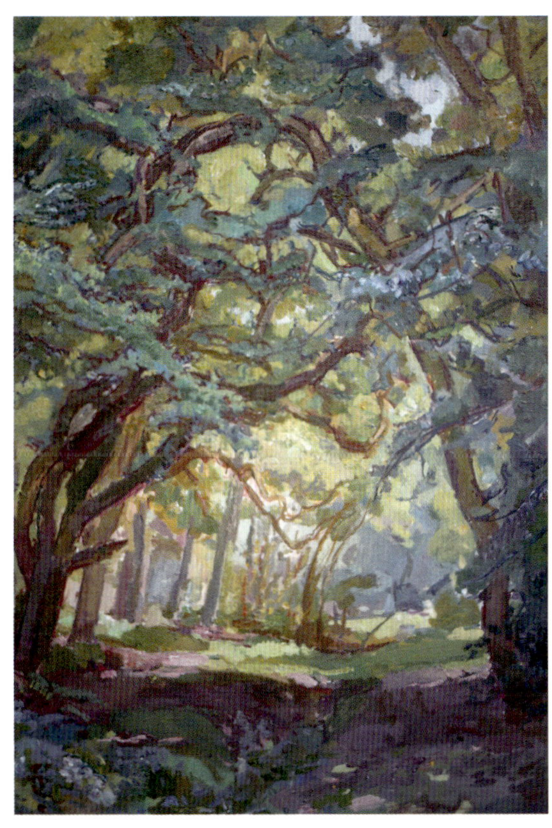

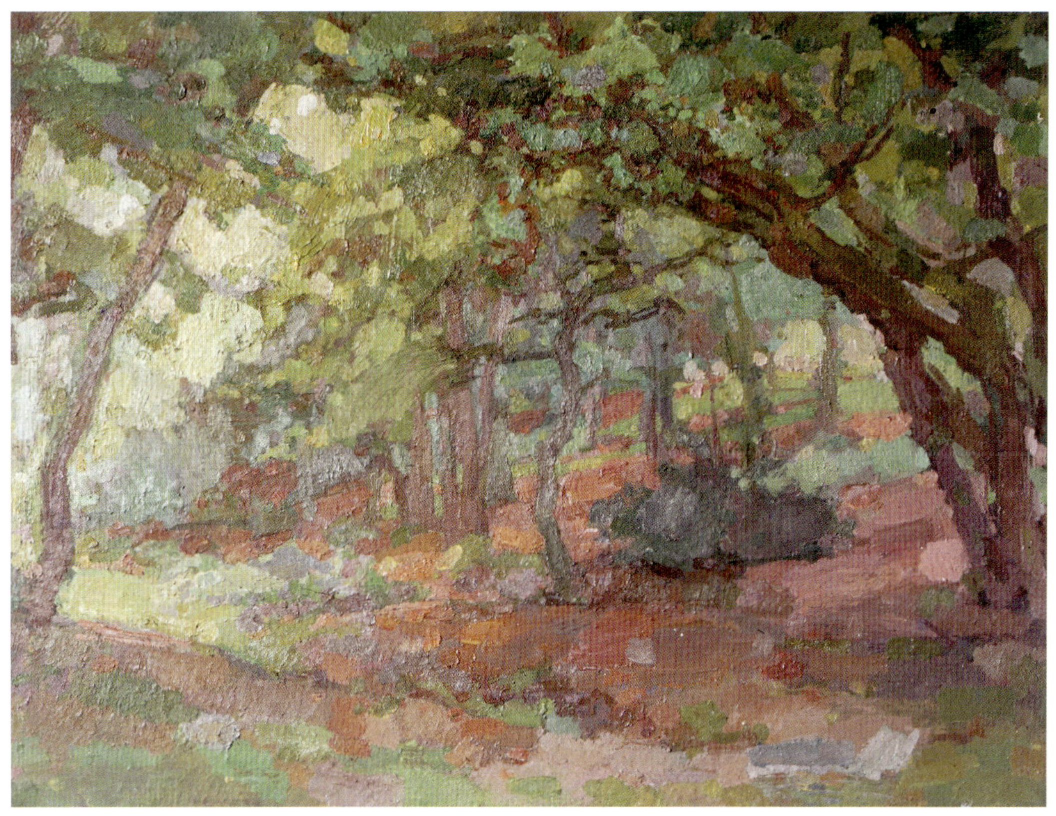

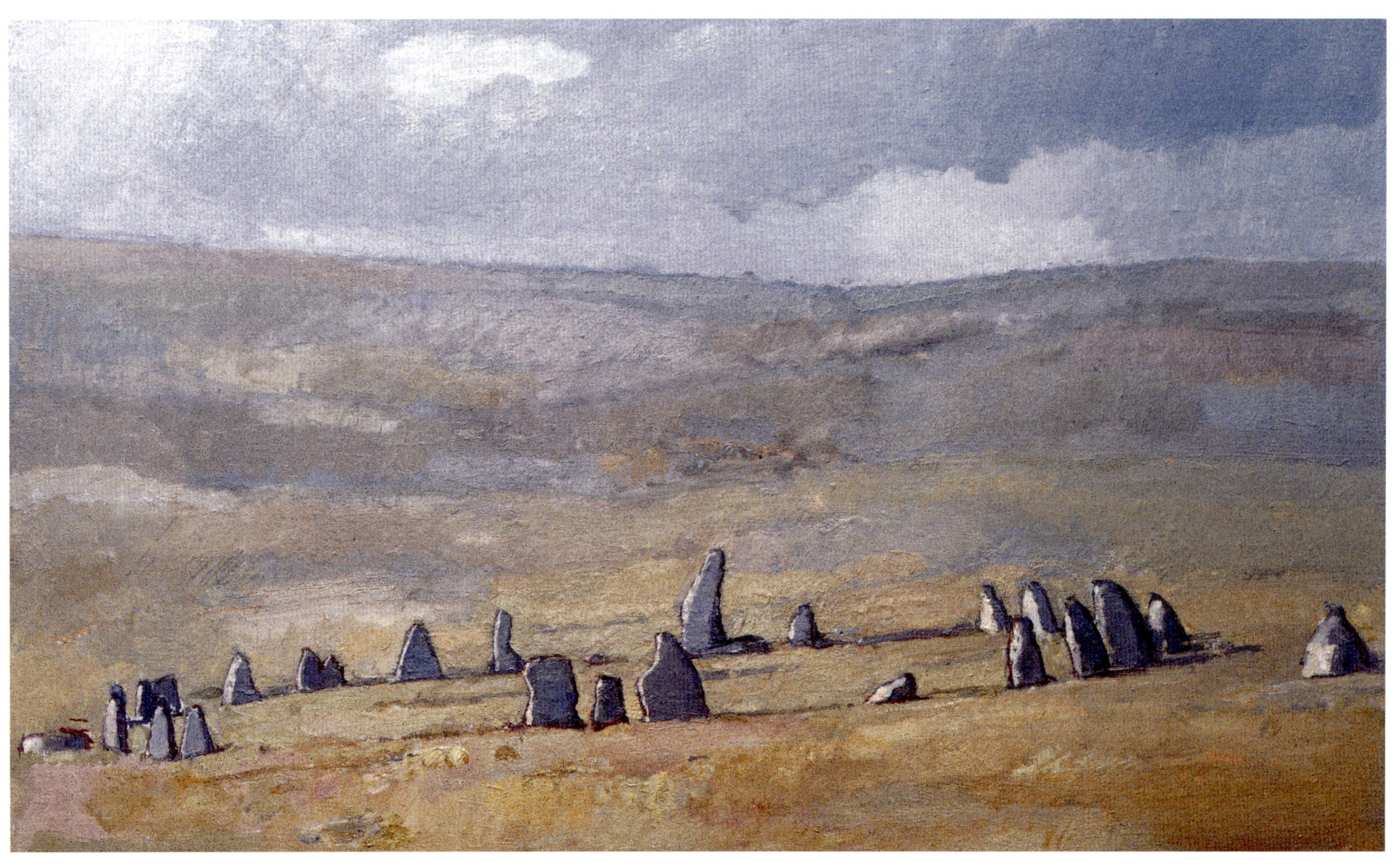

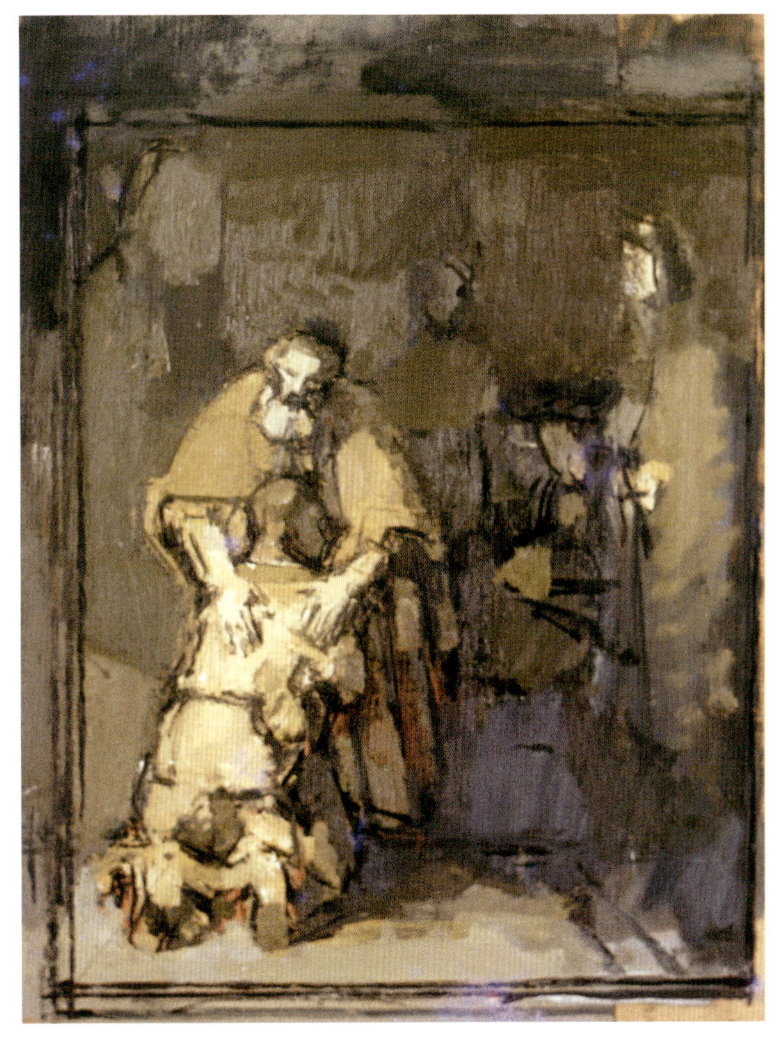

50
Scorhill Stone Circle, 1990
Oil on canvas, 46x76cms

51
After Rembrandt, 1981
Oil on board, 40.8x29.4cms

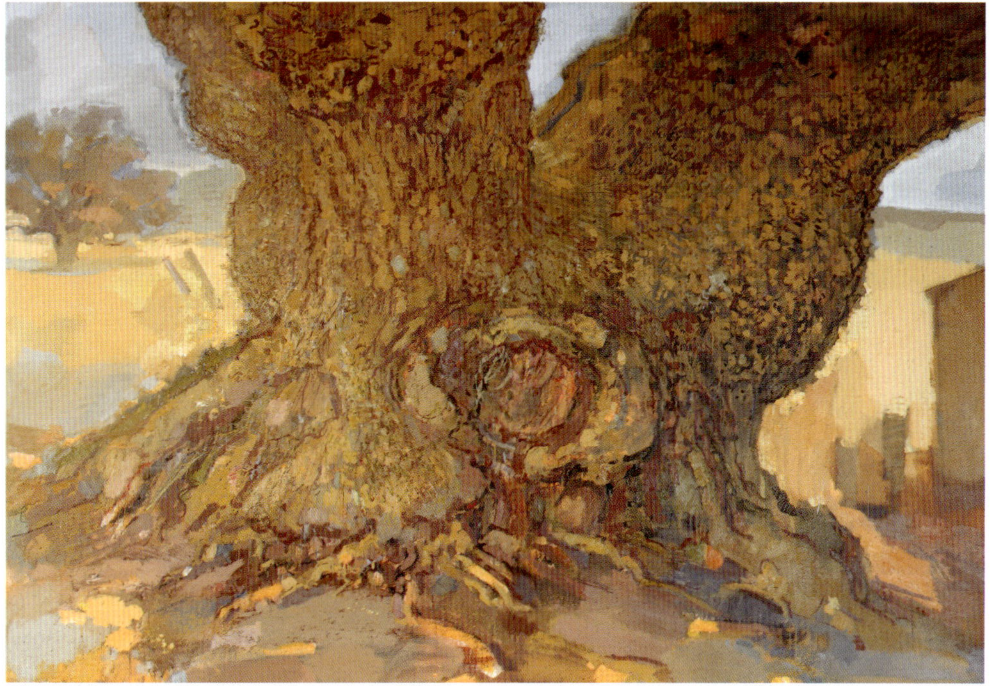

52
The Bole of the Oak, 1990–93
Oil on canvas, 165x239cms

53
The Bole of the Oak, 1993–96,
Oil on canvas, 165x239cms

The Bole of the Oak – there are two versions of this painting, both the same dimensions and each painted over three years, 1990–93 and 1993–96. In those days, teaching was a great interruption to working. Felcey would spend two days a week in London teaching at the Byam Shaw, but the disruption was in fact far greater than that to the daily work rhythm. They are both paintings of the tree outside Felcey's studio. Besides the obvious attractions of the massive trunk, Felcey was interested in capturing the space behind it. Of the second version he has said: 'I'm just trying to paint across the oak as though it's the world'. No small ambition.

54
Working Drawing for Bole of the Oak, 1993–96
Pencil on paper, 28x40cms

55
Bole of the Oak, 1993
Oil on board, 110x128cms

56
Beyond the Bole of the Oak, 1993
Acrylic on canvas, 179x224cms

57
Bole of the Oak, 1993
Acrylic on canvas, 140x160cms

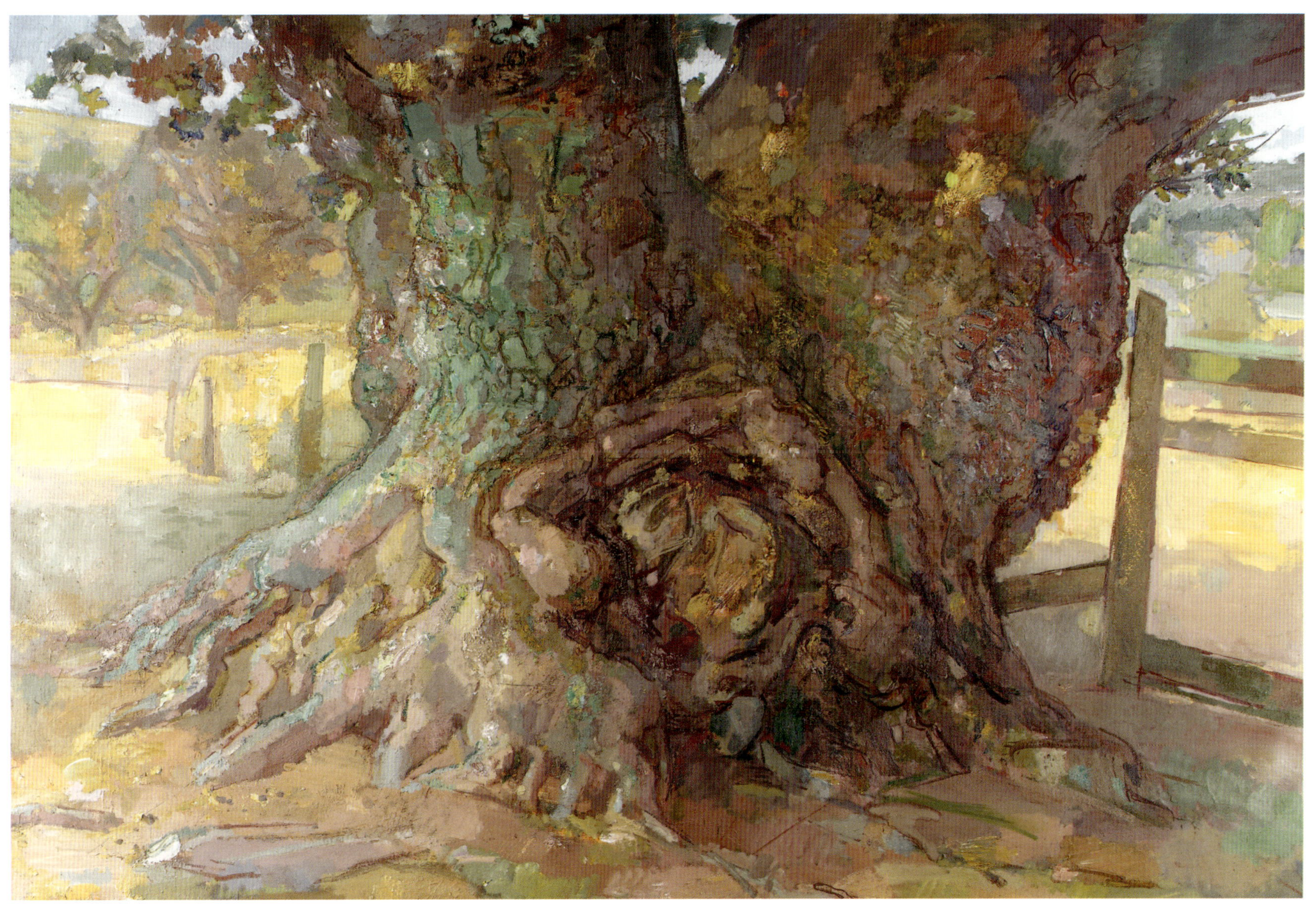

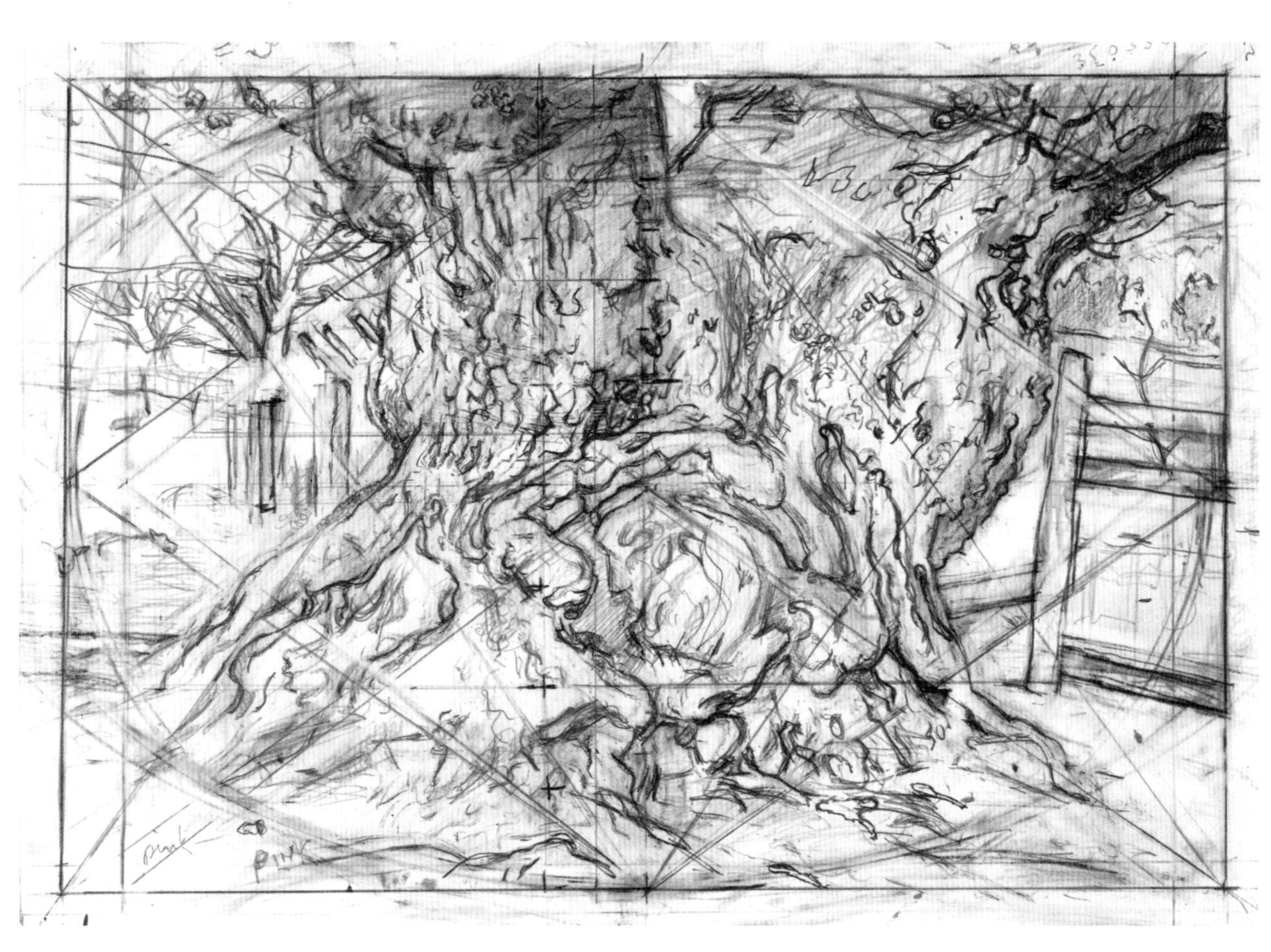

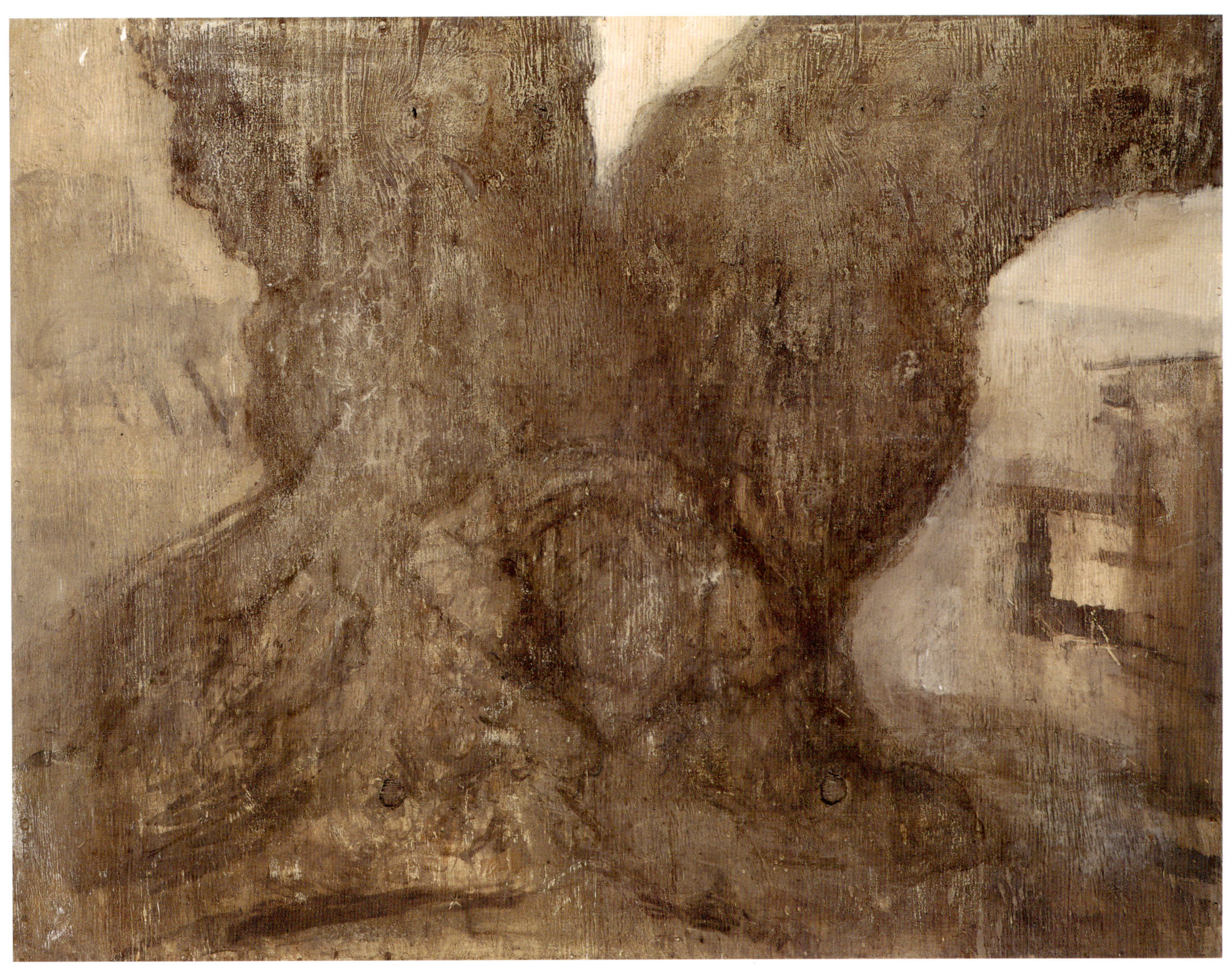

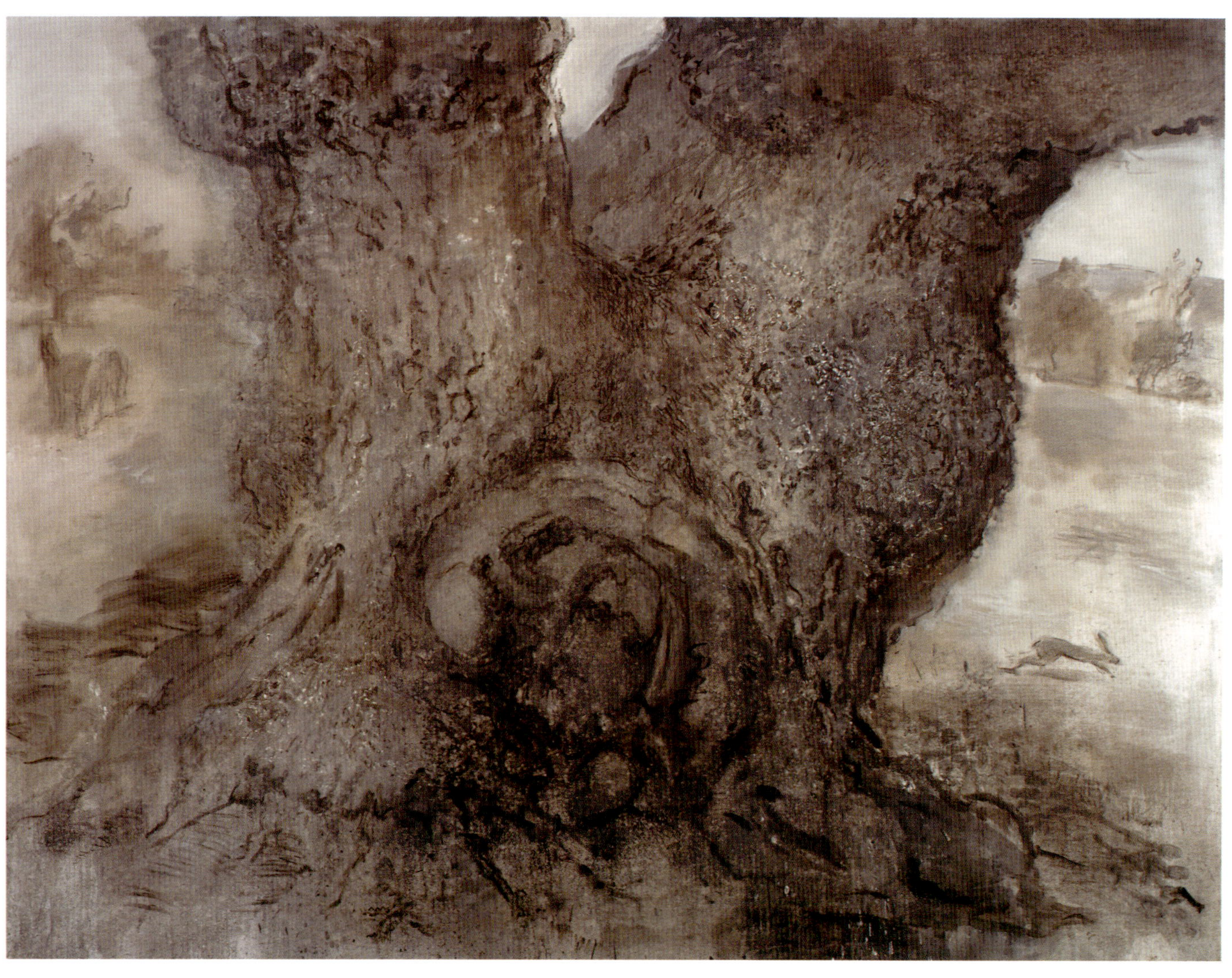

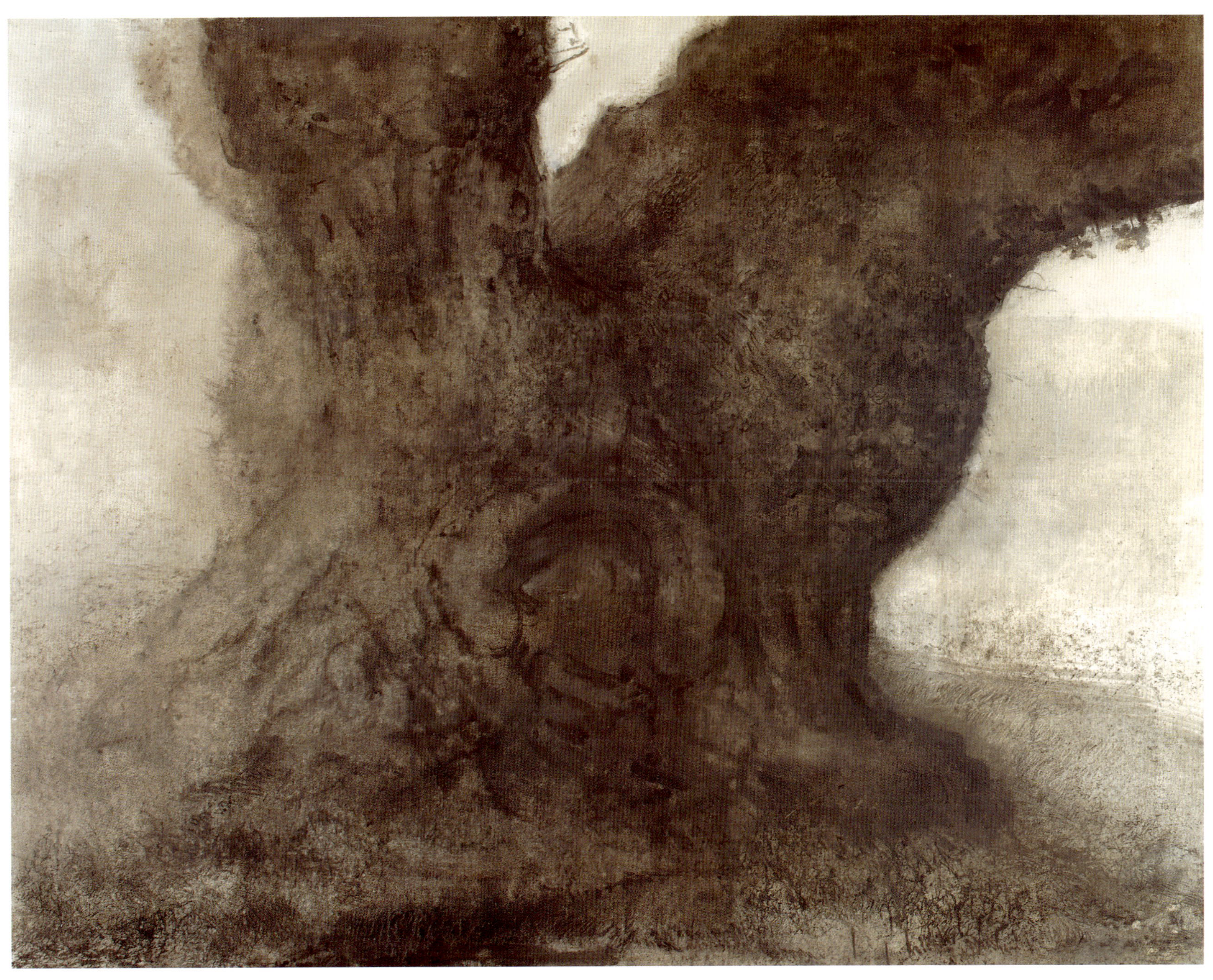

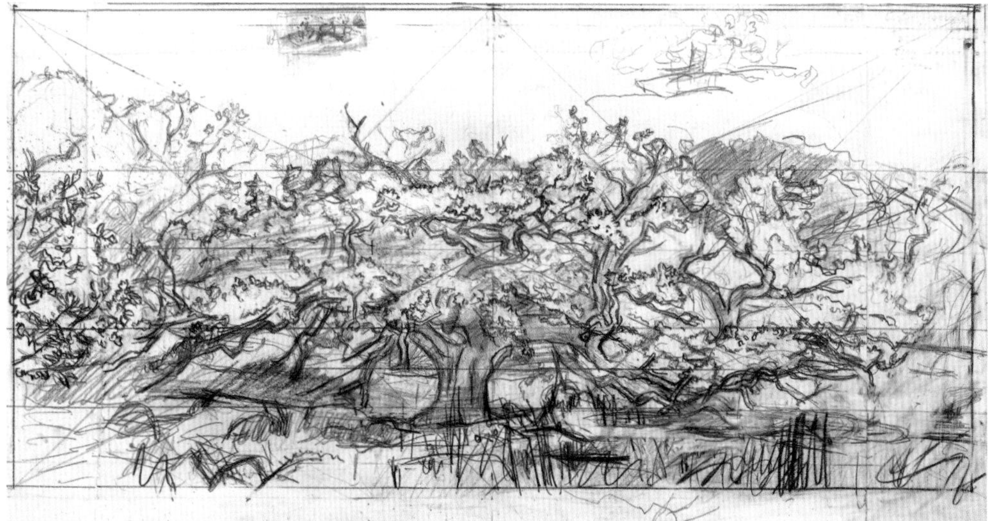

58
Working Drawing for Whiddon Oak,
Summer, 1998
Pencil, 30x60cms

59
Whiddon Oak,
Summer, No. I, 1997
Oil on canvas, 76x152cms

Whiddon Oak Summer Nos I, II & III. Felcey made three versions of much the same view of the Whiddon Oak in summer. The first dates to 1997 and shows the tree with early morning light coming through the foliage in a magical dappling of sunlight. The paint is dabbed on, applied in quite heavy impasto, as if crusted with light. The first is predominantly green. The second, painted the following year, appears to be blue, though the palette of its making included alizarin, green, ultramarine and yellow ochre. The third, also painted in the summer of 1998, is golden in appearance, depending on a palette composed of Indian yellow, cadmium yellow, burnt sienna, alizarin and cerulean blue. Felcey is a devotee of alizarin crimson because of its transparency. In this trio of paintings we are shown the three periods of summer: the early, succulent hopeful stage; the blue heat of maturity; and the burnt russet tones of high summer verging on autumn, all mellow fruitfulness.

60
Whiddon Oak,
Summer, No. II, 1998
Oil on canvas, 76x152cms

61
Whiddon Oak,
Summer, No. III, 1998
Oil on canvas, 76x152cms

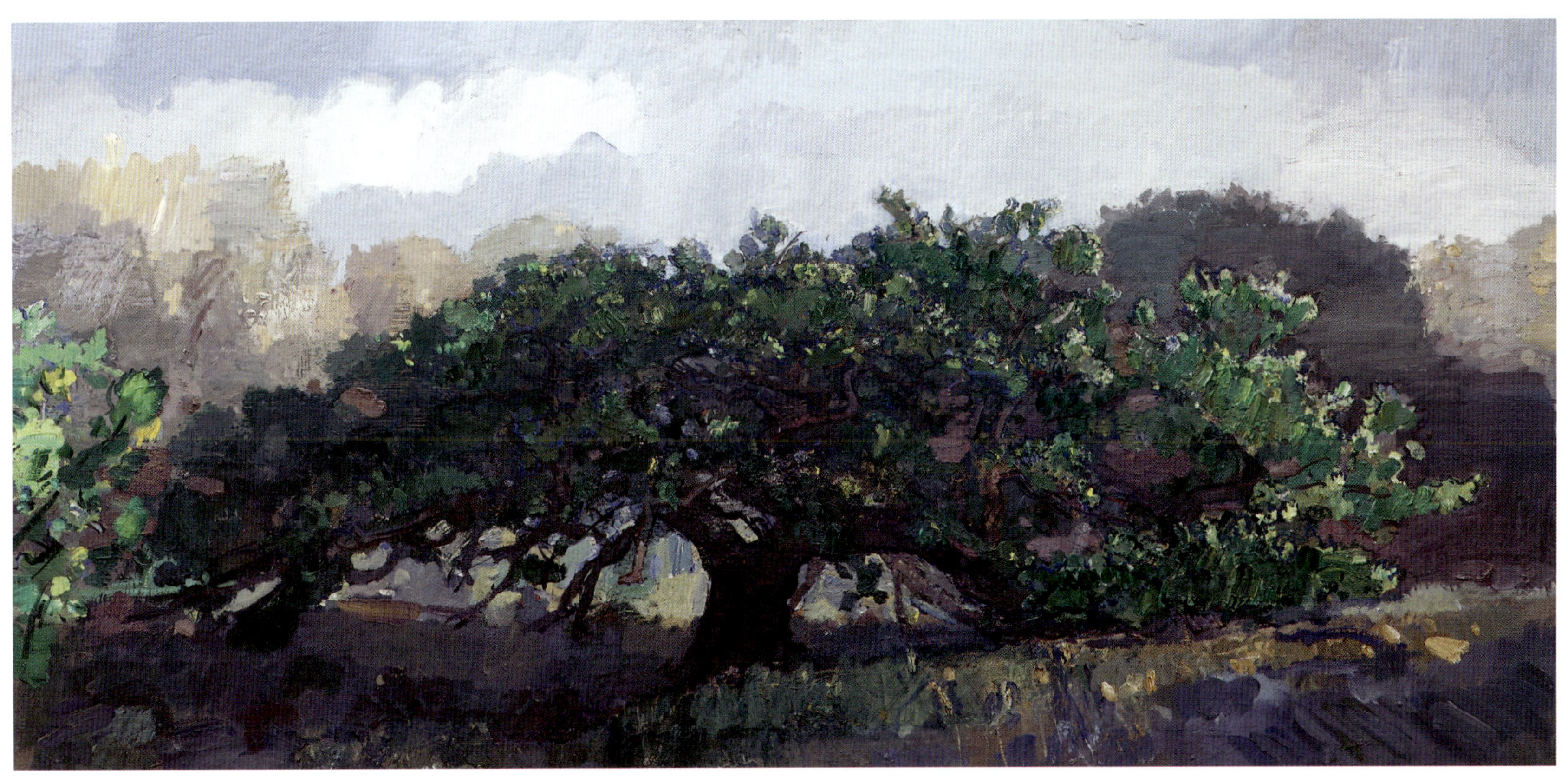

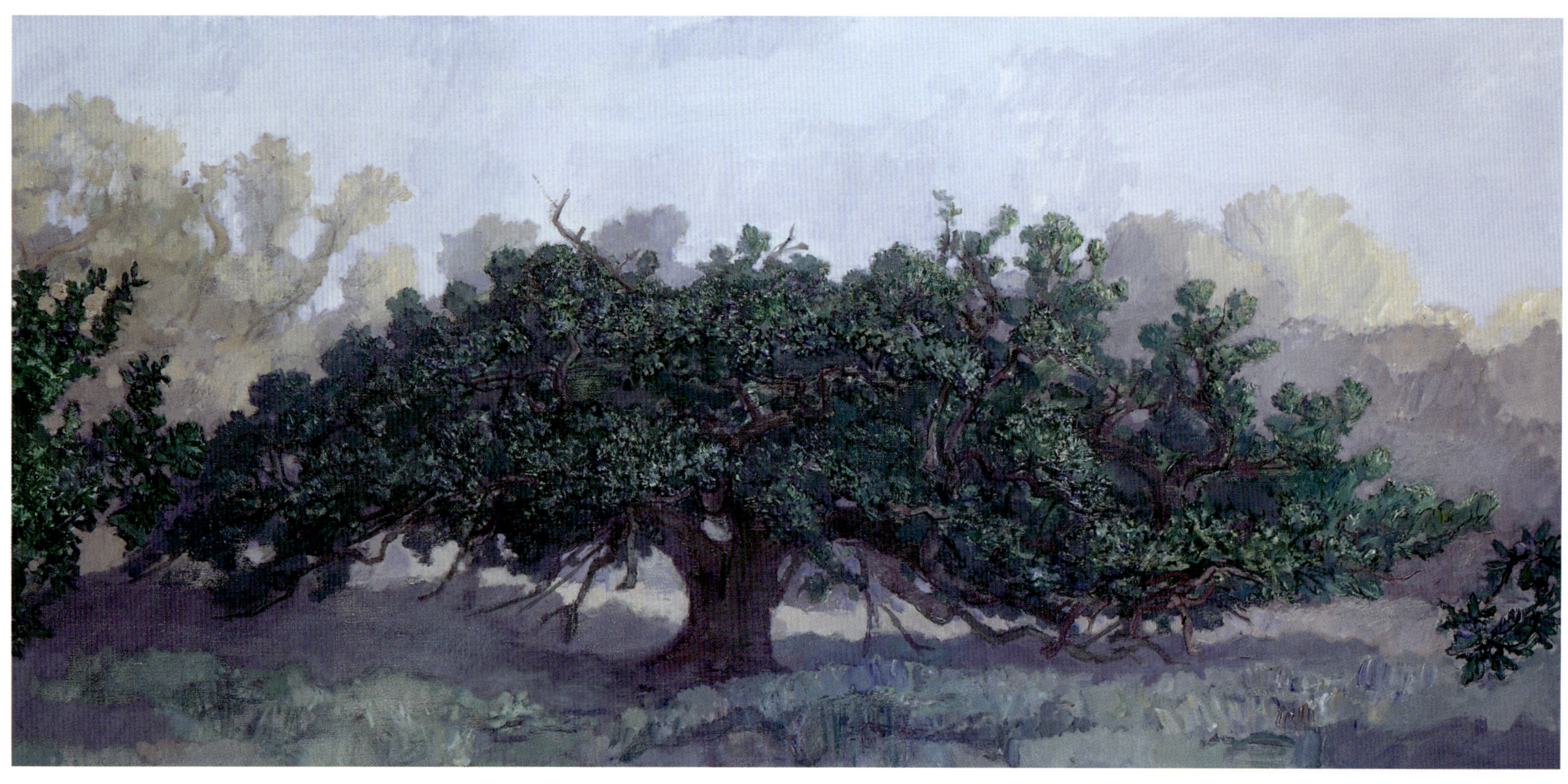

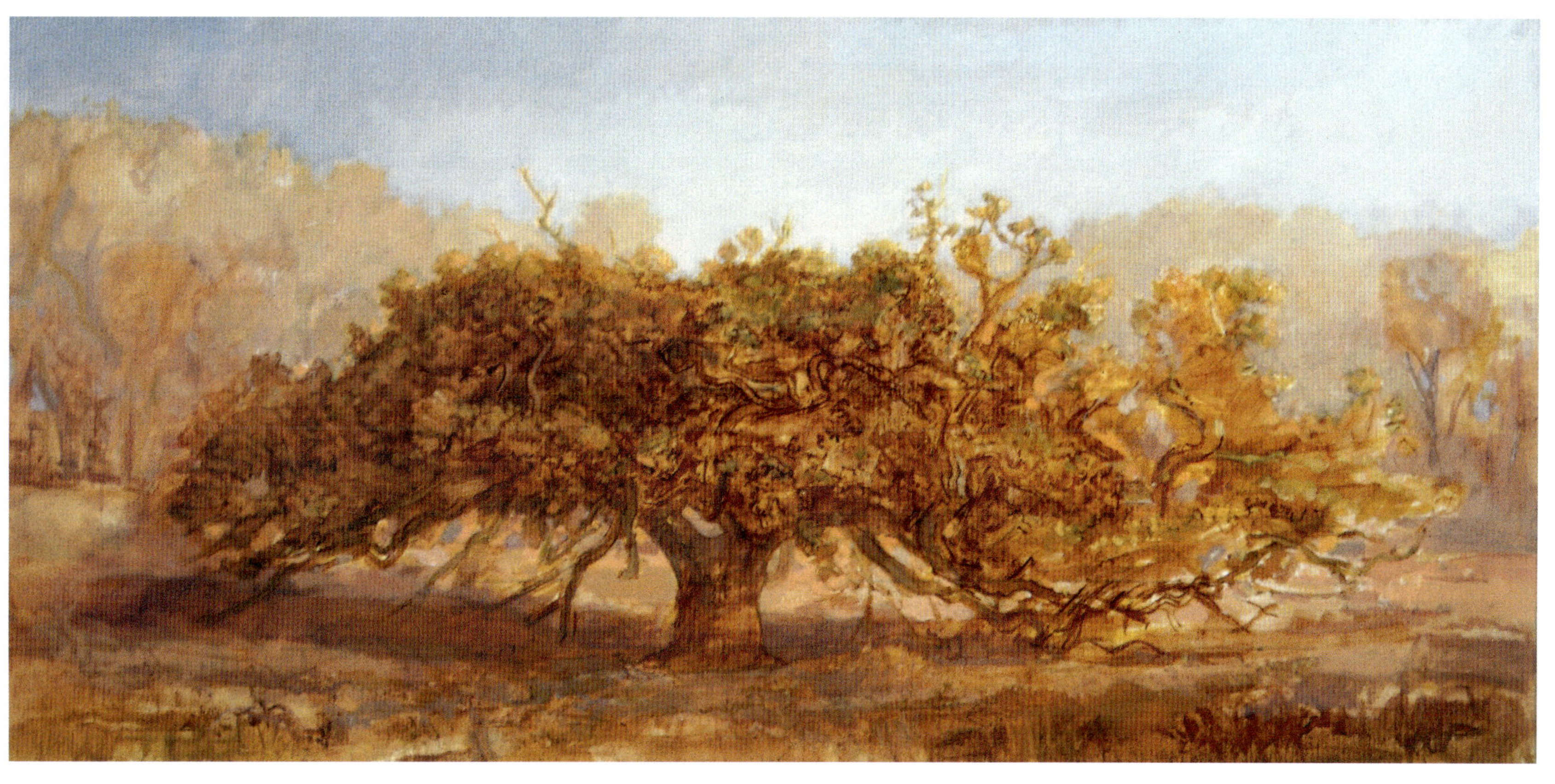

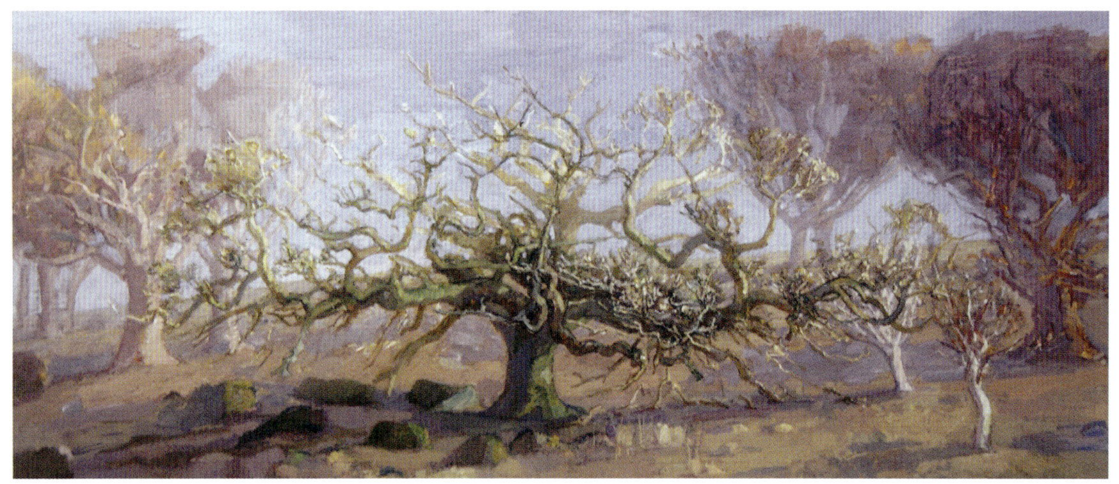

62
The Whiddon Oak, Winter, 1998-99
Oil on canvas, 103x237cms

The Whiddon Oak, Winter (1998-99) is a real contrast, writhing like Medusa's locks, more like a naked root system than branches, so stark and contorted are they. The lighting accentuates this effect: lit brutally by low raking light against a bright blue sky, the branches have nowhere to hide. The problem was to stop them moving about: it took Felcey a great deal of thought and effort, of trial and error, to make the picture still. It was a matter of locking all the individual elements of the composition together – the central tree with its smaller satellites and rocks – into a harmonious whole.

63
Whiddon Oak, Winter, 1997
Oil on canvas, 103x237cms

64
Studies for Winter Oak, 1997–98
Pencil on paper, 21x26.5cms

65, top
Whiddon Oak, 1998
Drypoint, 10.5x21.8cms

65, bottom
Working Drawing for Whiddon Oak, Winter, 1998
Pencil on paper, 38x80cms

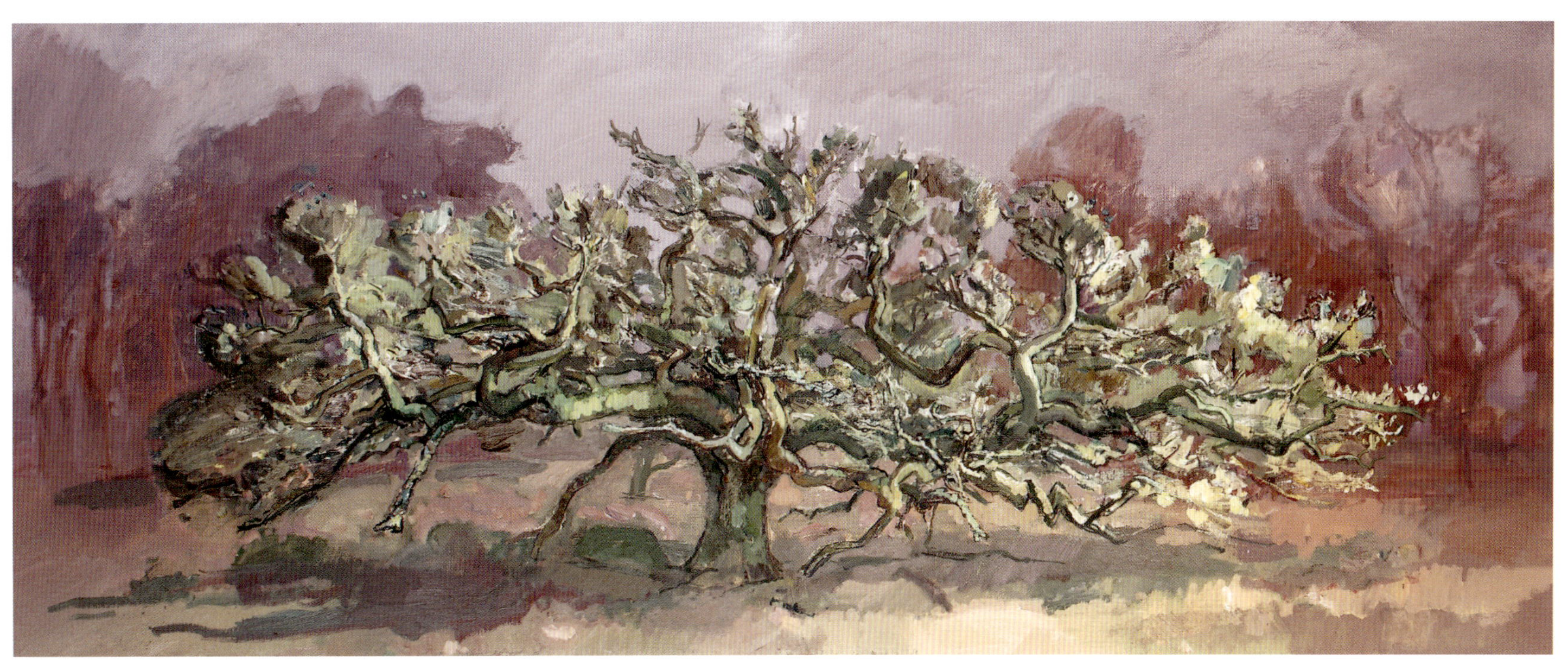

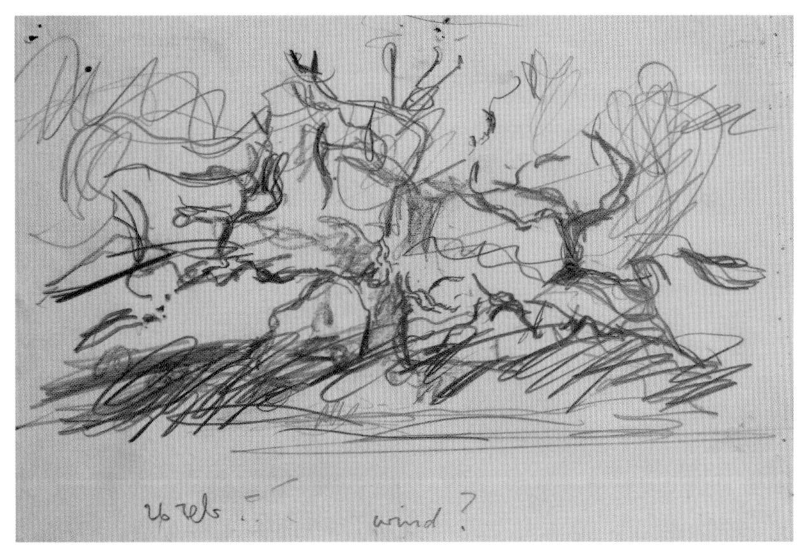
wind ?

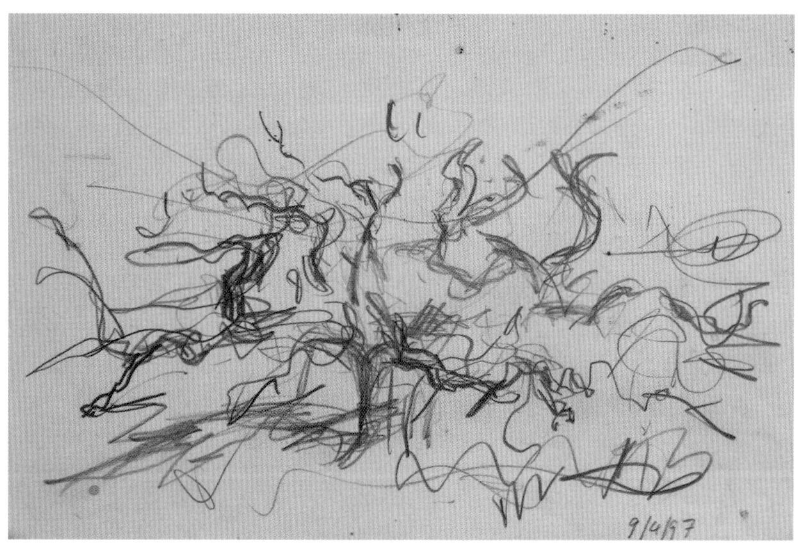
9/4/97

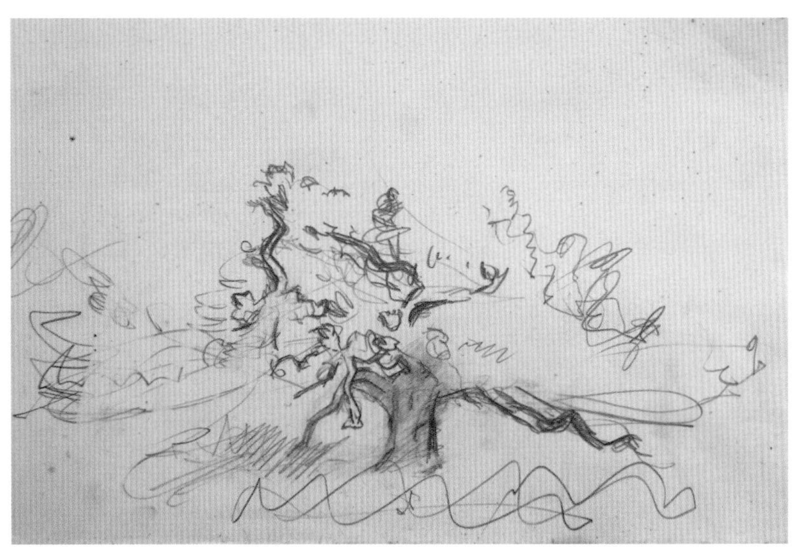

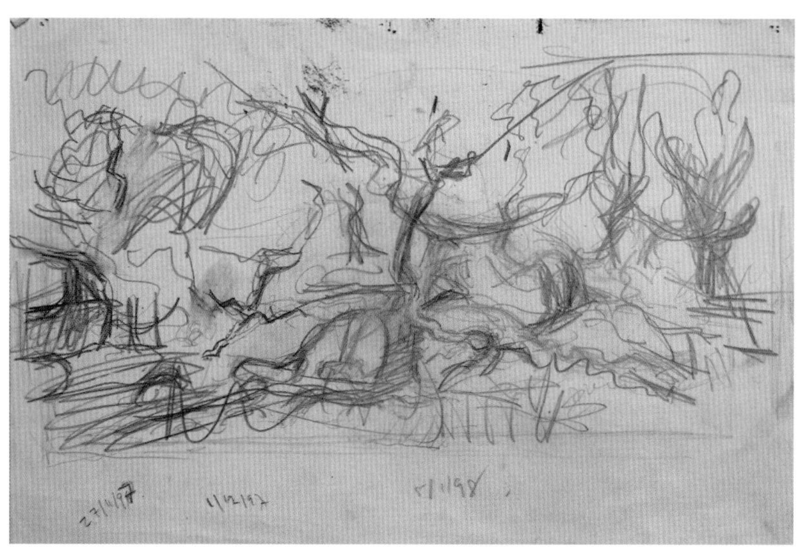

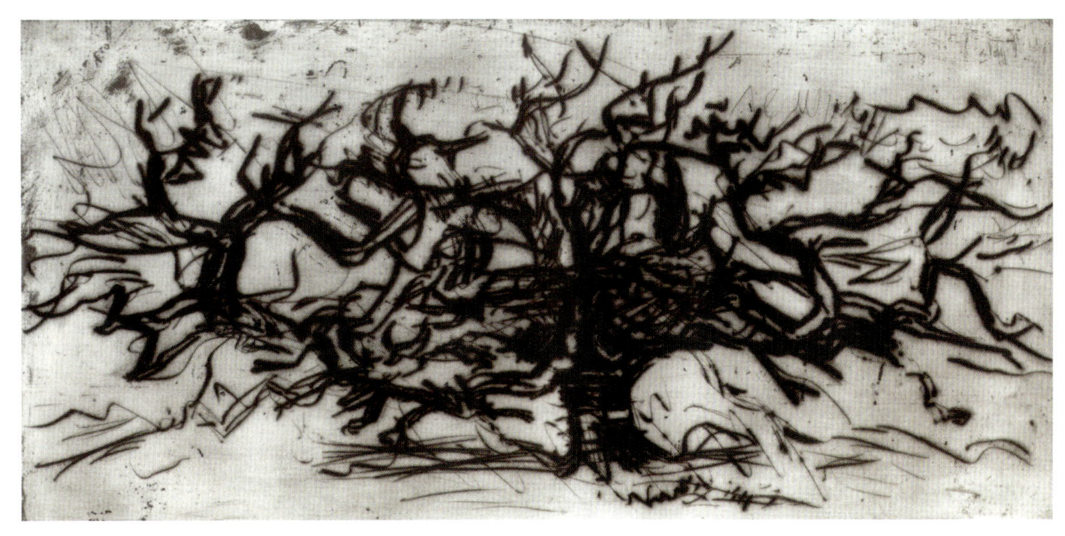

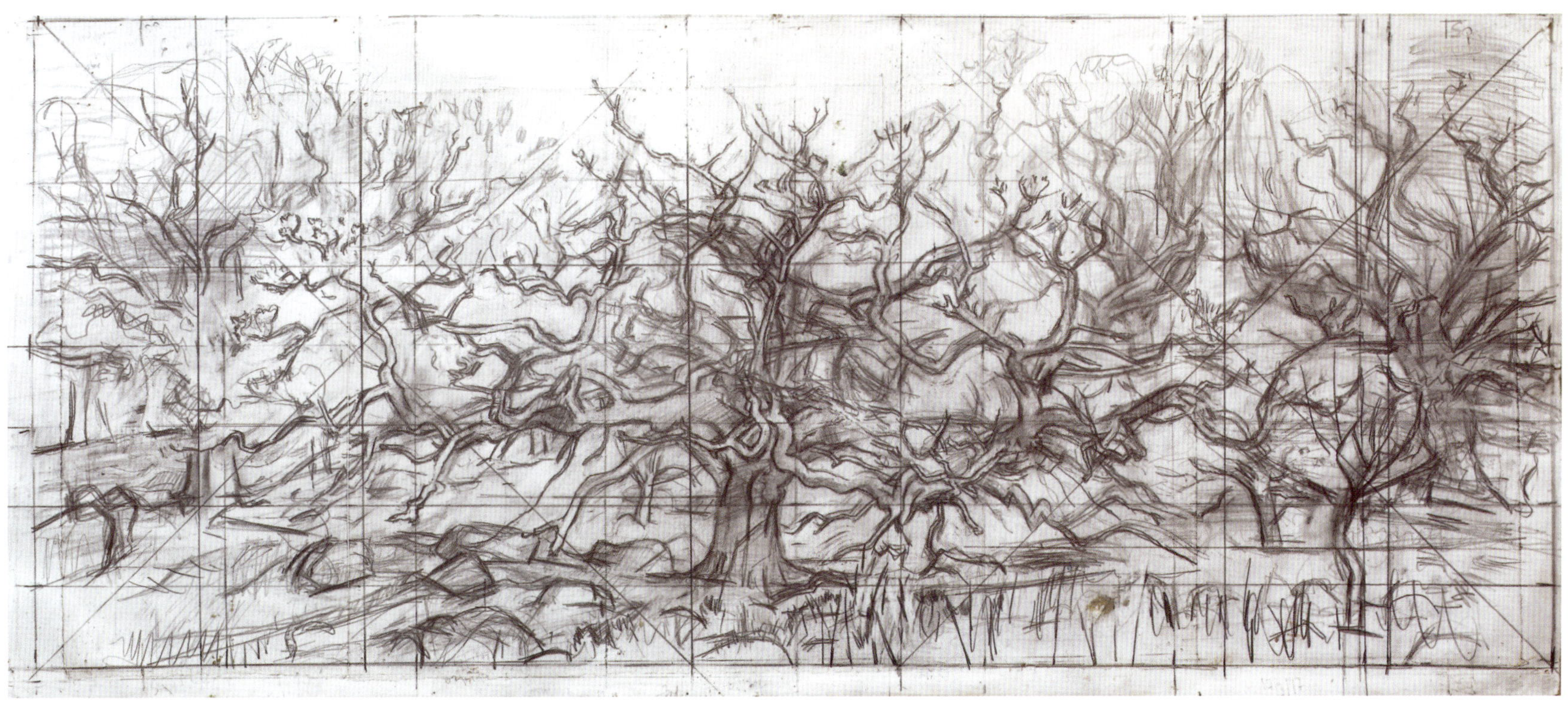

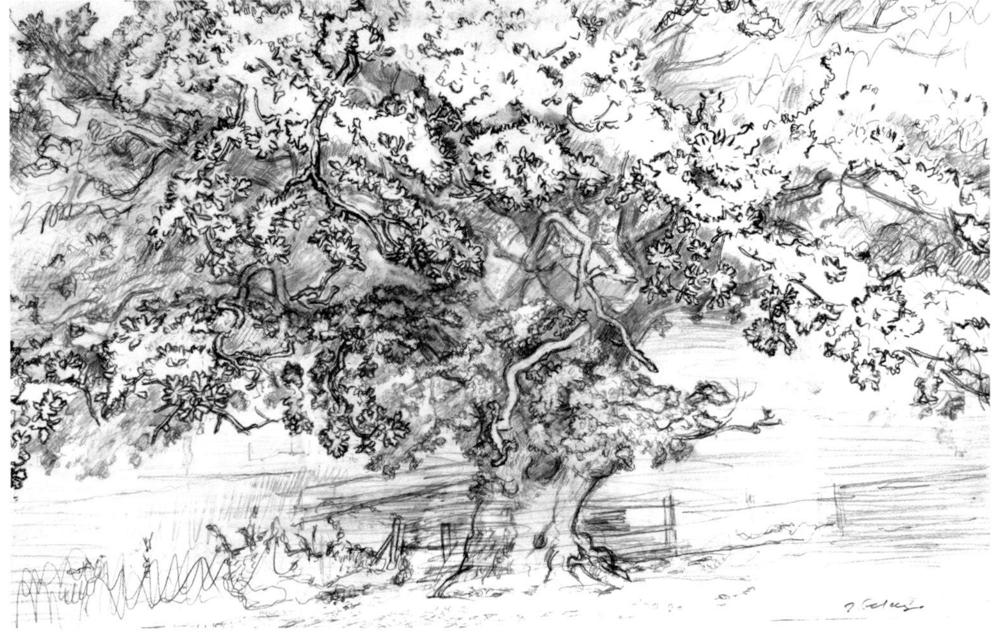

66

Drawing for Oak Embrace, 1996

Pencil on paper, 30x42.4cms

67

Oak Embrace, 1996

Oil on canvas, 116x183cms

Oak Embrace (1996) bears a familial resemblance to Uglow's succinct still life Cuddle – two pears (1985), which in turn resembles a couple embracing. But this is not a close stylistic parallel so much as a similarity of thought. Nor is it really to do with anthropomorphising the vegetable world. It's just another way of looking, a further layer of meaning and reference to be explored and enjoyed. Felcey's painting is about the idea of painting a frieze of leaves as well as the dome of the tree. The tree is all-embracing: it overspills the edges of the canvas on three sides and at the same time the serpentine curves of its branches beckon and lure. (Here the sharp-angled elbow-turns are gentled somewhat into a curvilinear embrace.) The tree has the appearance of a welcoming refuge.

At the same time as suggesting three-dimensional form existing in space, and deep space stretching out behind the tree, the under-drawing visible on the canvas emphasizes the picture surface (various diagonals are apparent to the bottom right of the picture, below the canopy). This accent on the two-dimensionality of the painting makes the frieze of leaves look for a moment like a rich tapestry: cf Two Oaks, Wistman's Wood (77). Felcey did not attempt to cover up these marks because to do so would be to put paint on the canvas that was not strictly necessary to his effects, and would therefore be inauthentic, or 'filling in'. He would rather the lines remain visible and the dialogue between flat surface pattern and form created in depth be given an extra twist in this way.

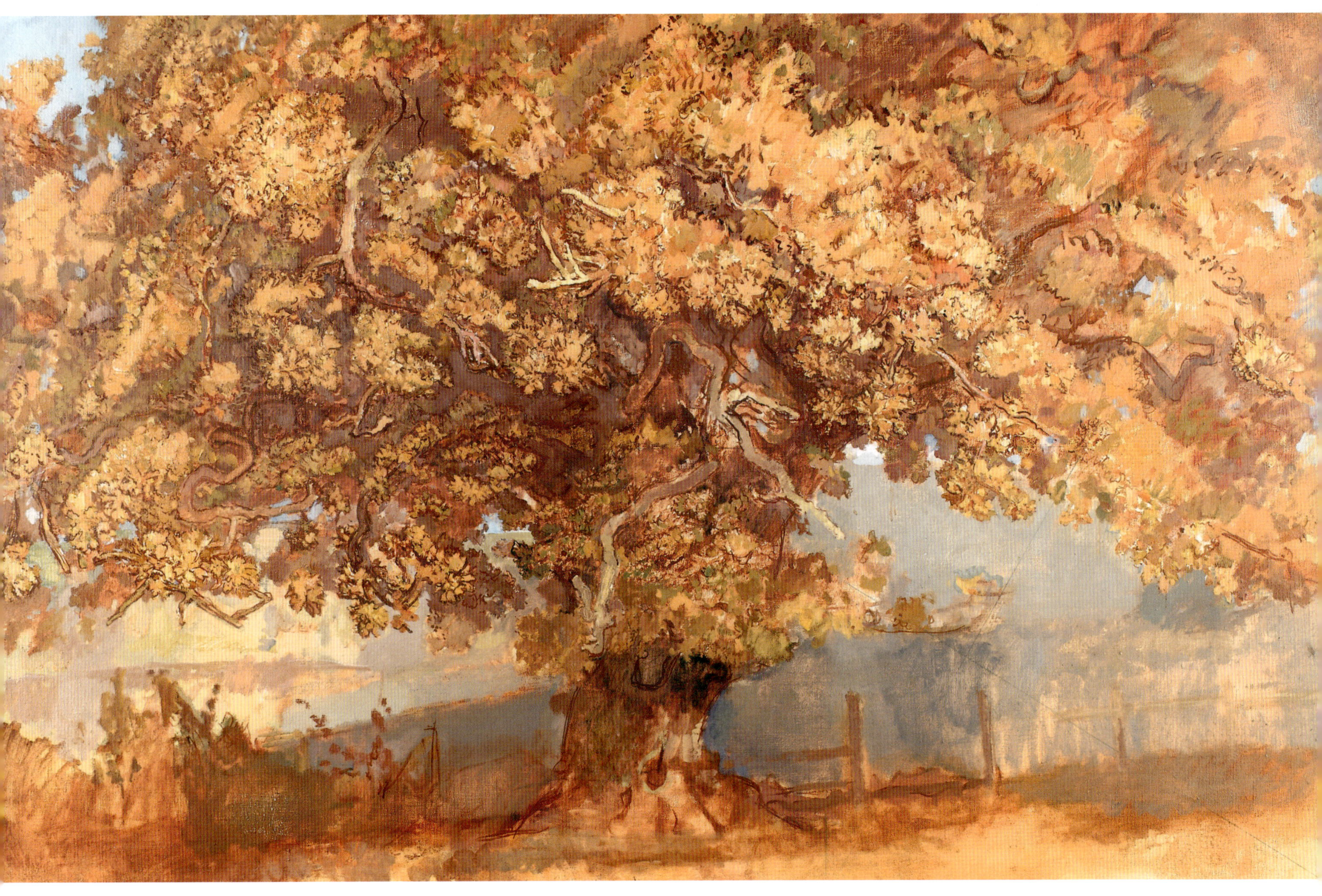

69
The Source of the Teign, 1998–99
Oil on canvas, 91x148cms

The Source of the Teign (1998–9) is one of several paintings on this subject, an oil on canvas depicting the point at which rises one of Dartmoor's principal rivers. The painting has an over-all golden clarity to it, a gin-clear light making the landscape appear to ride up towards you. Although it is properly recessive in space (the meander of the young river emphasizes this), there is also the feeling of the landscape flat on the surface of the picture, tipped up and confronting the viewer in a benign but implacable fashion. The sensation is doubled: of meeting a wall of landscape but also of falling into it. Here once again is Felcey trying to paint the moors as if they were the whole world – as he would paint across the bole of an oak with the same care and breadth of exactitude. At first sight the landscape looks like untouched open moor, but notice the ridged horizontal banding across it. These lines indicate that the area was a medieval industrial site: the hummocks of earth and stone would have been thrown up during the process of open-cast tin mining.

70
Working Drawing for Source of the Teign, 1998–99
Pencil on paper, 31x50cms

71, top
Source of the Teign, 1999
Oil on board, 30x40cms

71, bottom
Source of the Teign, 1998
Watercolour, 28x41cms

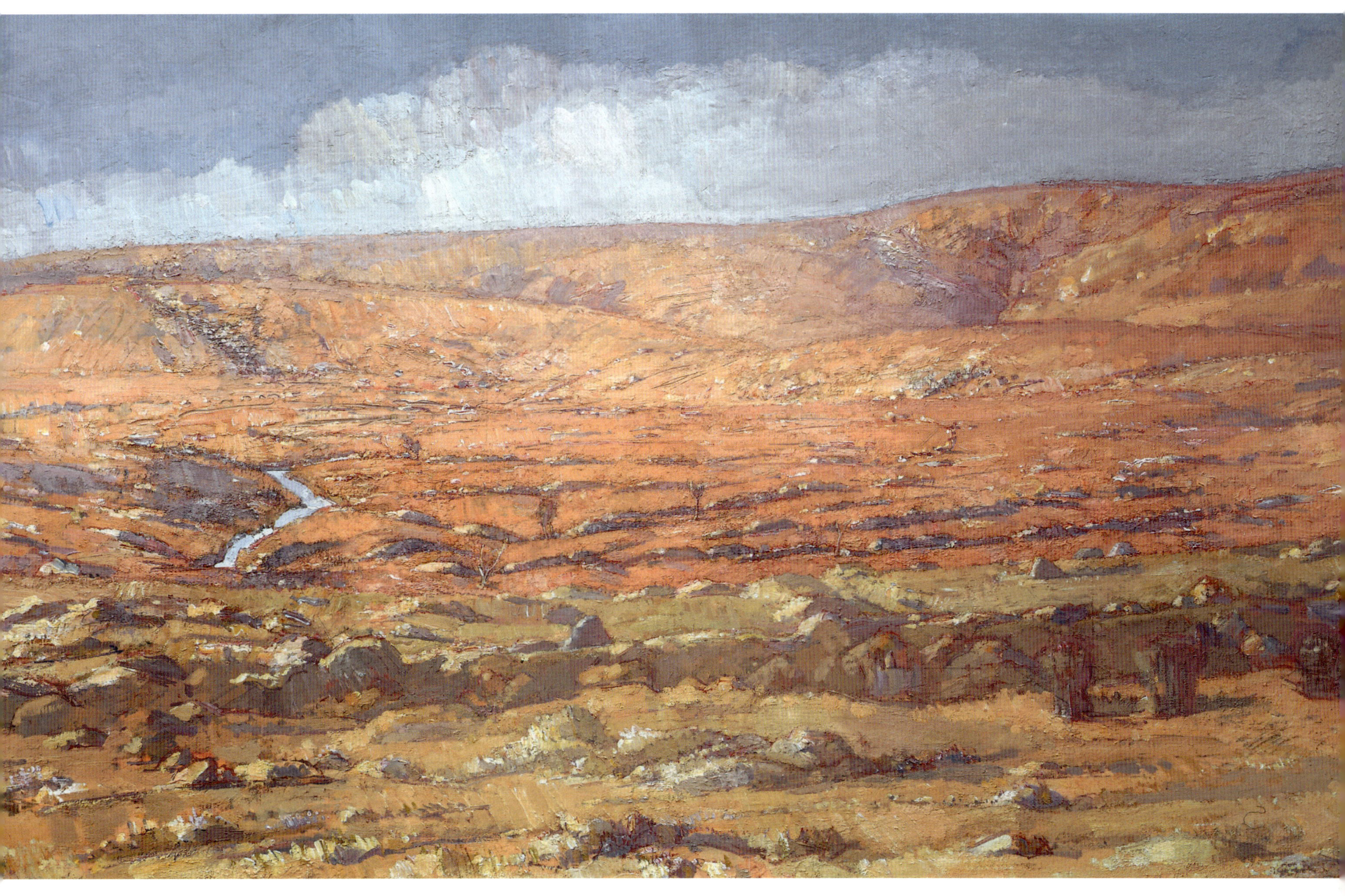

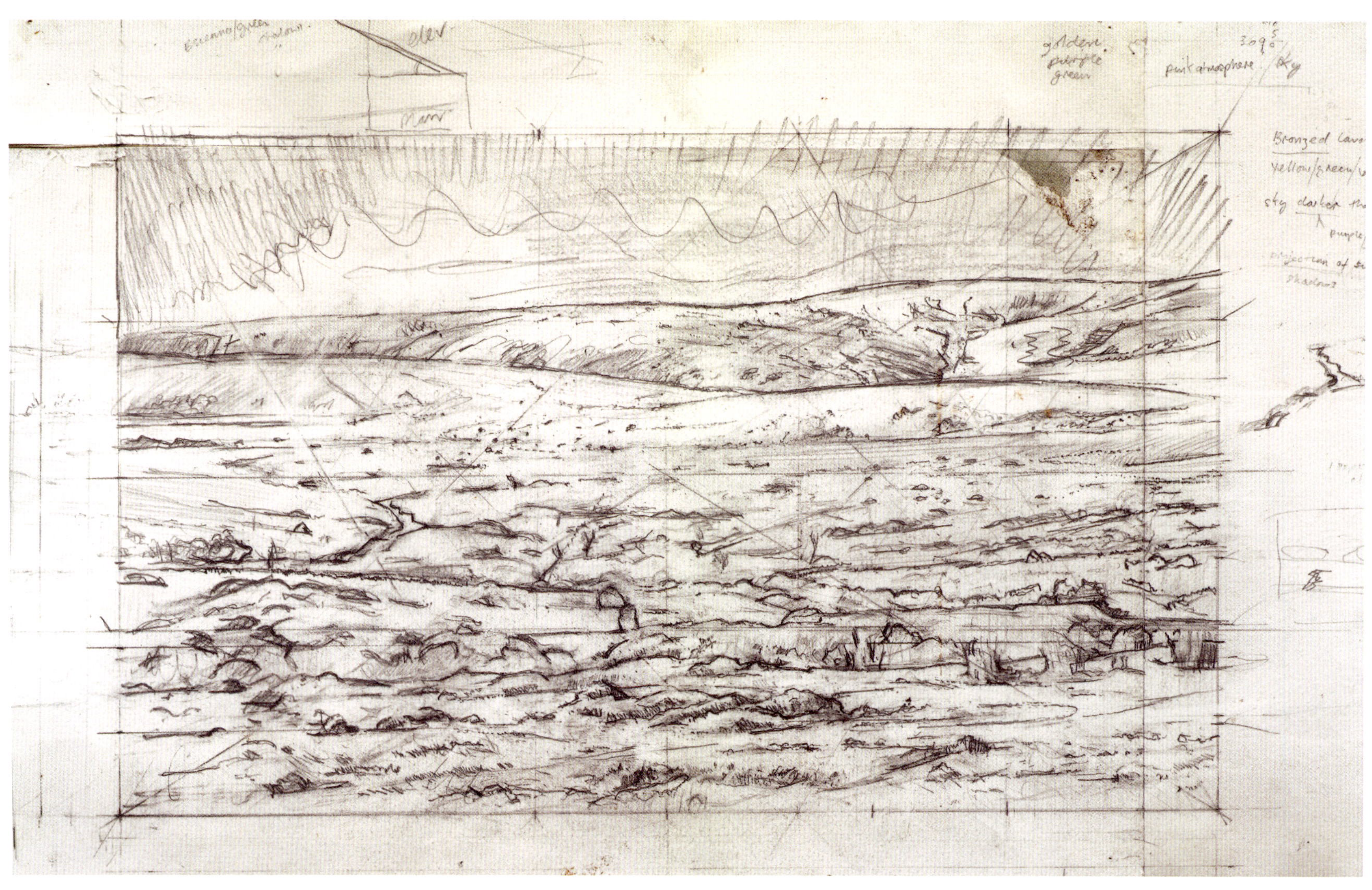

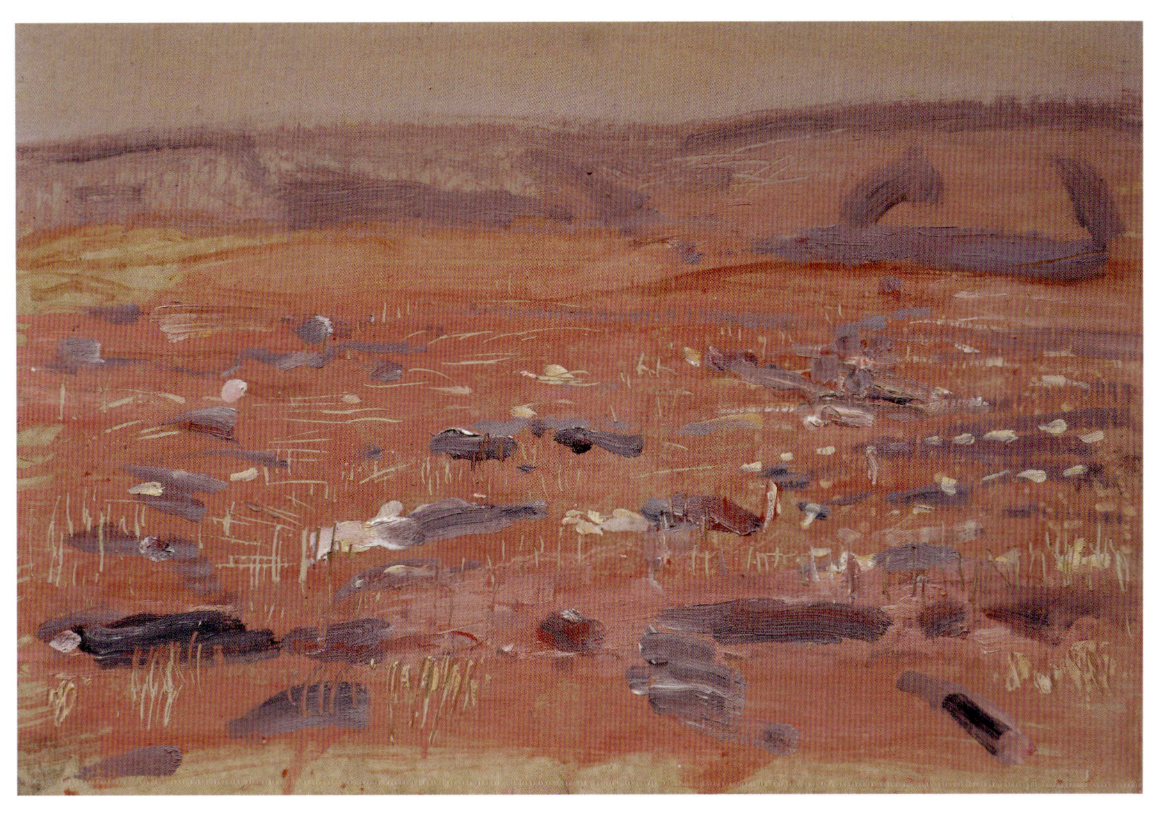

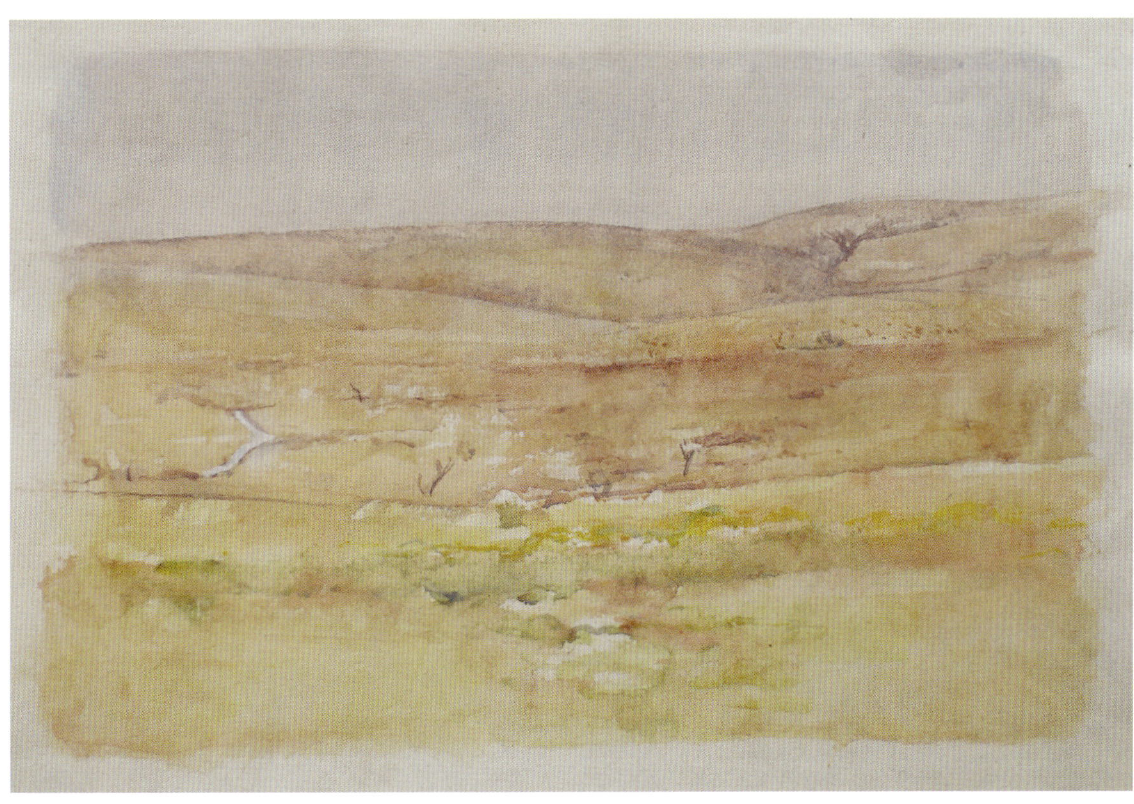

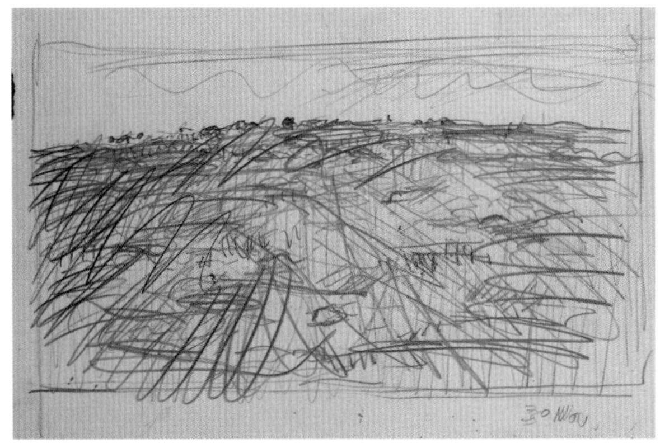
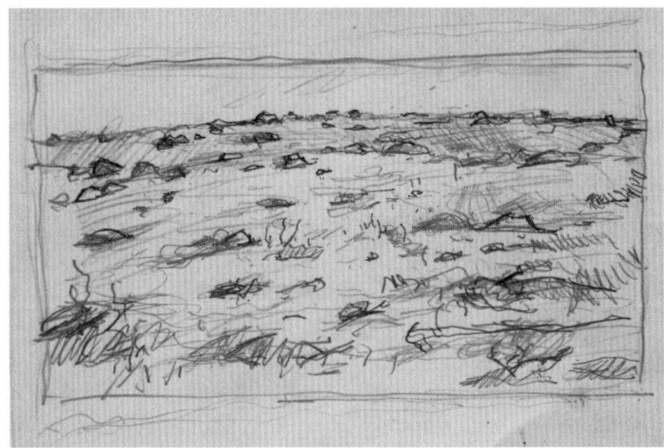
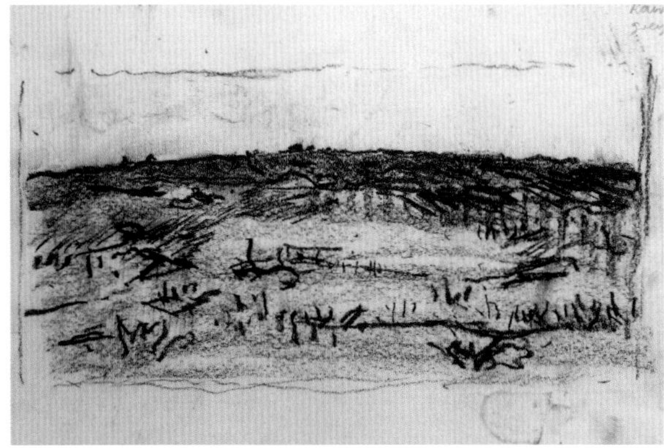
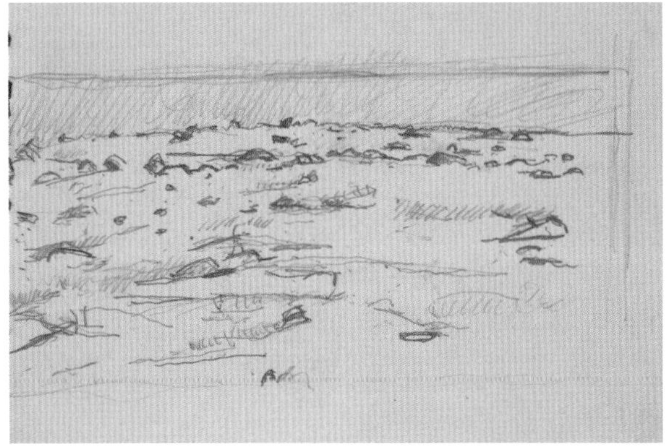

72
Studies for Quantum Landscape, 1999–2000
Pencil, Crayon on paper, 20x26cms

73
Quantum Landscape, 1999–2000
Oil on canvas, 91.5x183cms

Quantum Landscape (1999–2000). For this Felcey made a large drawing and dozens of smaller drawings as a way of summing up information on a daily basis. This painting takes its name from an idea Felcey had about our relationship to the landscape. 'Quantum' most usually refers to the quantum theory of physics (as opposed to the old Newtonian type), concerning the interconnected nature of the physical world. Felcey takes a stretch of moorland which is neither especially dramatic nor picturesque, and submits it to intense analytical scrutiny. Rocks and vegetation, with a high horizon line: a non-view if you like. Felcey comments: 'When one encounters a tree in the landscape, one is immediately aware of its presence (and it can be overwhelming), and one tries to bring one's own presence to that encounter. In choosing a subject like this open barren moor, with no discernible features and no immediate apparent interest, it somehow highlighted the fact that the interest in the landscape grew with one's own dialogue with it. In projecting into that space, feeling the distances between things – the more one could feel them internally, the more real they became out there. The subject seemed to me to be a marriage of the internal and external, almost as if the landscape didn't exist outside of oneself.' The point the picture makes is about the related nature of parts to the whole: we can only define landscape in relation to its constituent elements and to ourselves. In a painting we isolate a section of landscape, but it does not cease to be part of the greater landscape of England, which is still part of the world, and so on. The painting represents a particularly intense collision or encounter between the world out there and the internal world of the observer. That in turn – if it has any effect on us – reminds us of our own relationship to our environment.

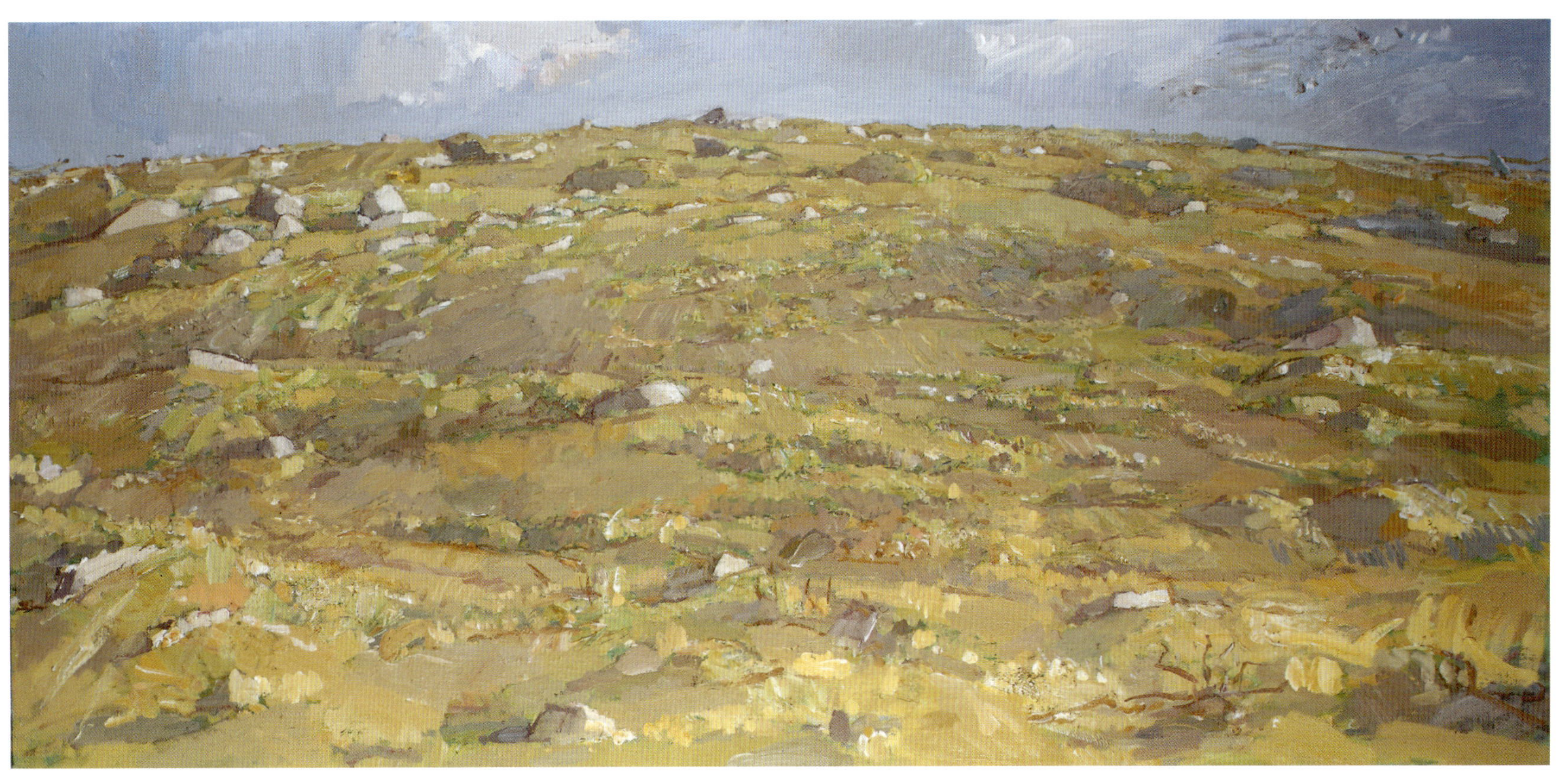

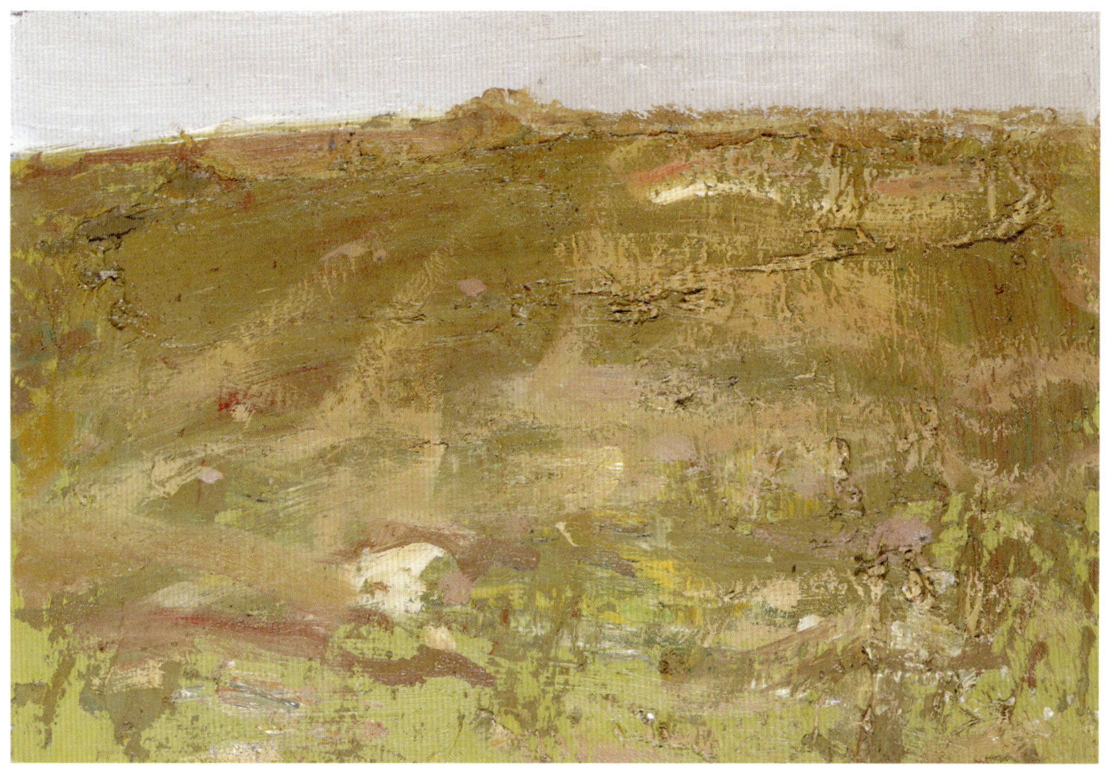

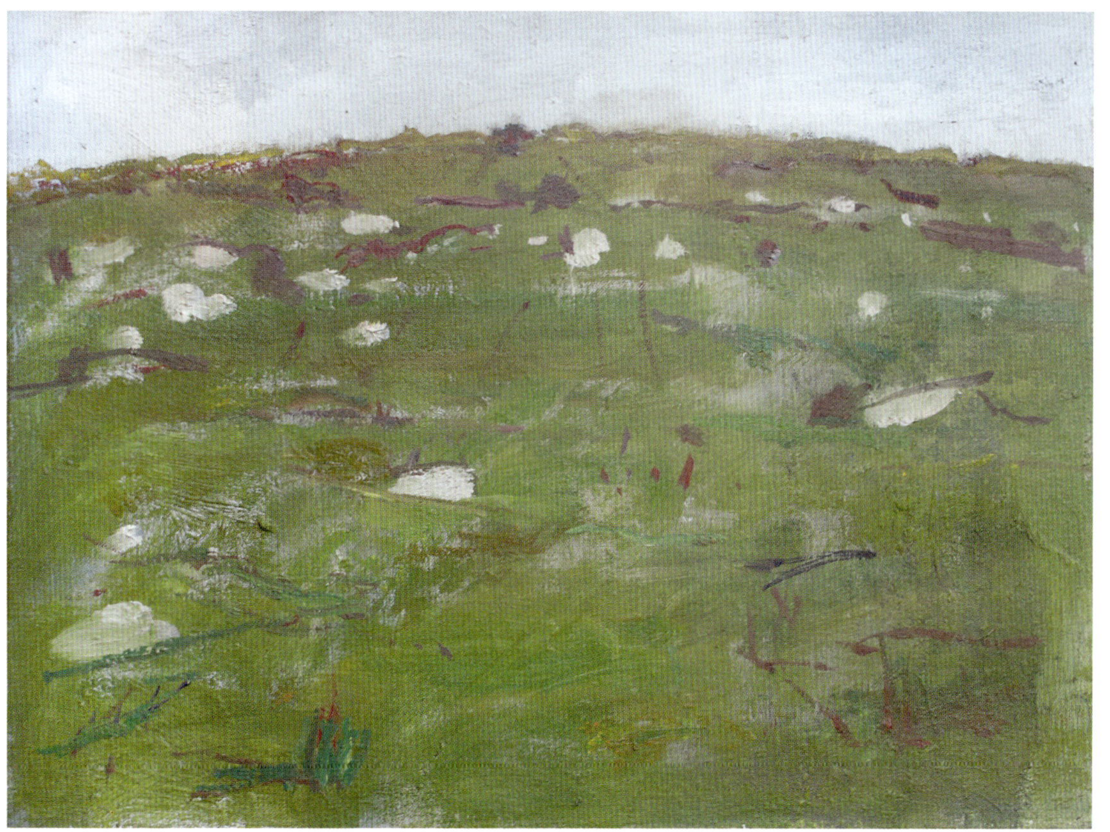

74, top
Throwleigh Common Study, 1999
Oil on board, 23x33cms

74, bottom
Throwleigh Common Study, 1999
Oil on canvas, 31x41cms

75
Throwleigh Common, 2000
Ink on paper, 60x80cms

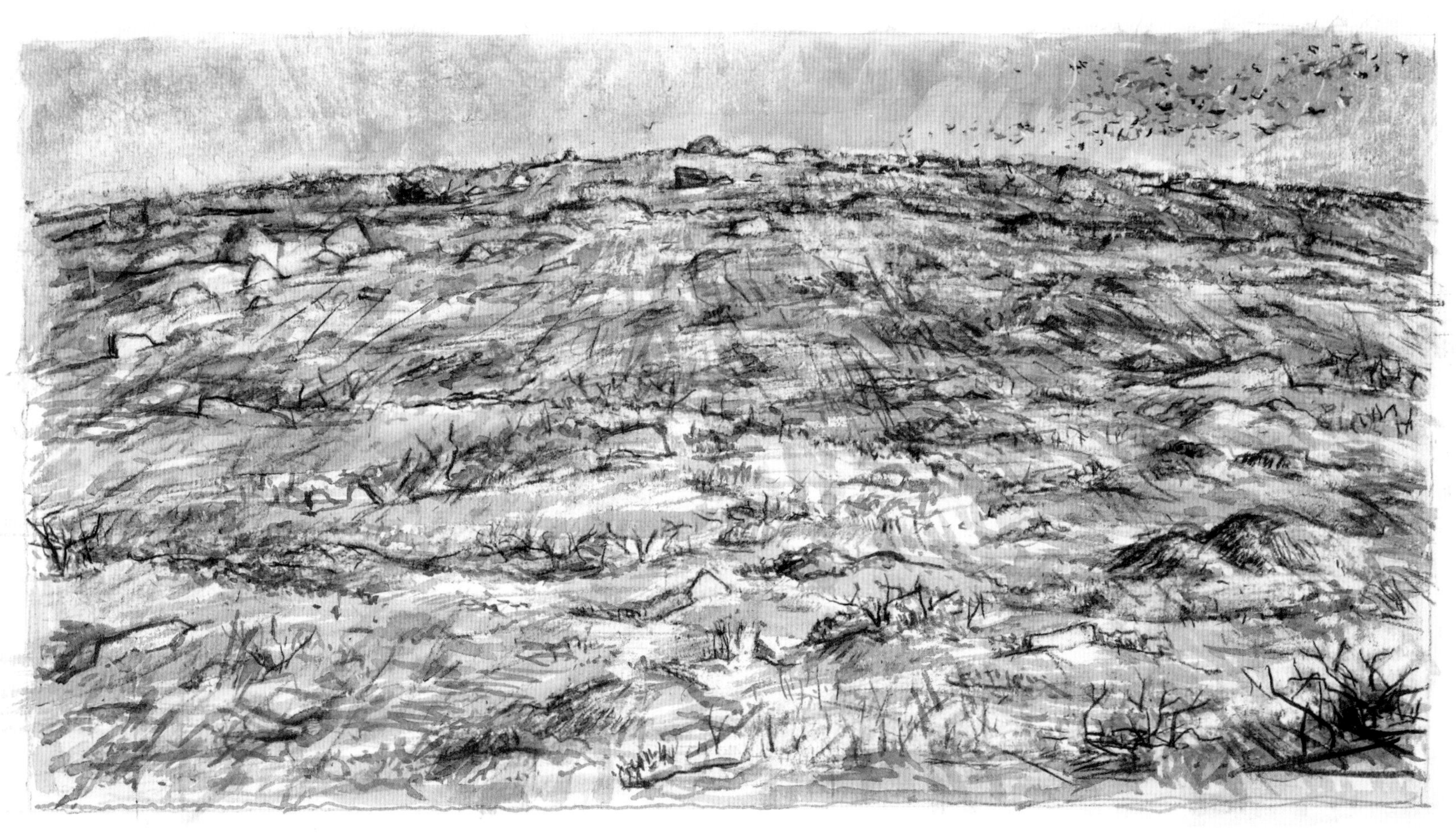

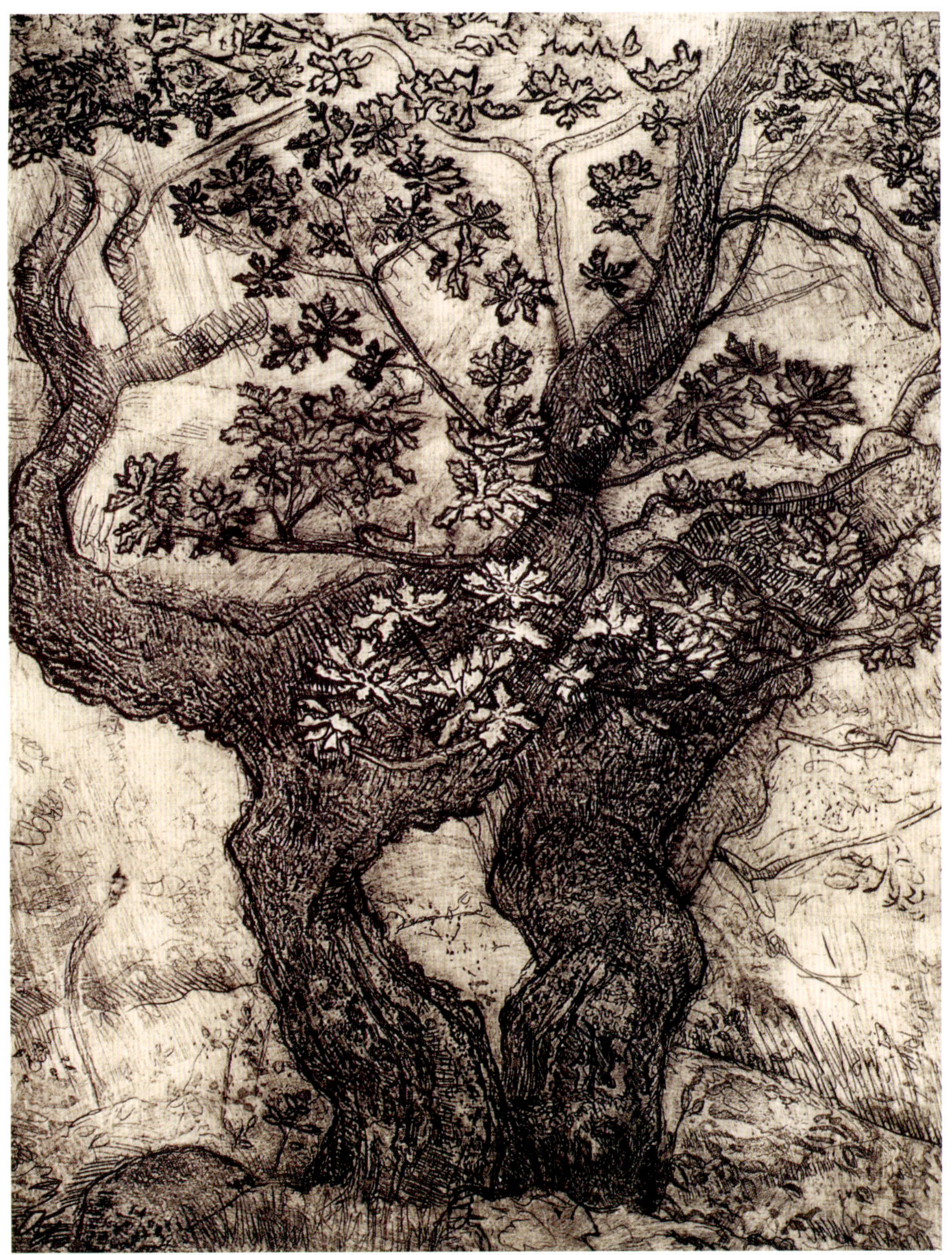

76

Two Oaks at Wistman's Wood, 1996
Etching, 33x25cms

77

Two Oaks, Wistman's Wood, 1995
Oil on canvas, 122x115.5cms

Two Oak Trees, Wistman's Wood (1995) has a tapestry-like presence. Felcey comments: 'It's got a decorative quality, it's very much like a pattern, more so than usual, which is to do with separating the tree shapes from the background. It's in a very simple key: red/yellow, red/gold, that's like a tapestry. Things are the same scale throughout the picture. I suppose I wanted a different kind of particularity in the way that the leaves are repetitive and obviously not visually drawn but drawn as patterns. You don't feel this painting is so laborious – fancy having to draw all those leaves – it's exuberant.'

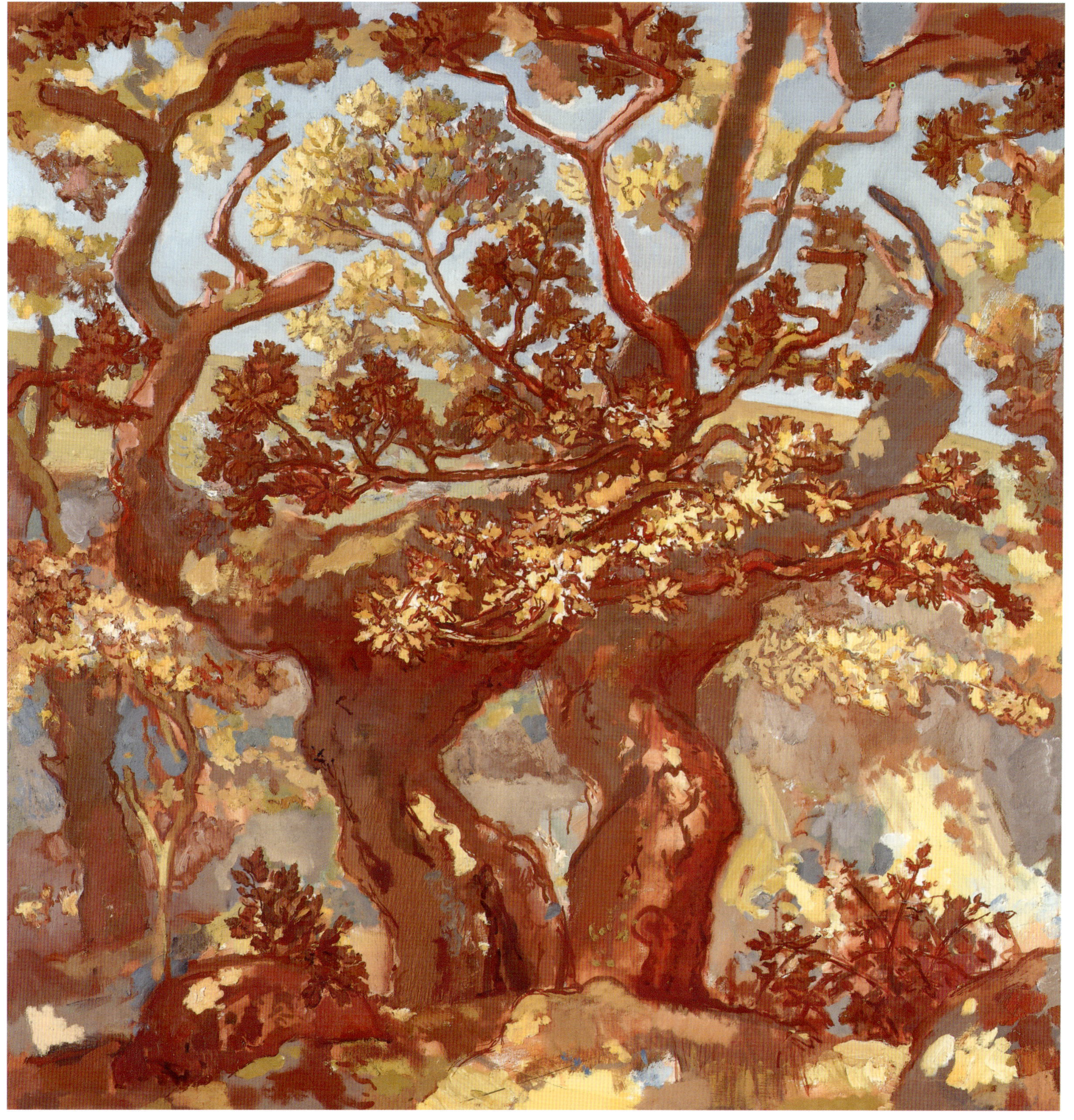

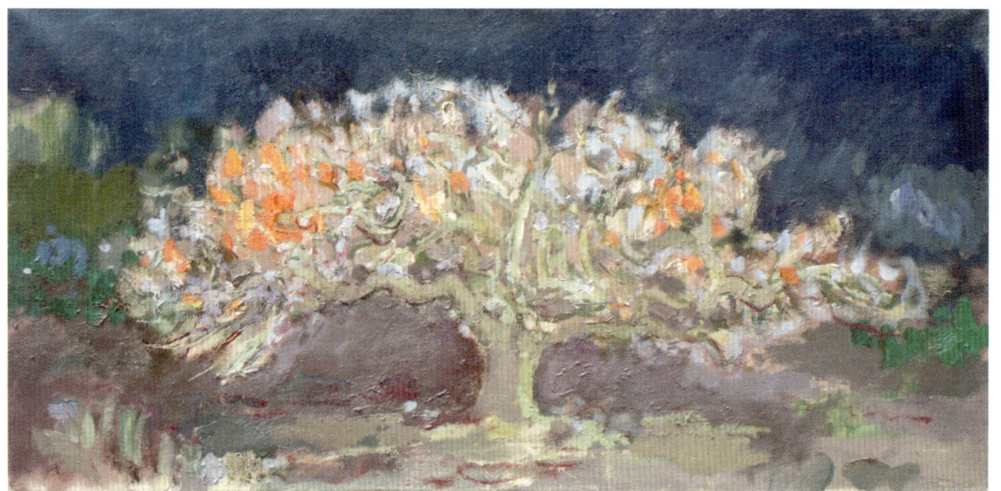

78
Whiddon Oak, Sunset, 2007
Oil on canvas 56x112cms

79
Oak, Sunset, 1987–97
Oil on oak panel, 25x39.2cms

Oak, Sunset caused Felcey terrible trouble and went on for about 10 years. It's actually painted on a slab of oak about 1¼ thick. It depicts that autumn moment when the trees have turned. 'I suppose one reason this painting took so long, is that I couldn't make my mind up about the light I wanted. It ended up being about the light of the setting sun being trapped within the tree, a mirror of the sun. I imagined the light not to be hitting the tree but being emanated from it, and I think this is a recurring theme throughout my work, that is, of colour and form emanating light. Of course I'm very much indebted to Adrian Stokes for these ideas, but it also comes from Indian/Persian paintings and their exquisite use of colour.'

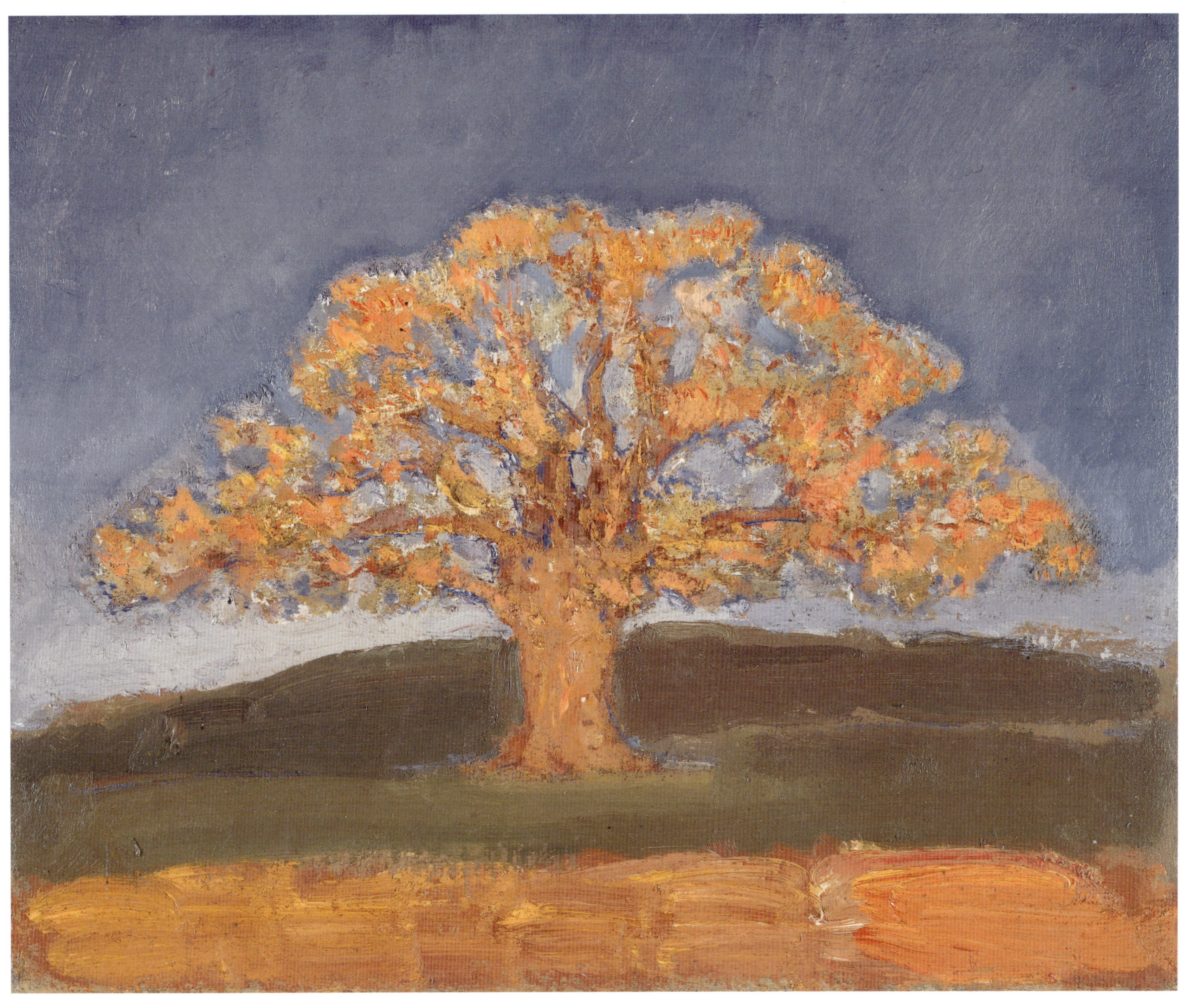

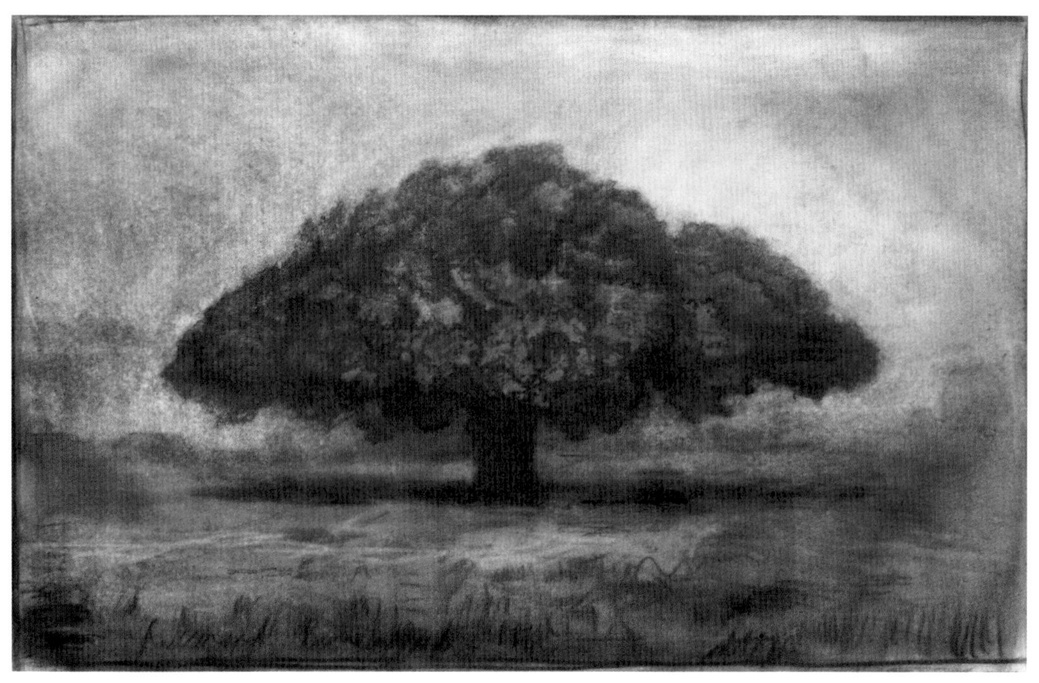

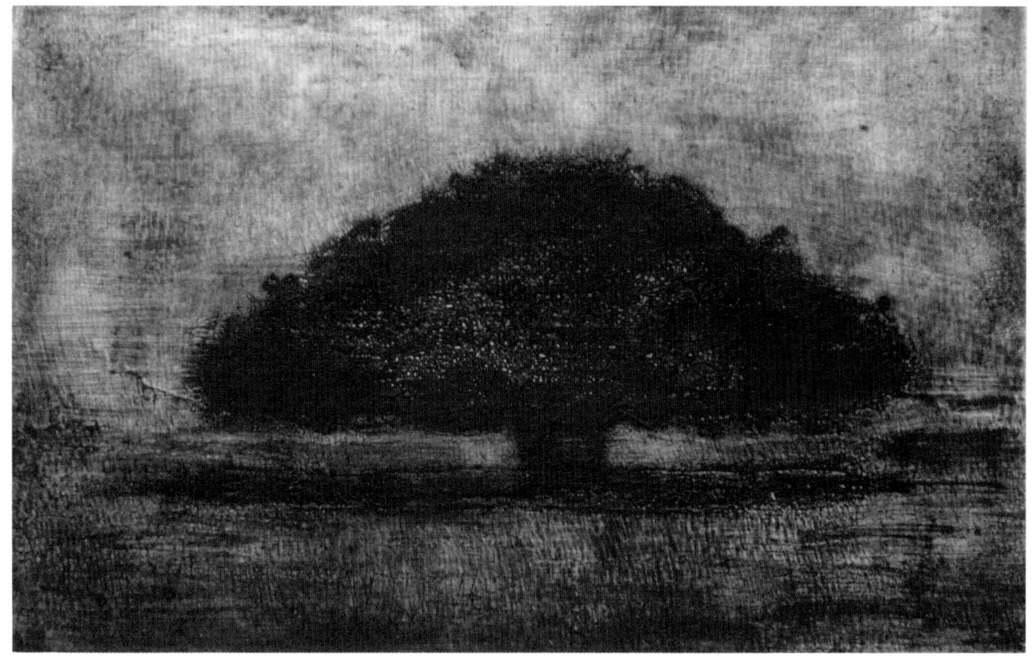

80, top
Remembered Oak, 1993
Mixed media on paper, 76x102cms

80, bottom
Remembered Oak, 1998
Etching, 17x26cms

81
Field Oak, 1993
Oil on canvas, 90x180cms

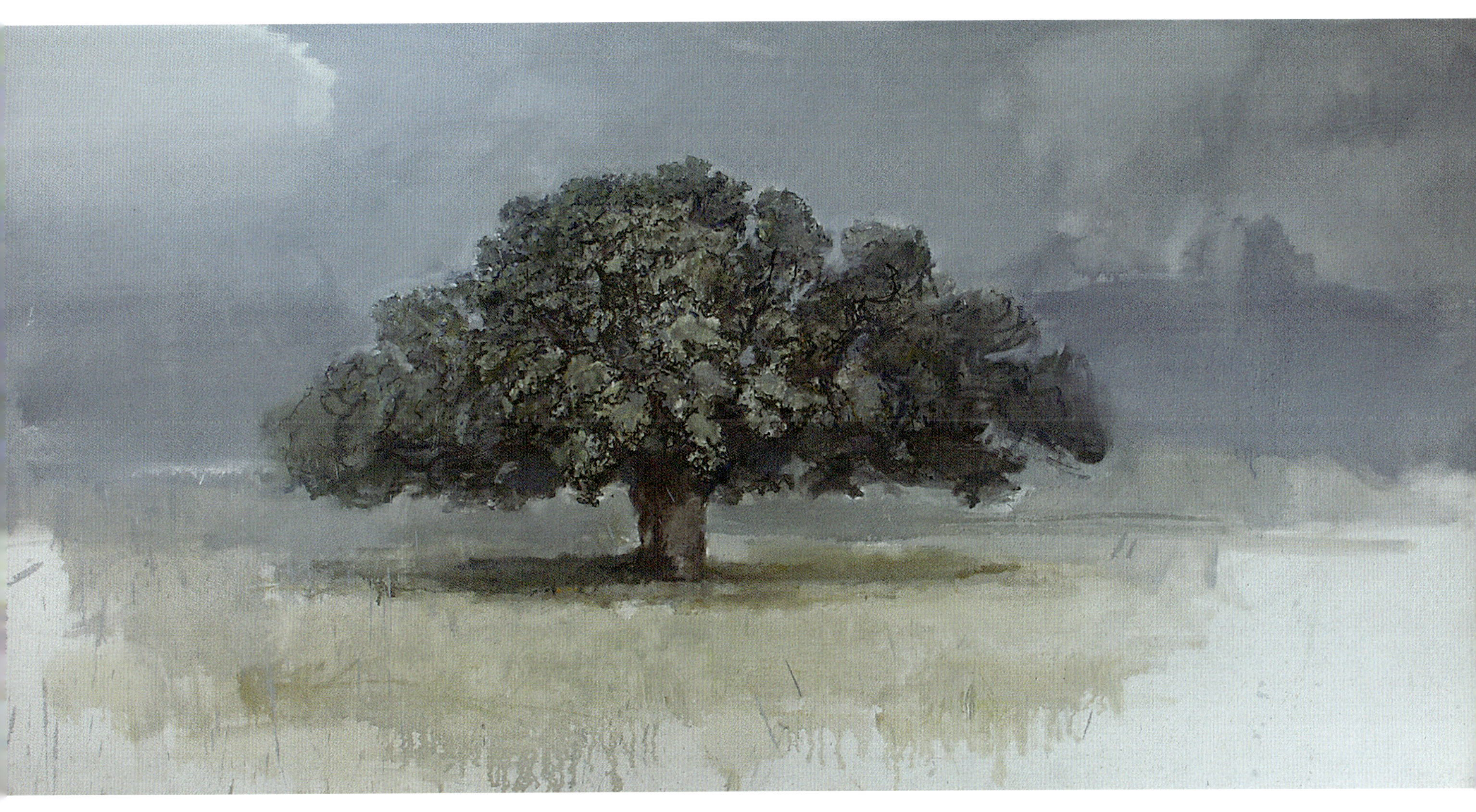

83

Procumbent Oak, 1993–6

Oil on board, 94x243cms

Procumbent Oak (1993–6), is rather Mediterranean in aspect, like an ancient vine or olive tree coiling down the stony terraces of some Italian hillside. Again a section had to be added onto the right-hand side. This should not be seen as a early miscalculation on Felcey's part, but rather as an ability to allow the painting to grow and develop organically, and for his interpretation to develop too, rather than remaining static and becoming compromised. The ground is lighter than the sky on the left, darker on the right, as read from left to right traditionally. Actually, what is now the right-hand side of the painting was cut off from its original place on the left and re-positioned, so that the picture had some sort of balance. The rectangle was originally a double square, but the geometry was once again susceptible to change. The long shallow diagonal which now drives the painting's dynamic is surprisingly satisfying as well as elegant.

84, top

Procumbent Oak, 1995–98

Etching, 45.5x80cms

84, bottom

Study for Procumbent Oak, 1996

Charcoal on paper, 45x110cms

85

Devon 1993 photograph © Chris Chapman

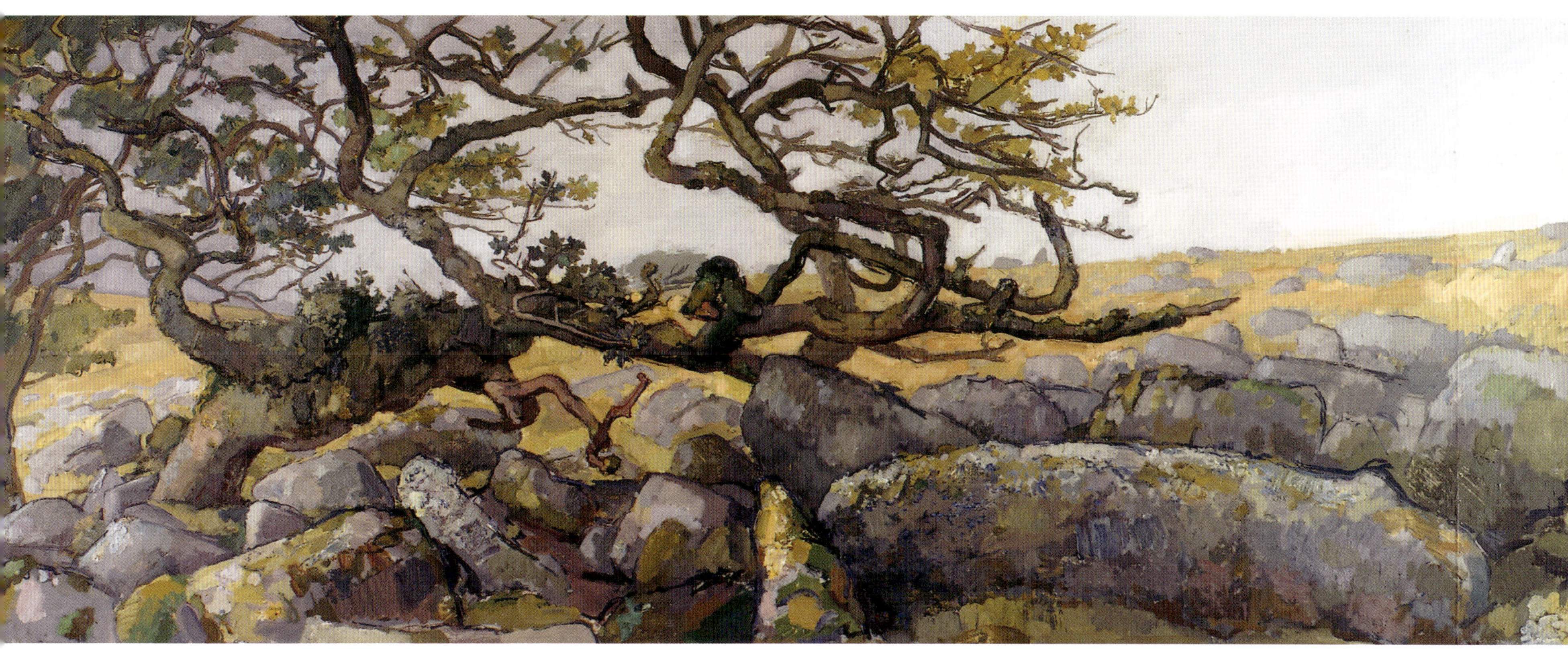

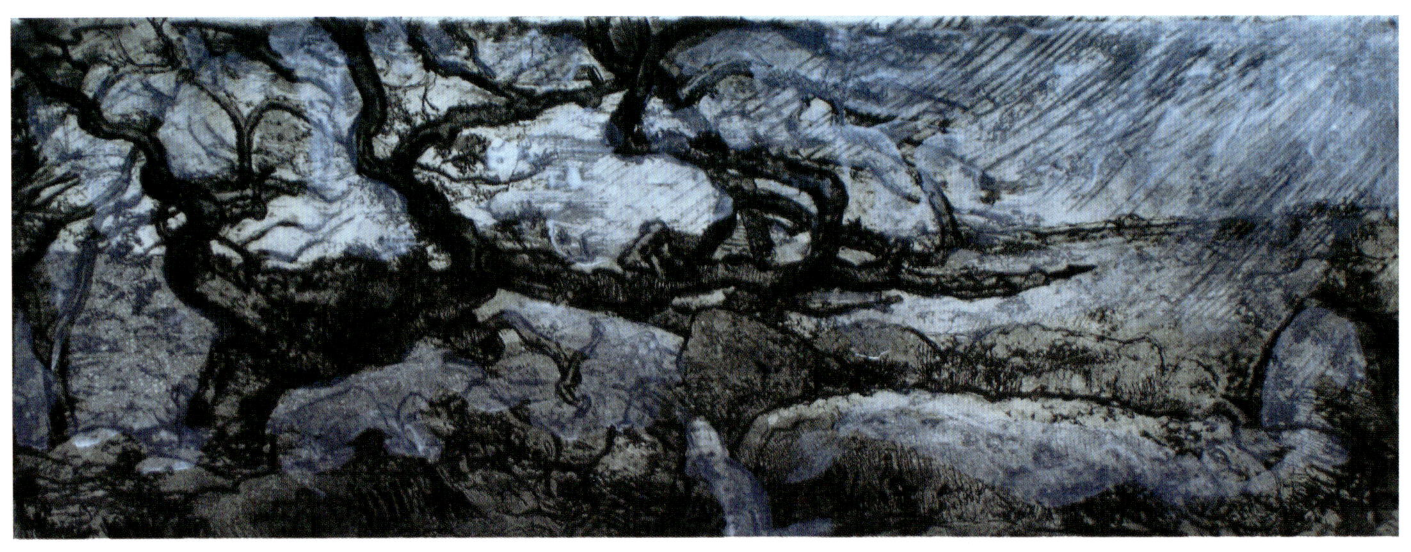

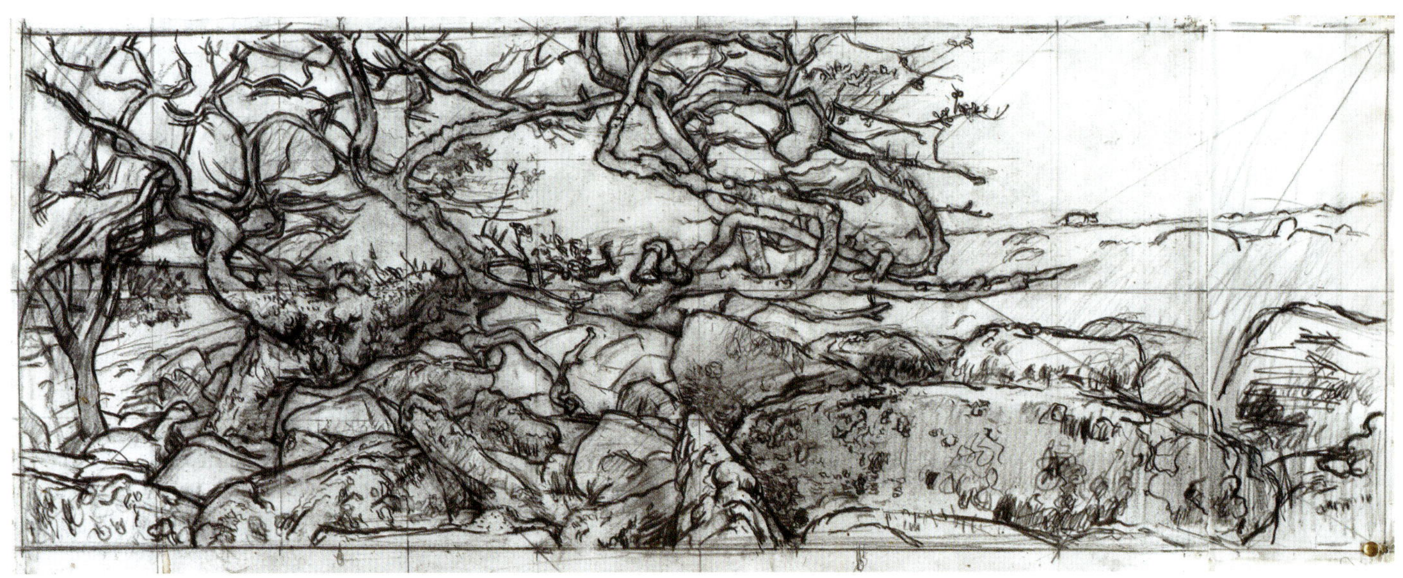

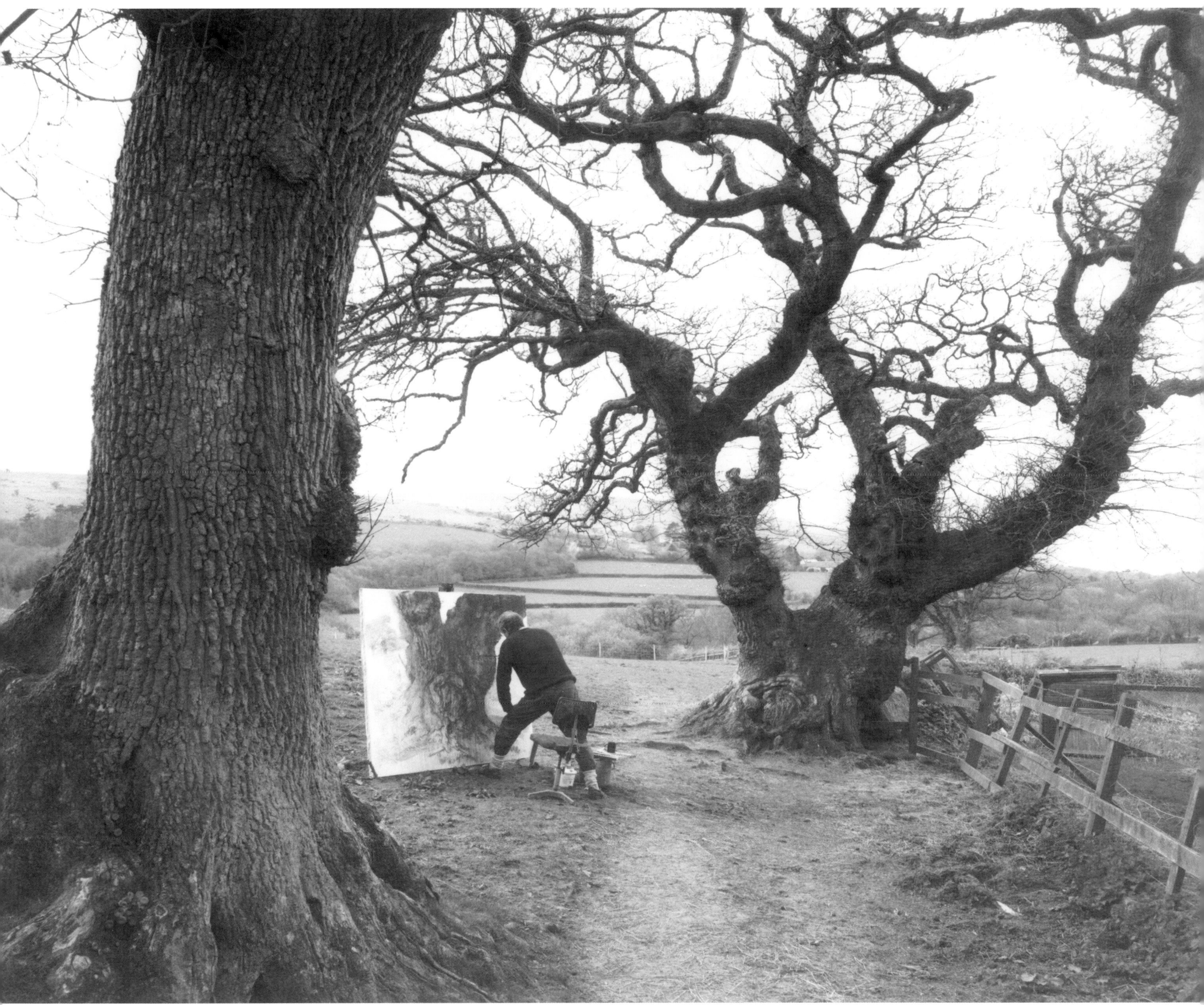

87
Whiddon Oak, Summer, 1996
Oil on canvas, 90x189cms

88
Radiant Oak, 1999
Oil on canvas, 60.5x122.5cms

89
Luminous Oak, 2005
Oil on canvas, 54x84.3cms

90, top
Deer Park Encounter, 2005
Mixed media on paper, 76.2x147.3cms

90, bottom
Whiddon Oak, Autumn, 1996
Acrylic on canvas, 90x180cms

91, top
Whiddon Oak Moonlight, 2000
Oil on canvas, 46x80cms

91, bottom
Whiddon Oak Winter, 2005
Charcoal on paper, 60x90cms

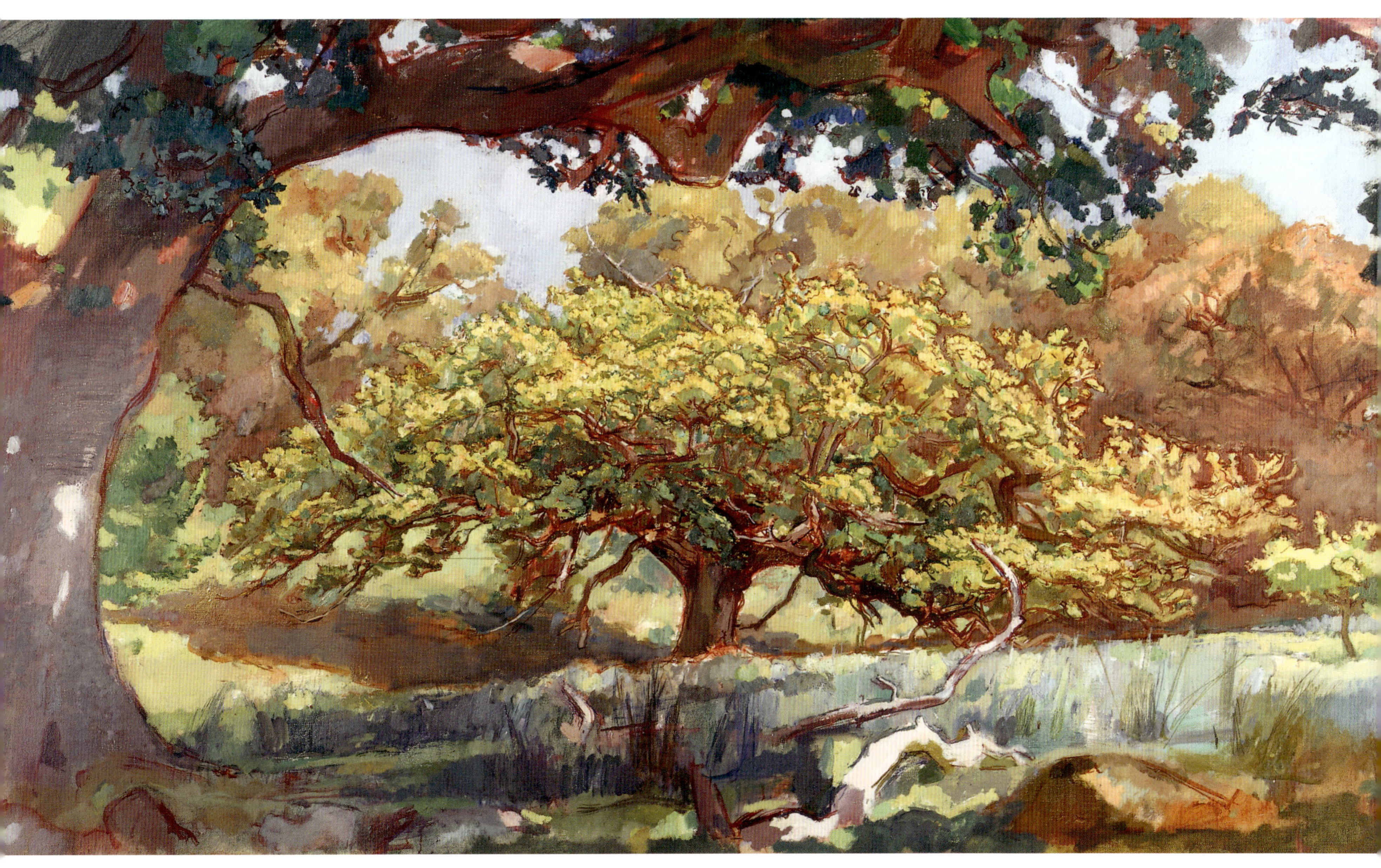

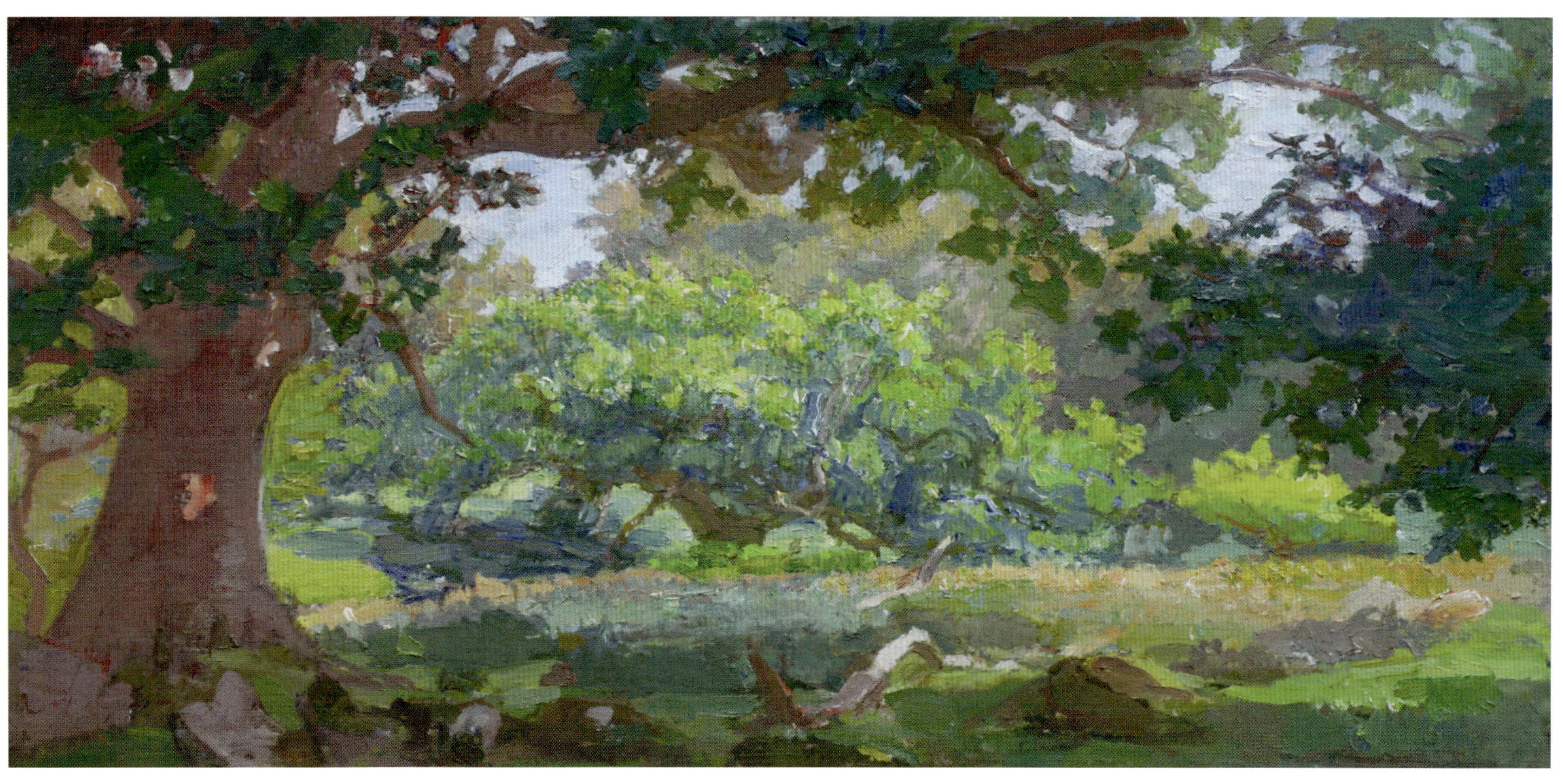

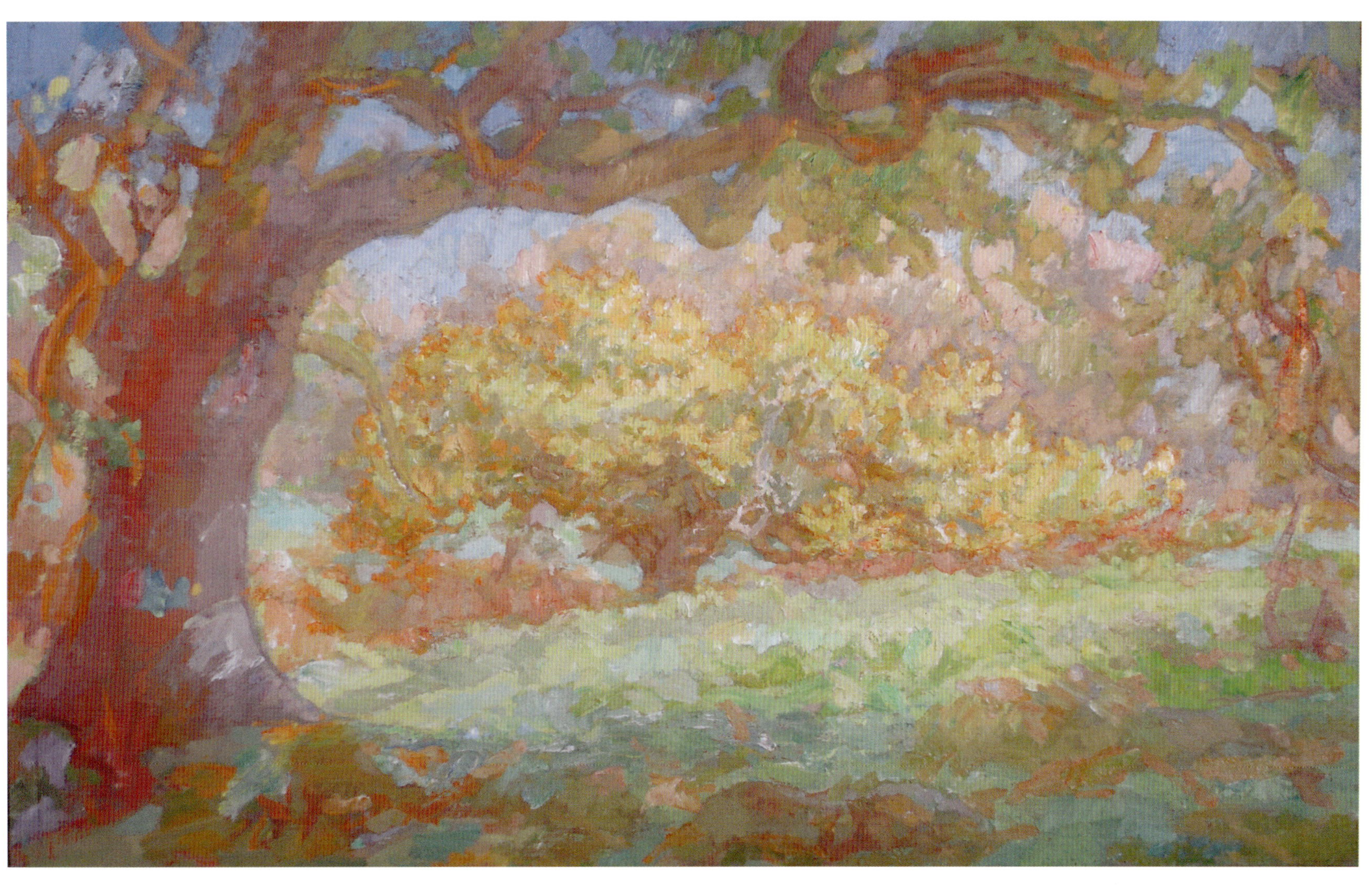

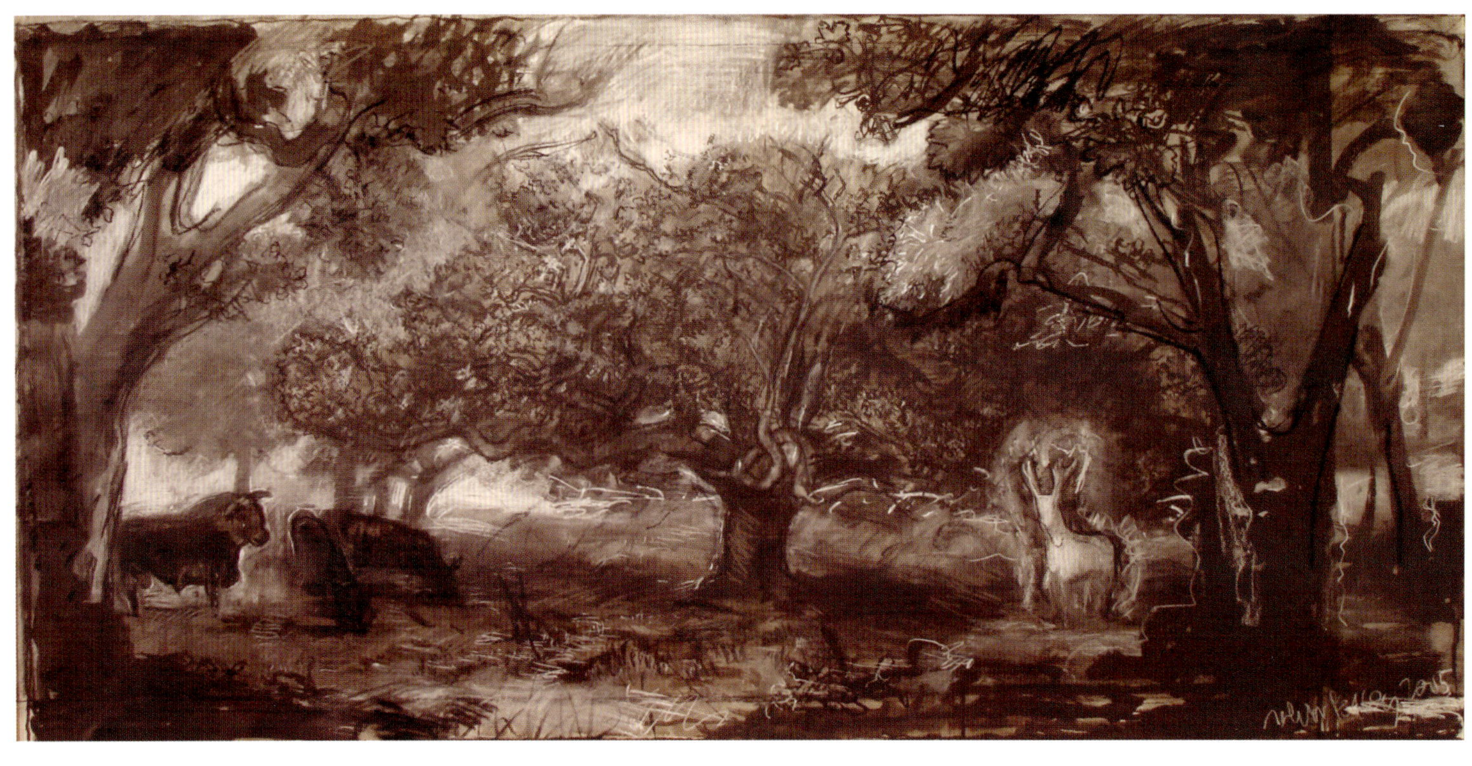

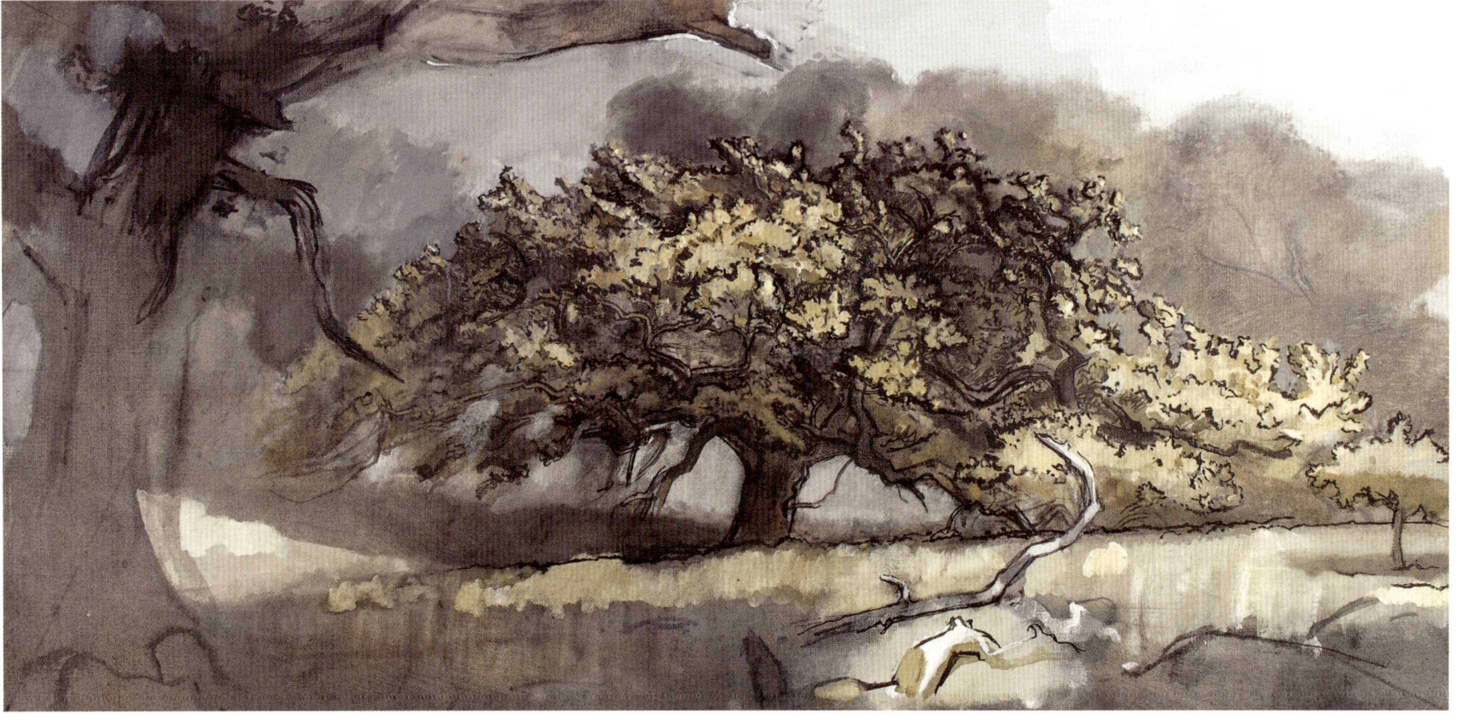

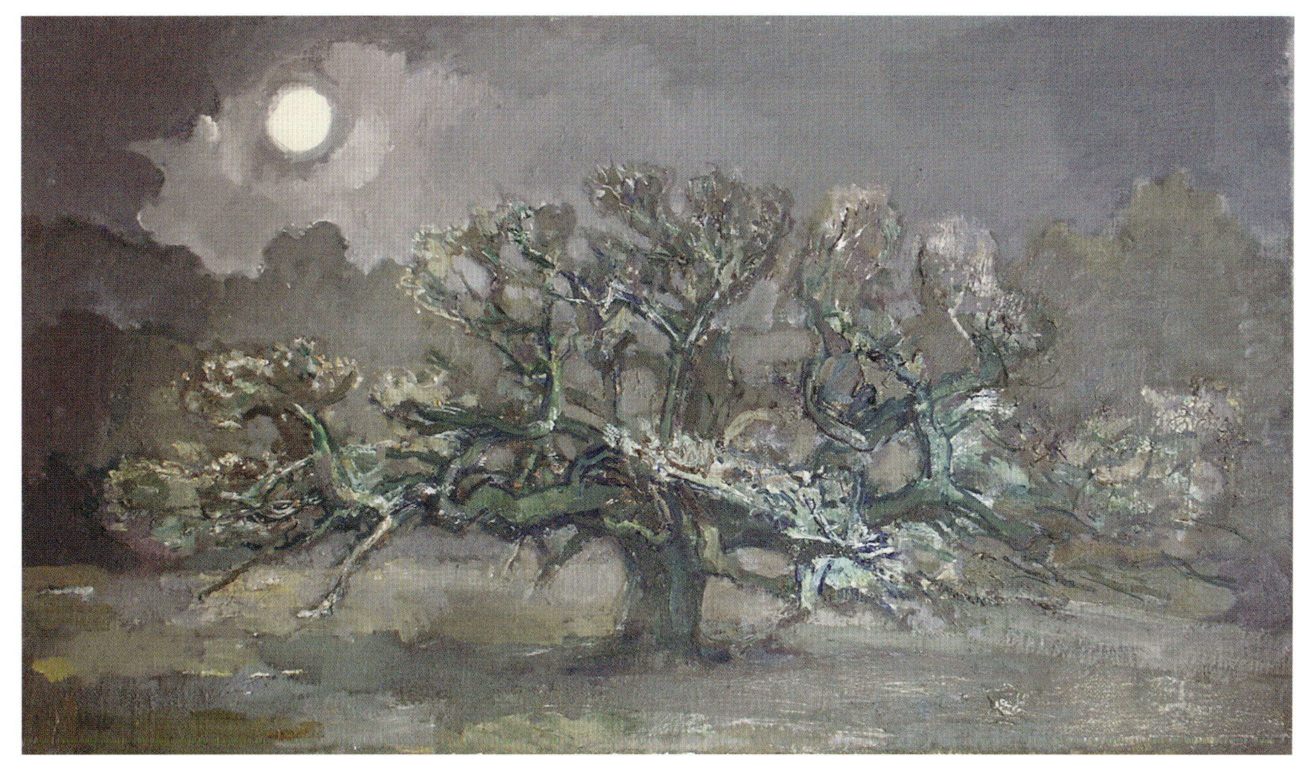

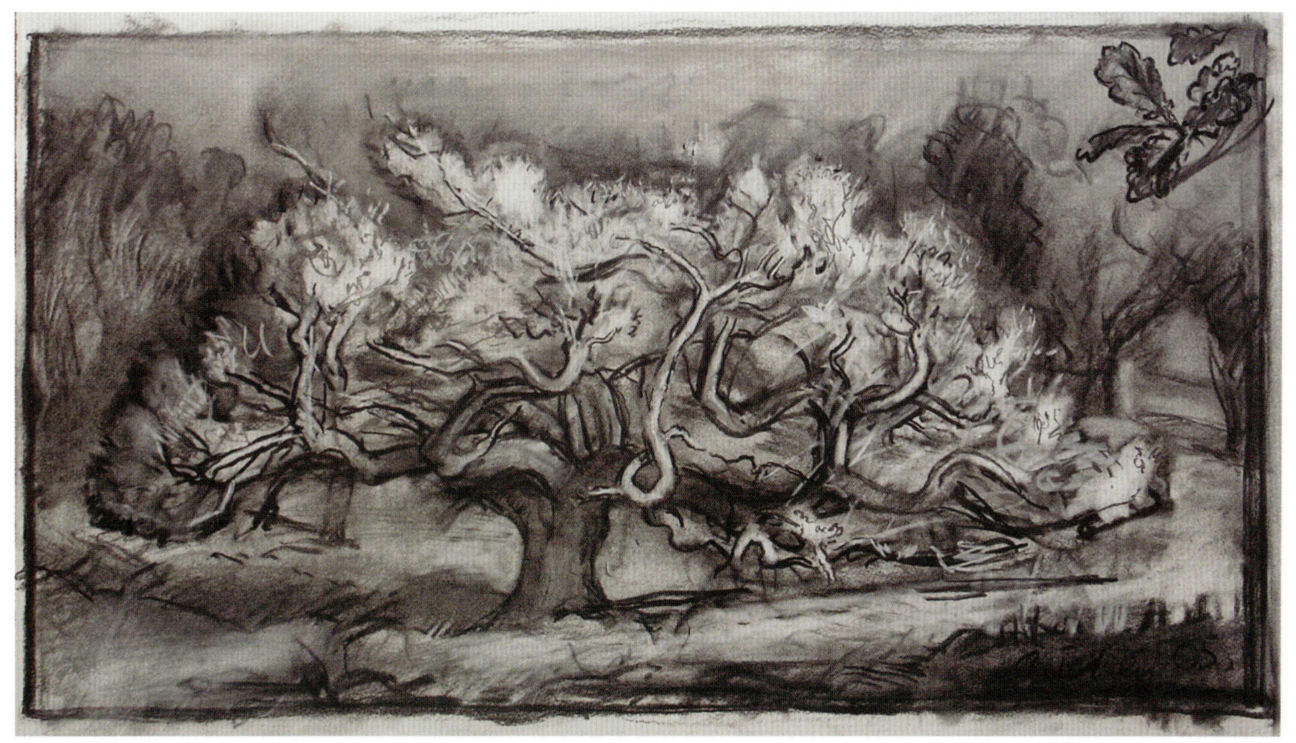

93

Allegory, 2005–06

Oil on canvas, 46.5x61.5cms

Allegory (2005–6) is a magical picture containing a mythical white deer like a unicorn. 'Initially it started as being about an encounter in the deer park between an albino deer and a bull', says Felcey. 'There was an albino, though I never saw it. I did start a drawing of cattle underneath the trees, then I put the deer in as well. It started about that then just developed and took on a life of its own. I used a five foot drawing of a horse and then made the others up. There's a snake around the tree. The horse has seen the snake but the albino deer is not aware at all of this. And the stork – I'd just been in Spain and seen storks flying – they look absolutely magnificent. But I don't know what it all means.

'I always think I'd like to paint compositions {in other words, something he's composed or made up}. I wanted a very alert horse here, this one with its ears back is frightened, but it's also partly to do with the whole fan shape of the ears. It's a kind of abstract thing and yet it has meaning. You don't know which comes first – they both come together. I spent a long time trying to paint those tree trunks – the essential space through there, the big funnel of the painting.'

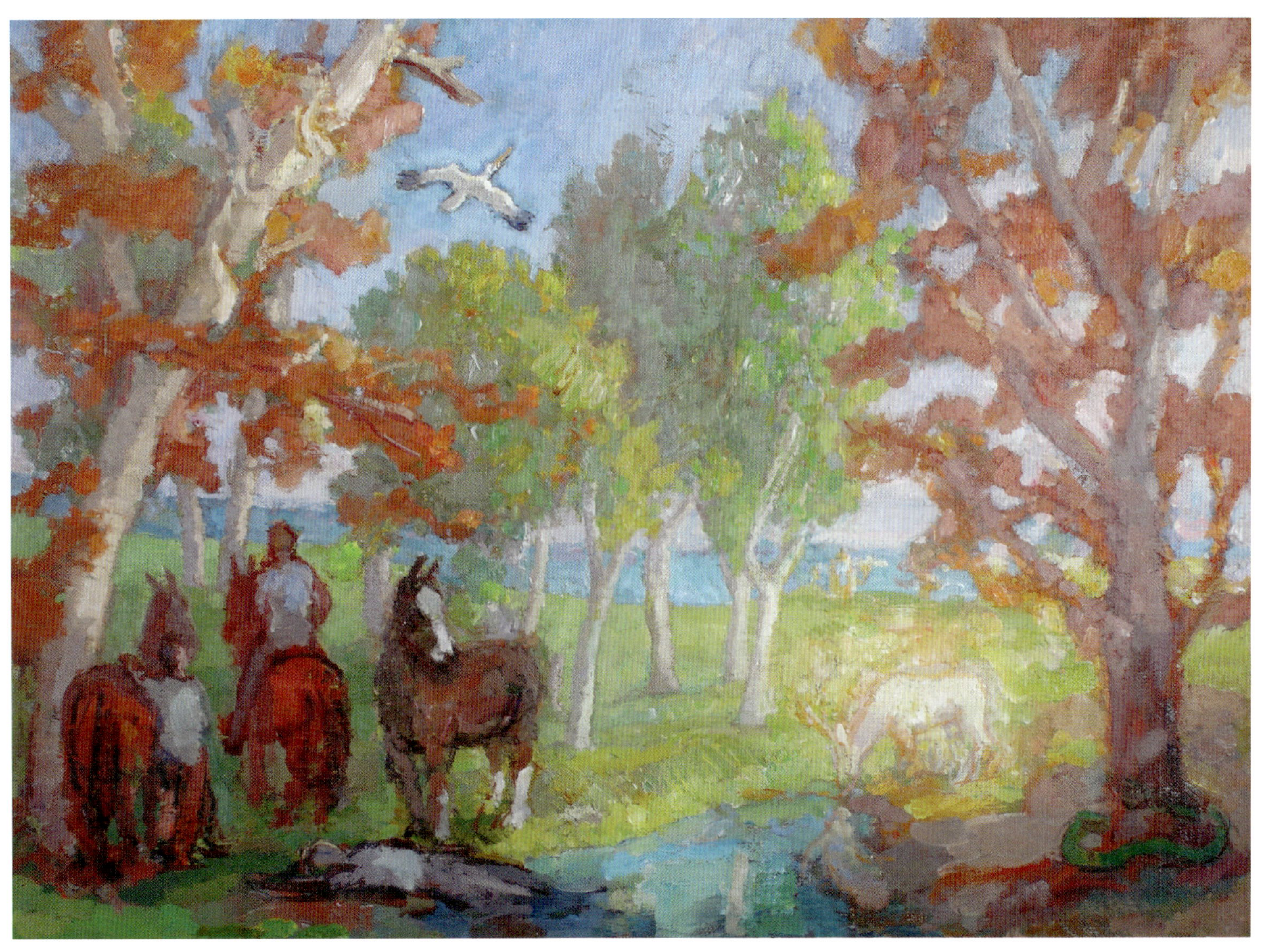

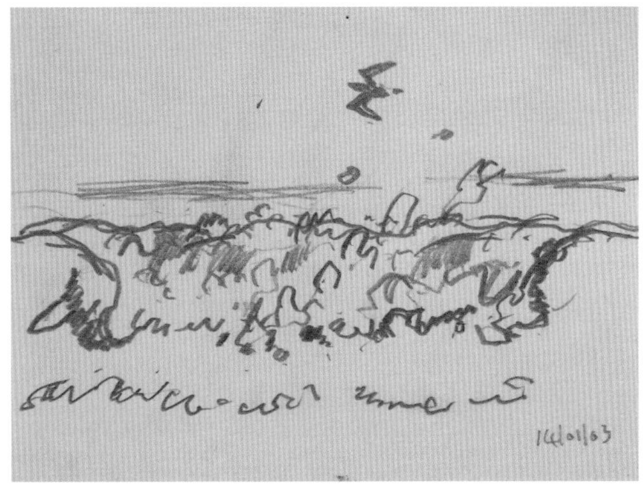

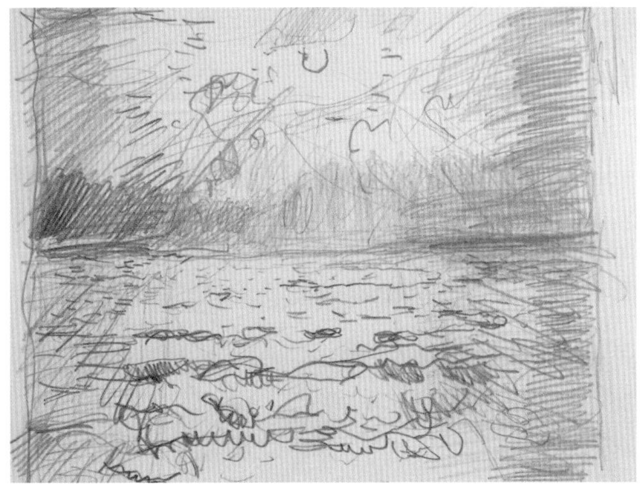

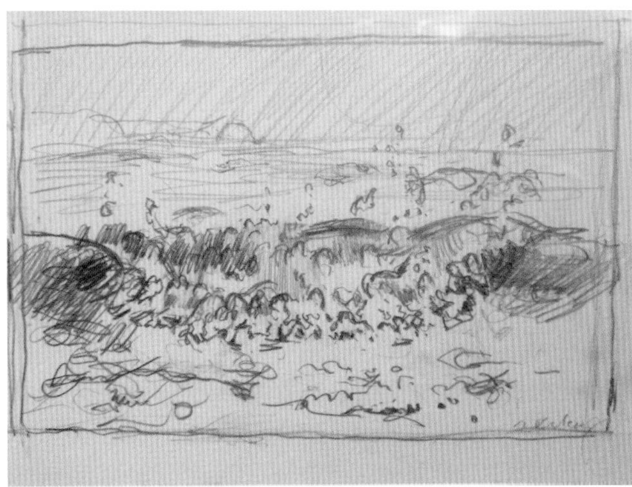

94
Wave pencil studies, 2001–03
Oil on board 20x30cms

95
Wave No. I, 2001
Oil on canvas, 99.1x129.5cms

96
Wave No. I, 2002
Etching and aquatint,
17.1x25cms

97, top left
Wave, Widemouth, 2000
Oil on board, 20x33cms

97, top right
Portscatho Wave Study, 2001
Oil on canvas, 21.5x30.5cms

97, bottom left
Wave Study, 2002
Oil on board, 25x35cms

97, bottom right
Sun Through the Wave, 2001
Oil on board, 22x30cms

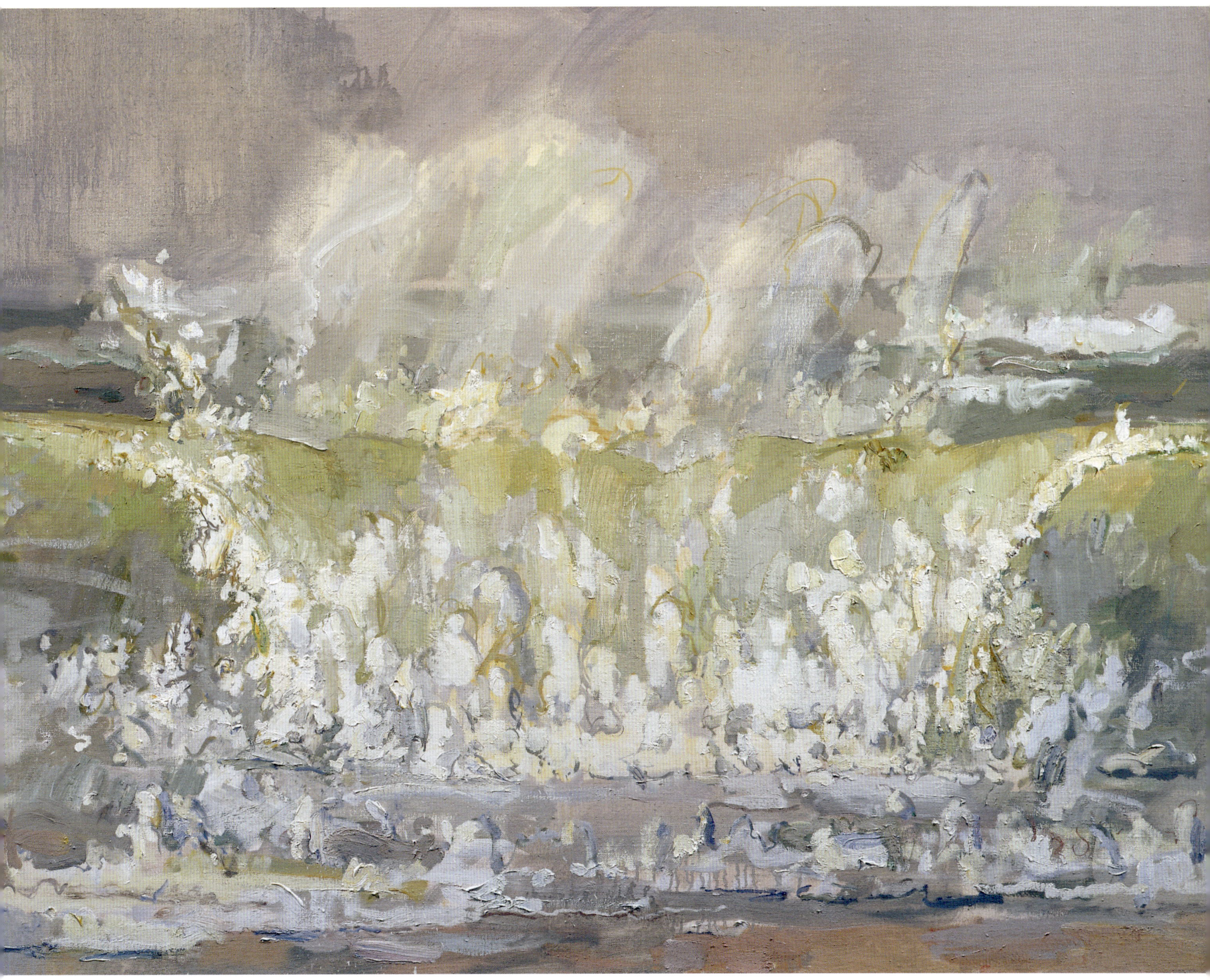

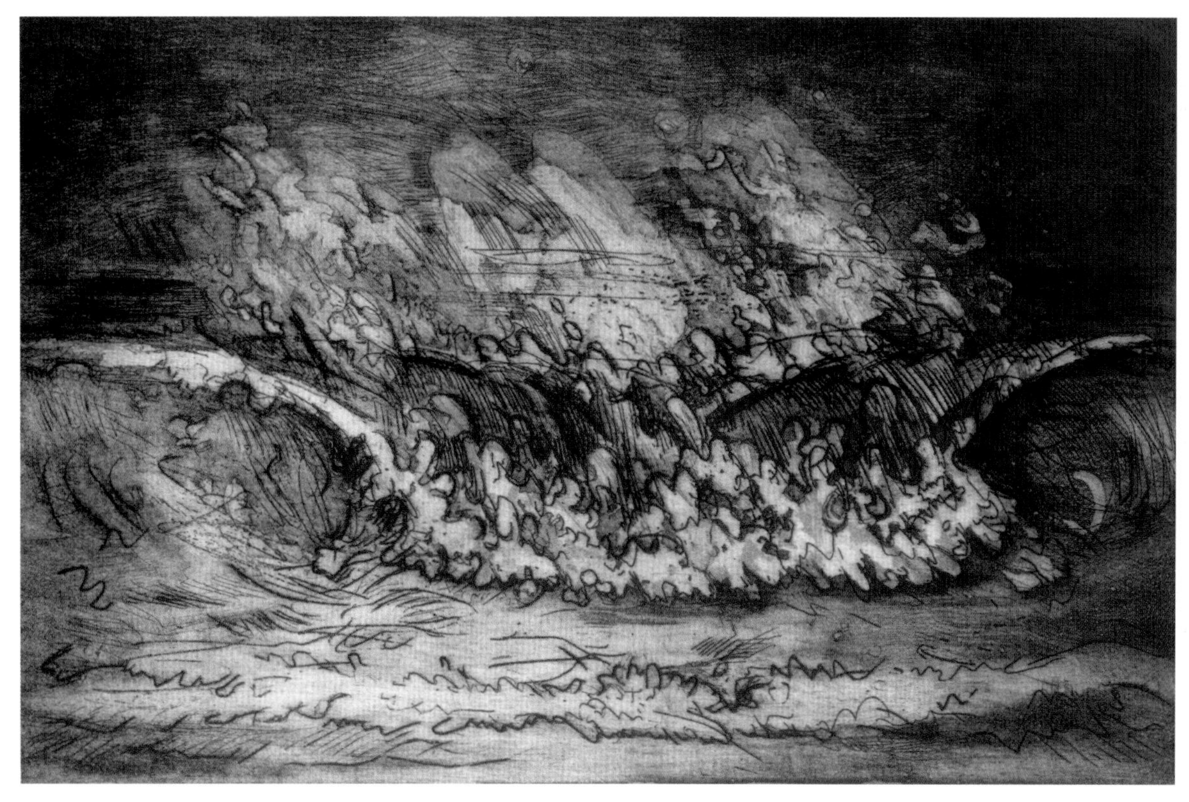

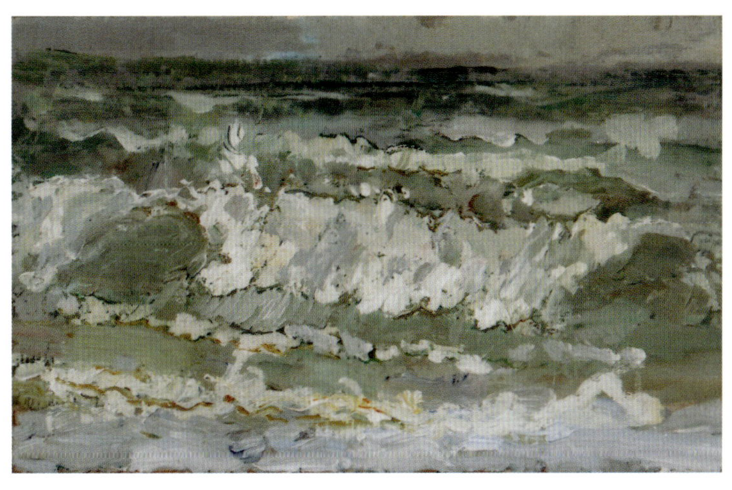

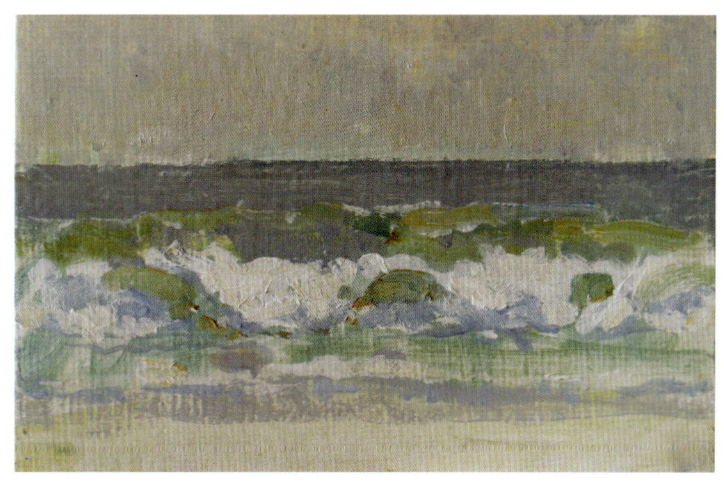

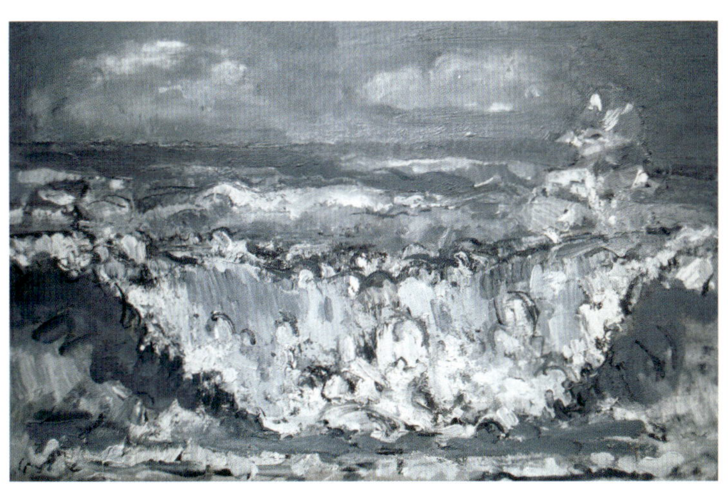

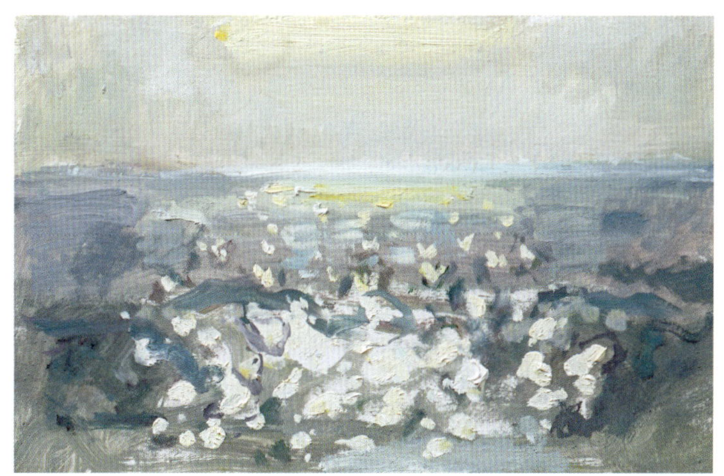

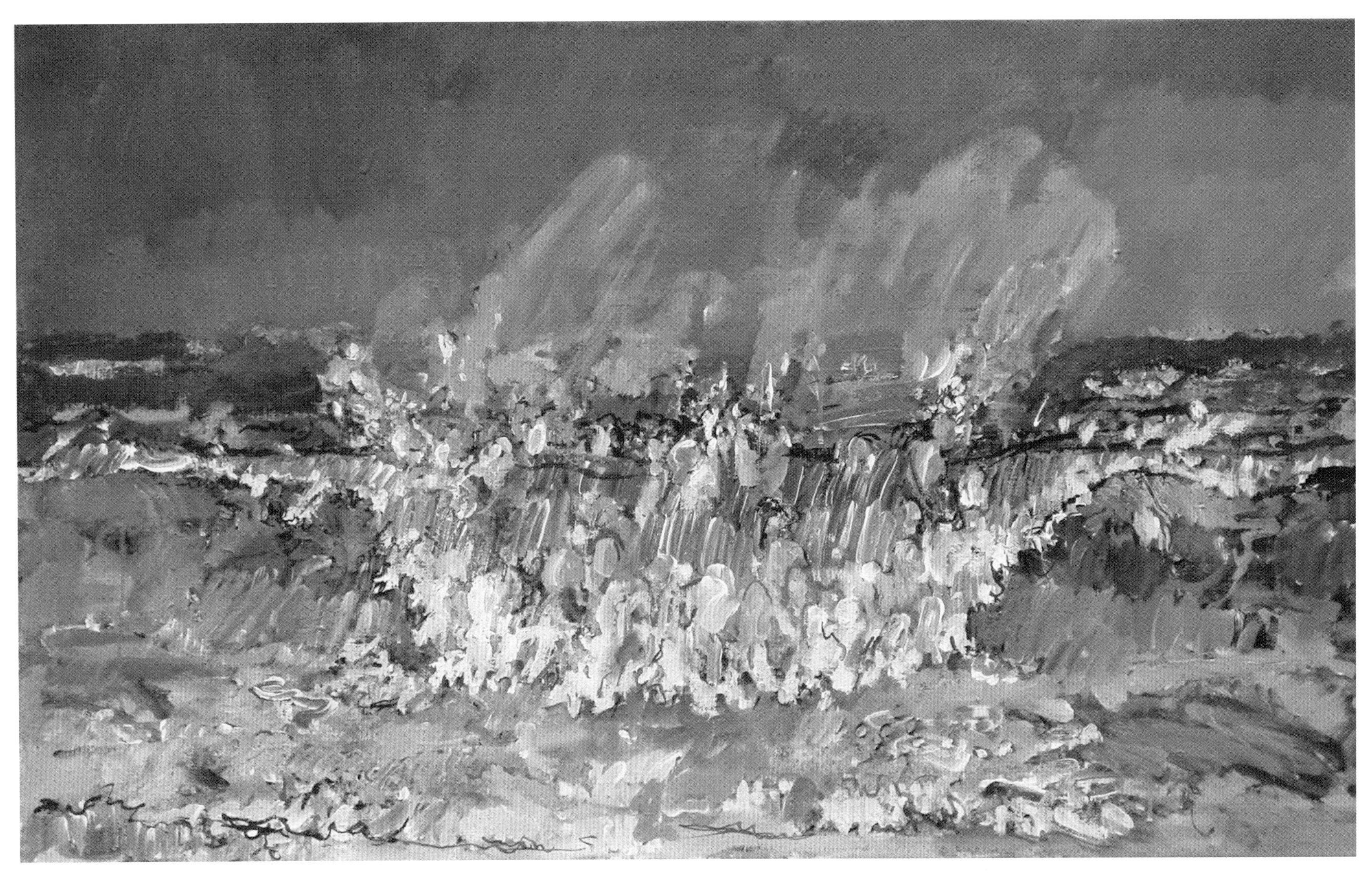

98
Wave and spray, 2000
Acrylic on canvas, 90x150cms

99
Wave, 1993
Japanese ink on paper, 29x56cms

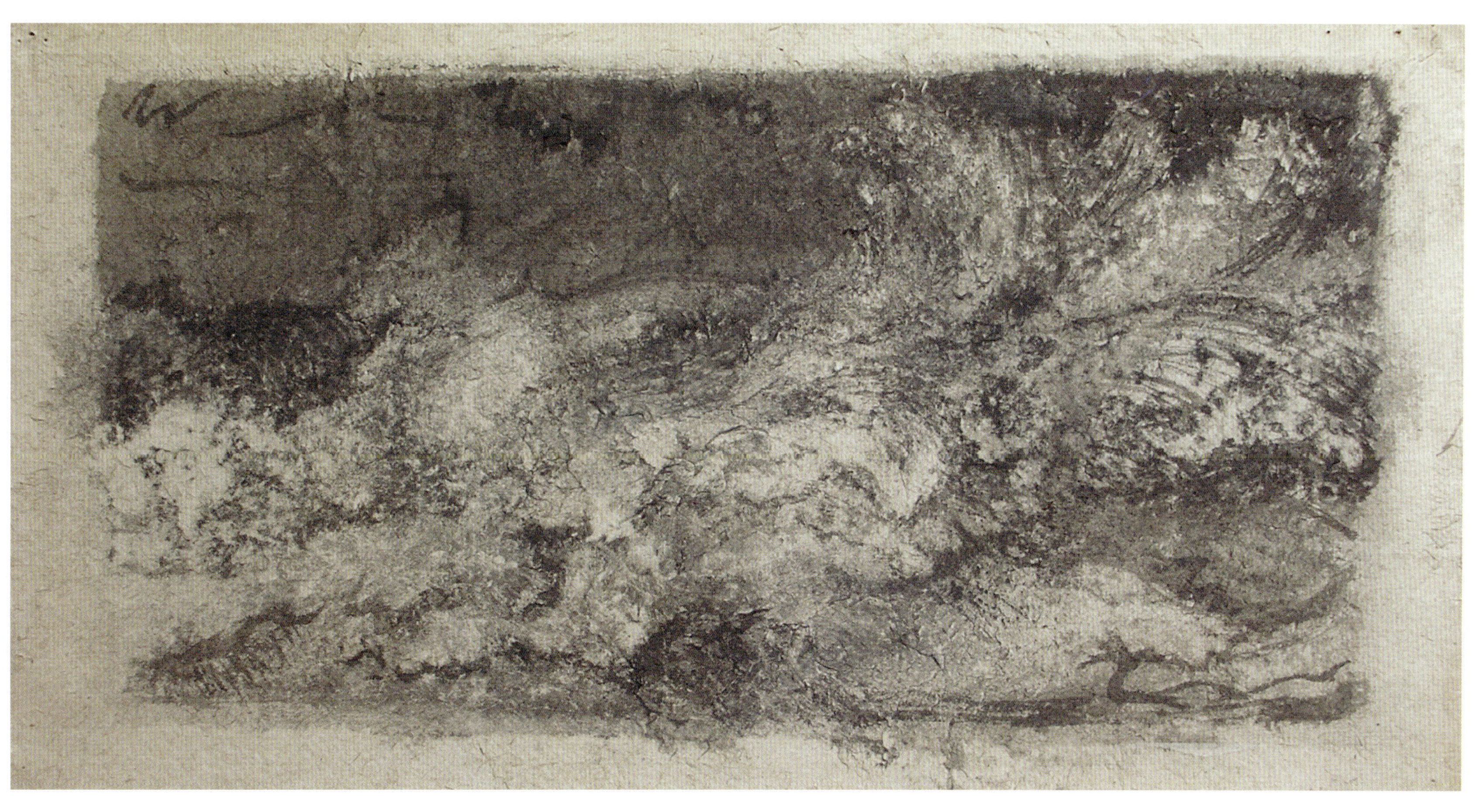

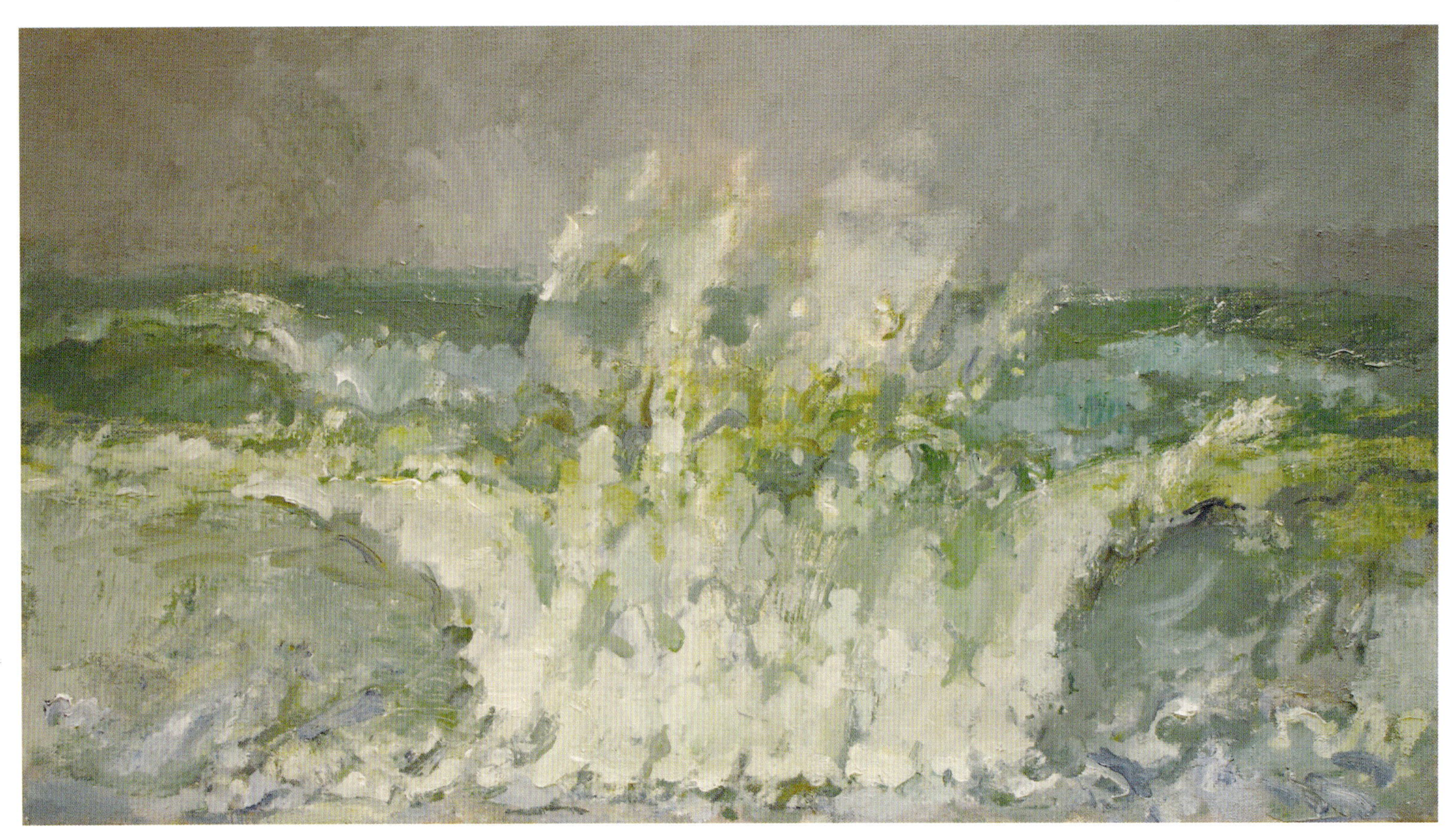

100
Incoming Wave, 2001
Oil on canvas, 61x107cms

101
Wave No. 2, 2001
Oil on canvas, 99.1 x 129.5cms

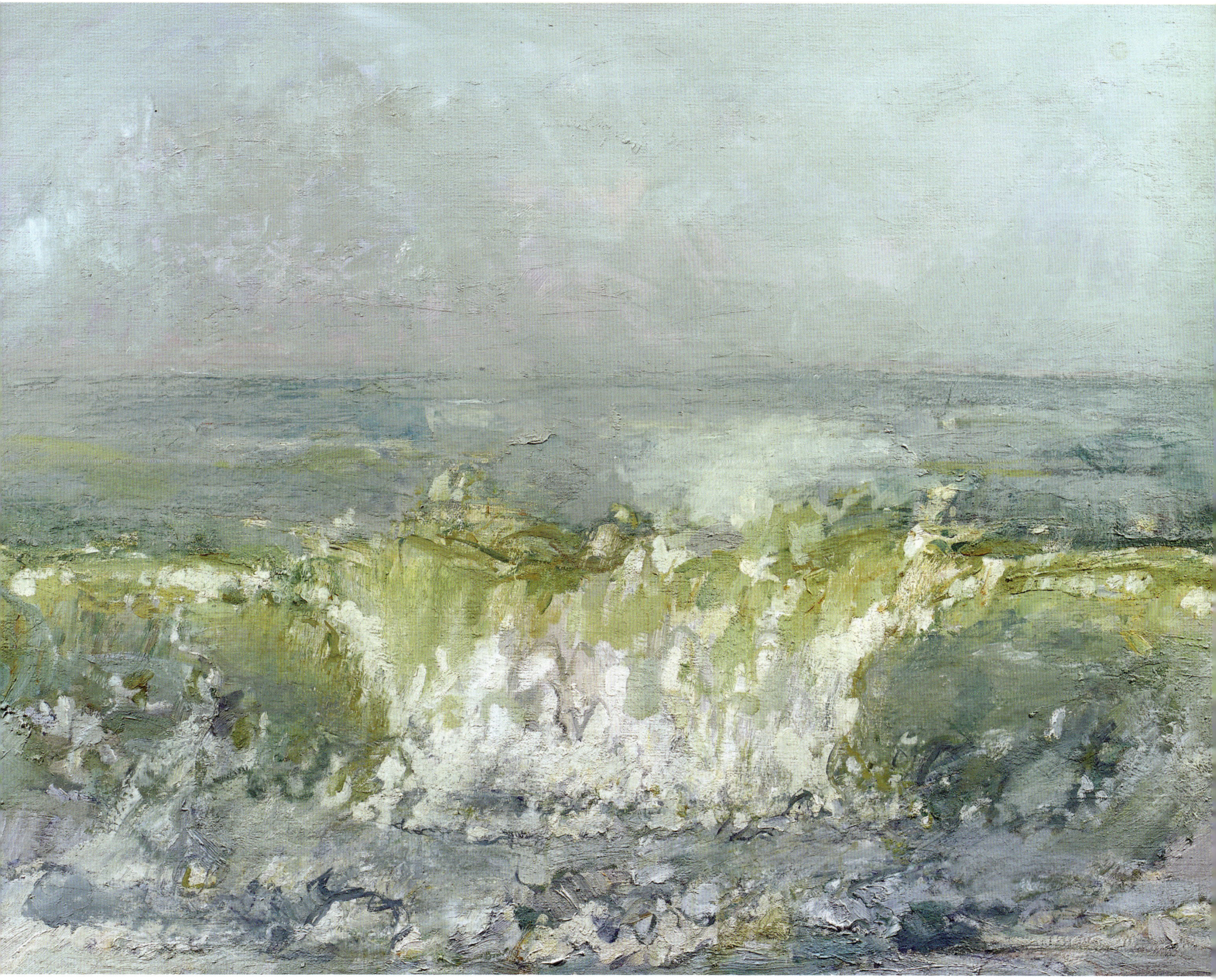

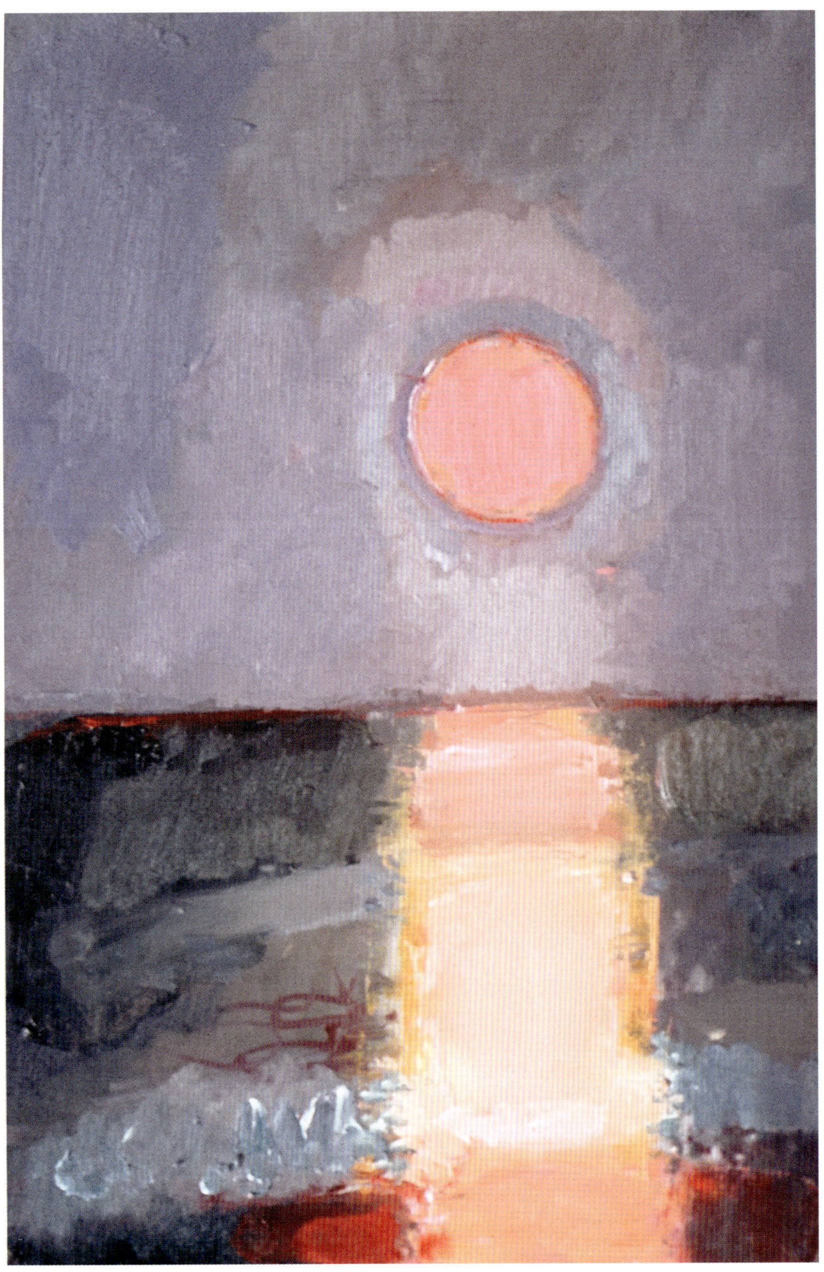

102
Moonrise over the sea, 2002
Oil on board 35x20cms

103
Yorkstrasse, Berlin Night, 2001
Oil on canvas, 130x100cms

Yorkstrasse, Berlin Night (2001) was painted during Felcey's brief sojourn in that city, and depicts the view from the balcony of his apartment. It evolved at the same time as drawings of the studio looking out at Yorkstrasse and the church on the corner of Mansteinstrasse. Space is articulated through the lights permeating the more solid darkness: the vertical strips of lighted windows and the search-light from Potzdammerplatz going across the sky. The paint application looks speedy but it's a very settled image. 'If the whole idea's there then that's it really', says Felcey. It's not like finishing off or tying up loose ends. 'One of the difficulties about trying to make that painting was trying to illuminate darkness, to bring palpable light to the dark and yet keep full value to the local colours – the red of the traffic lights, or the orange, or the blue and green sign of the station.' There's a nice trickly quality of the paint – very thin colour which makes a satisfying contrast with more densely worked areas. Felcey admits that most of his pictures start like that, but get painted over. 'However long the painting goes on one still wants it to actually be physically paint on the surface of the canvas – those thinner mixtures do just read as paint as well as light.'

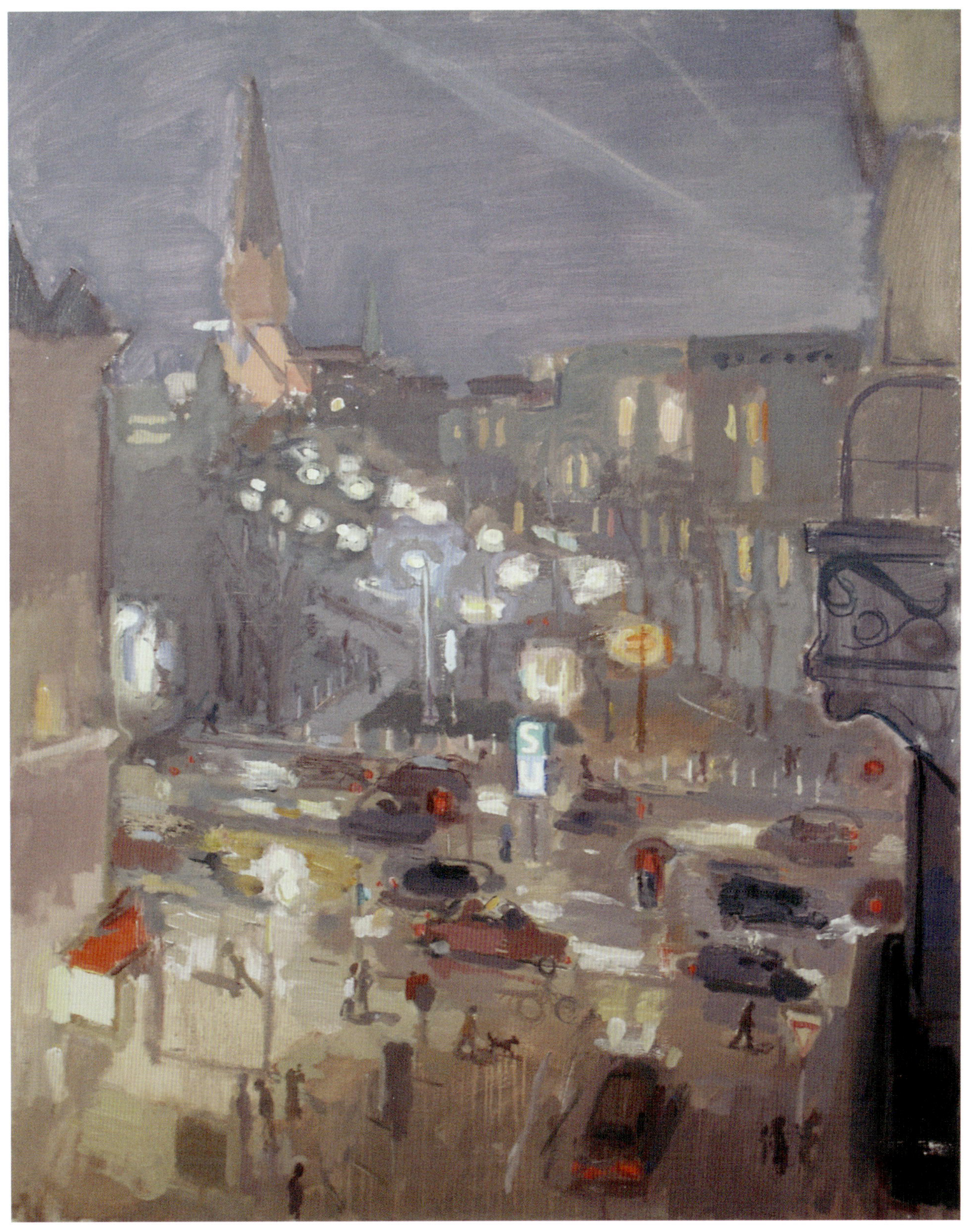

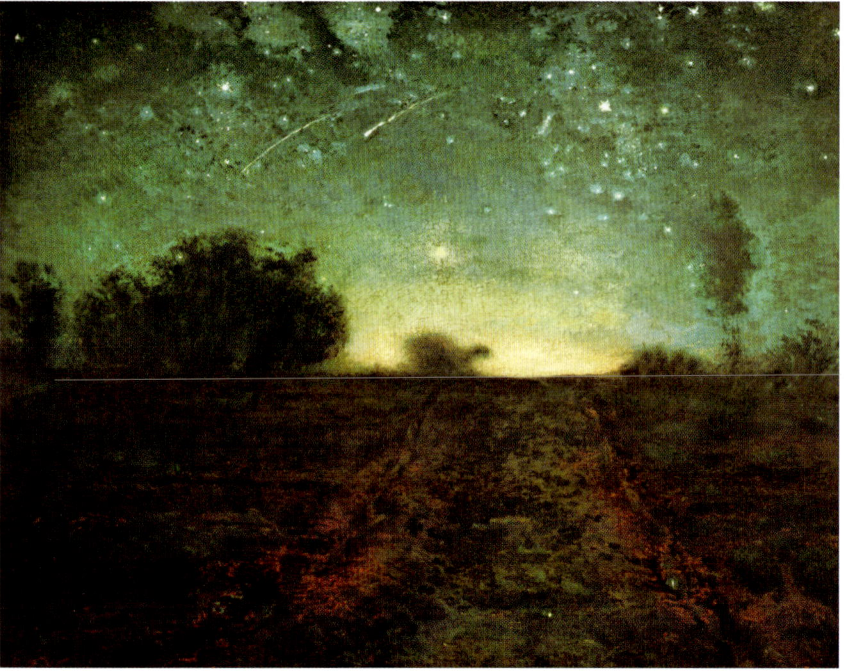

104
Starry Night, J. F. Millet, 1855–67, 65x81cms

105
Starshine, Moonshine, Earthshine, 2006–07
Oil on canvas, 60x120cms

Felcey comments: 'When I started this painting I didn't know about the beautiful phenomenon of the sickle moon chasing the setting sun. I thought that was just some phenomenon of the sun, but actually it's the sun shining on the earth reflecting back onto the moon. So it is earthshine – the dictionary definition is wonderful: the ashen light on the moon caused by the reflection of the earth.' Of course, one can't attempt a painting of the night without thinking of J. F. Millet. Generally he is somebody who is very important for me – an incredible draughtsman and wonderful colourist. His 'Starry Night' is sublime. There's an absolute galaxy of stars in a diagonal thrust behind the hill. Even a shooting star. Felcey says: 'I did initially use the drawings for Throwleigh Common in the painting. I've often painted pictures of night but I wanted to try to paint a more complete space, so I wanted something to hinge the invention of the colours of the night on, something physically to relate it to.'

Notice the water taking reflections so that the sky comes into the ground. 'I like the idea of when you're looking at the painting you think "Oh, is this a hill or is it the arc of the earth?" I was thinking about Giacometti and that palpable idea of the space. That's certainly what you feel at night, much more than in daylight, when things are out there, separate. At night you are enveloped in the space. That's such a wonderful feeling.' The colours are emphatic: distinctive blue-grey-brown rocks on a grey-green ground, and green-haloed stars on a purplish grey sky. If it doesn't have quite the same grandeur or unity of conception as Night Moor (which was painted next), it does possess a wildness and ardour, due in part to the use of dark red outlining objects and giving them a real force.

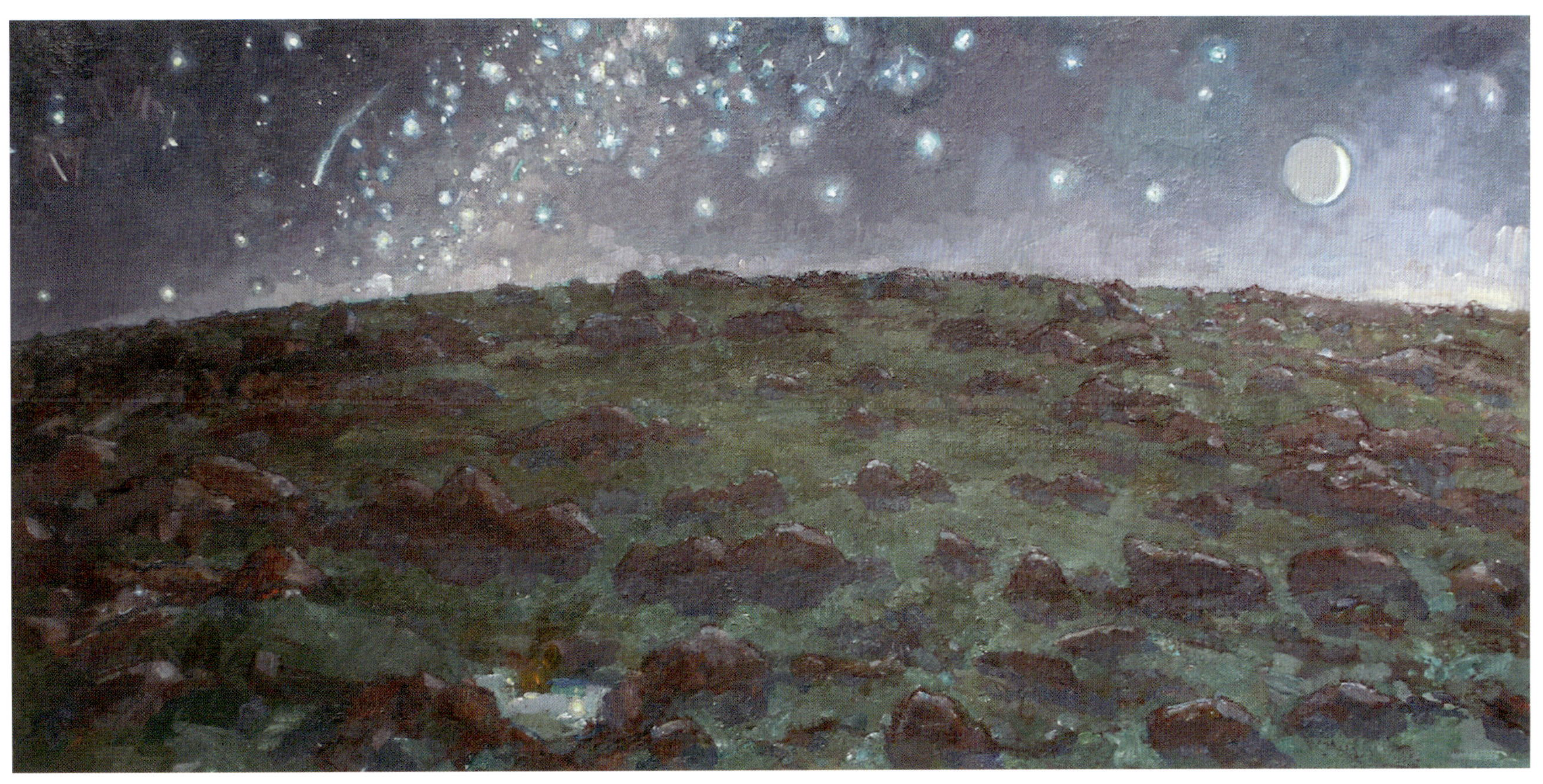

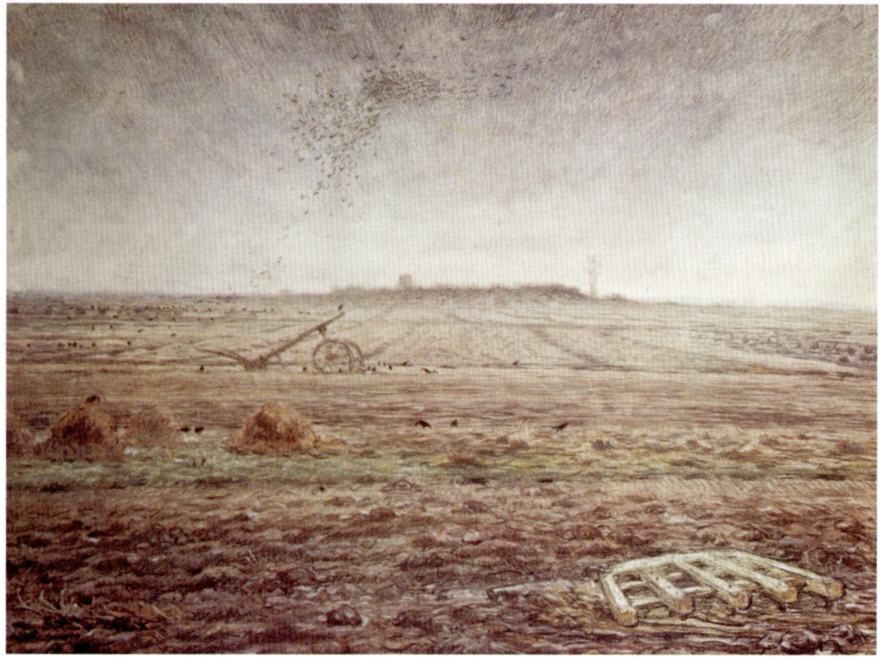

106
Winter with Crows, J. F. Millet
Pastel, 70x94cms

107
Night Moor, 2006–07
Oil on board, 104x122cms

Night Moor (2006–7) was begun after Starshine but overlaps with it. It's a big night painting with stars and a shooting star crusted and jagged into the darkness of night, enhaloed in viridian, yellow, blue. The earth is alive with pulses, dark colours, a richness of browns. Contour lines are in black, there's also lots of blue and touches of green (this is the idea of bringing the sky down to the earth again). Although Felcey usually keeps the night paintings to monochrome, this one burgeoned with colour. There's quite a lot of blue in the land, for instance: some of the drawing is in black, some in Prussian blue. The rhythm in the sky goes through the landscape as well as the sky appearing behind the moor. The land also looks more like a choppy sea, or rather, it has the feeling of sea. It's an altogether more elemental painting, with a conspicuous surface tension. The paint is very physically on the surface. It has to work as both surface and space.

108, top
Night Moor with Two Trees, 2006
Oil on canvas, 60x90cms

108, bottom
Night Moor drawing, 2007,
Mixed media on paper, 80x100cms

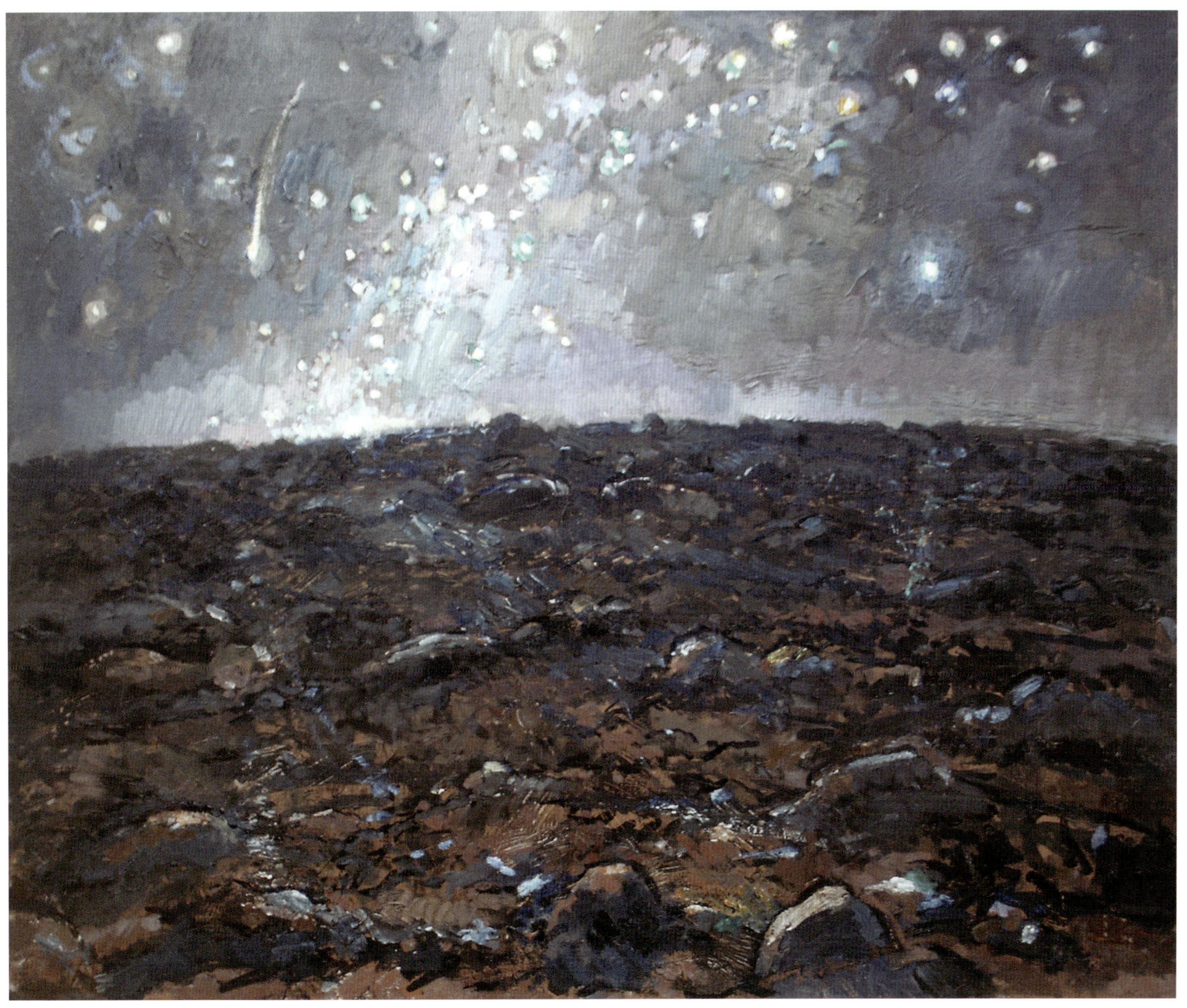

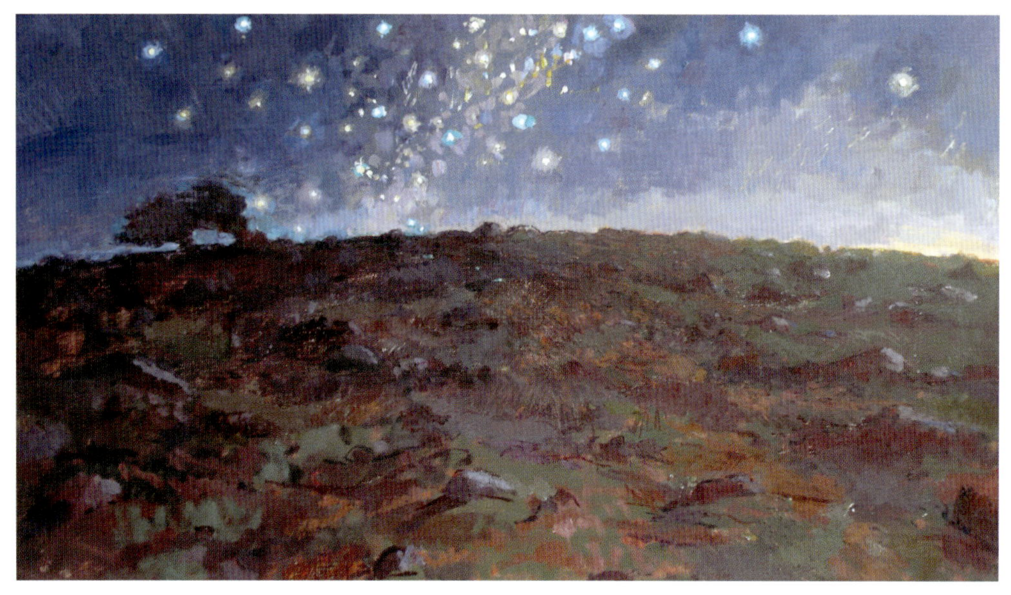

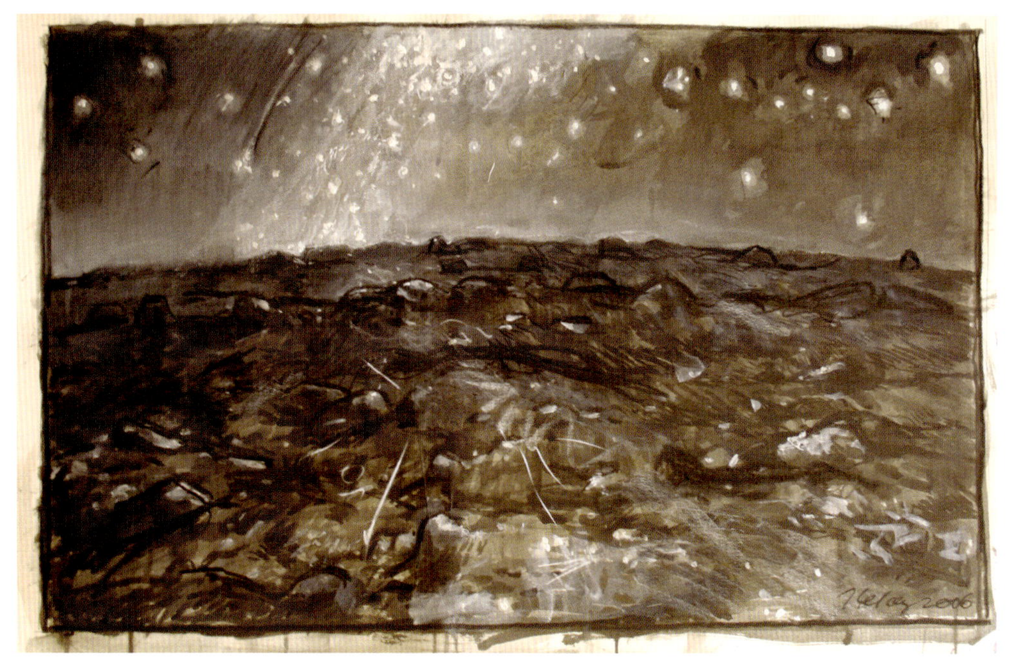

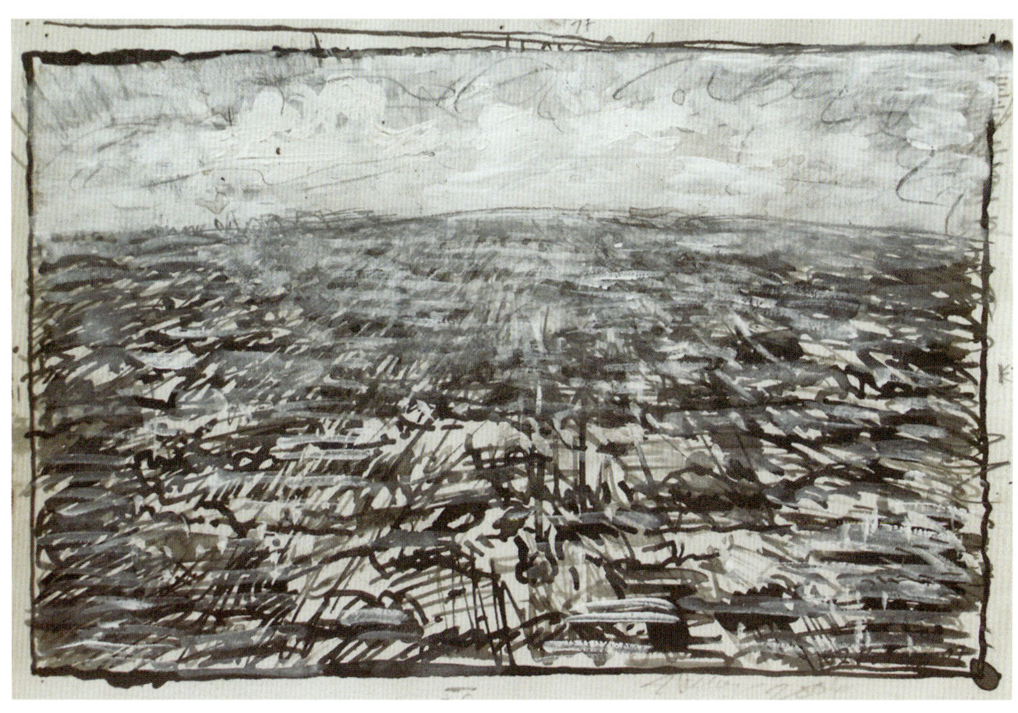

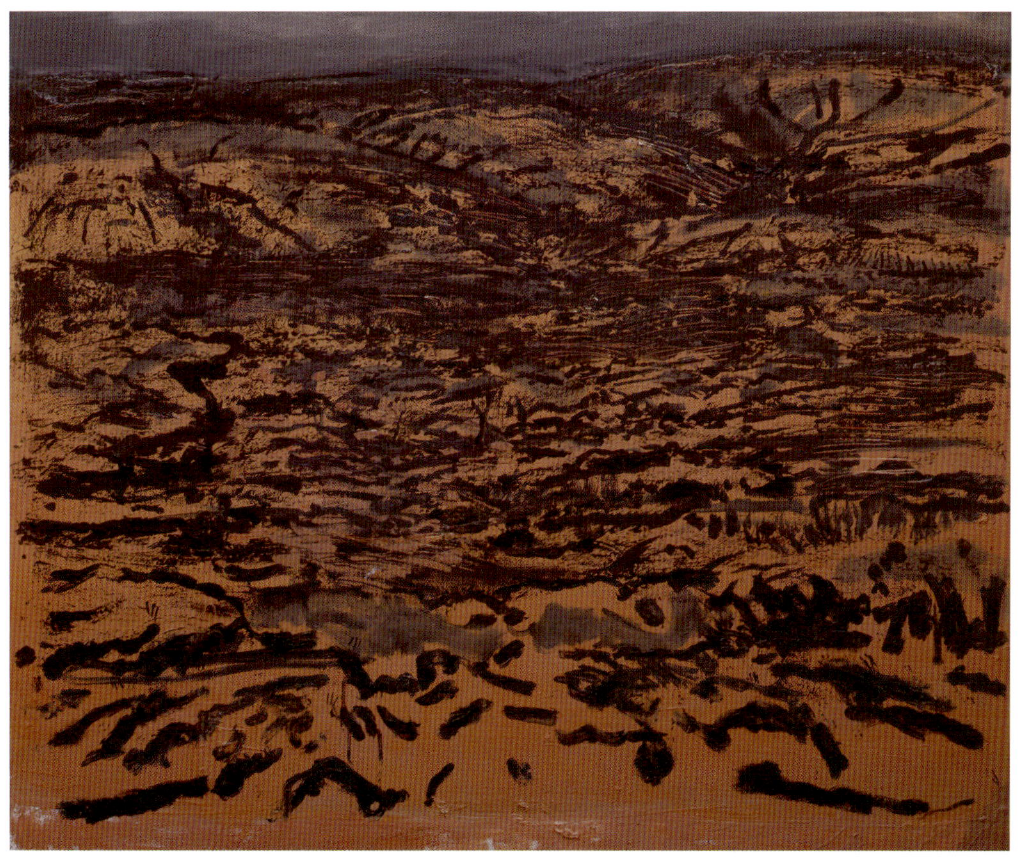

109, top
Moor Landscape, 2006
Mixed media on paper, 17.5x27.5cms

109, bottom
Moor Landscape, 2000
Oil on board, 104x122cms

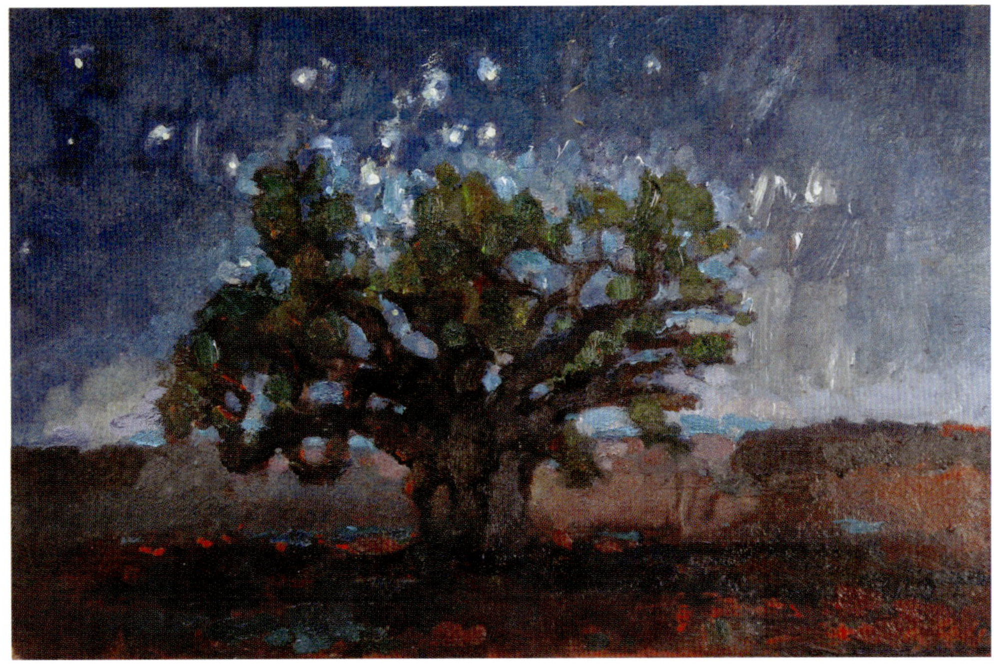

110
Oak and Stars, 2007
Oil on board, 26x33cms

111
Gorse Burning at Night, 2007
Oil on board, 91.5x122cms

Gorse-burning at Night (2007) Felcey comments: 'Gorse-burning takes place in early spring: a renewing of the land by burning off the bracken and gorse. There are fire-breaks. Sometimes you see the whole hill here alight, it's pretty extraordinary.' Again, it's not the sort of subject you can draw but he does look into the wood burner a lot, and he might make drawings of flames in the fire-place. The subject is more remembered and imagined, re-created. 'Some of the bits of drawing came from the moor pictures – about the rocks and things. This painting is about a diagonal movement coming down. Two pictures that I thought of – maybe this sounds like a loose connection – are Brueghel's The Blind Leading the Blind and Goya's Third of May, the reverse of the illumination in that. When I started these paintings I didn't think of any connection they might have with the wave paintings.' Yet they do have a rhythmic similarity, making another continuity within his work.

112
Night fire study, 2007
Oil on board, 31.5x40cms

113
Moor Fire, 2007
Oil on canvas, 60x90cms

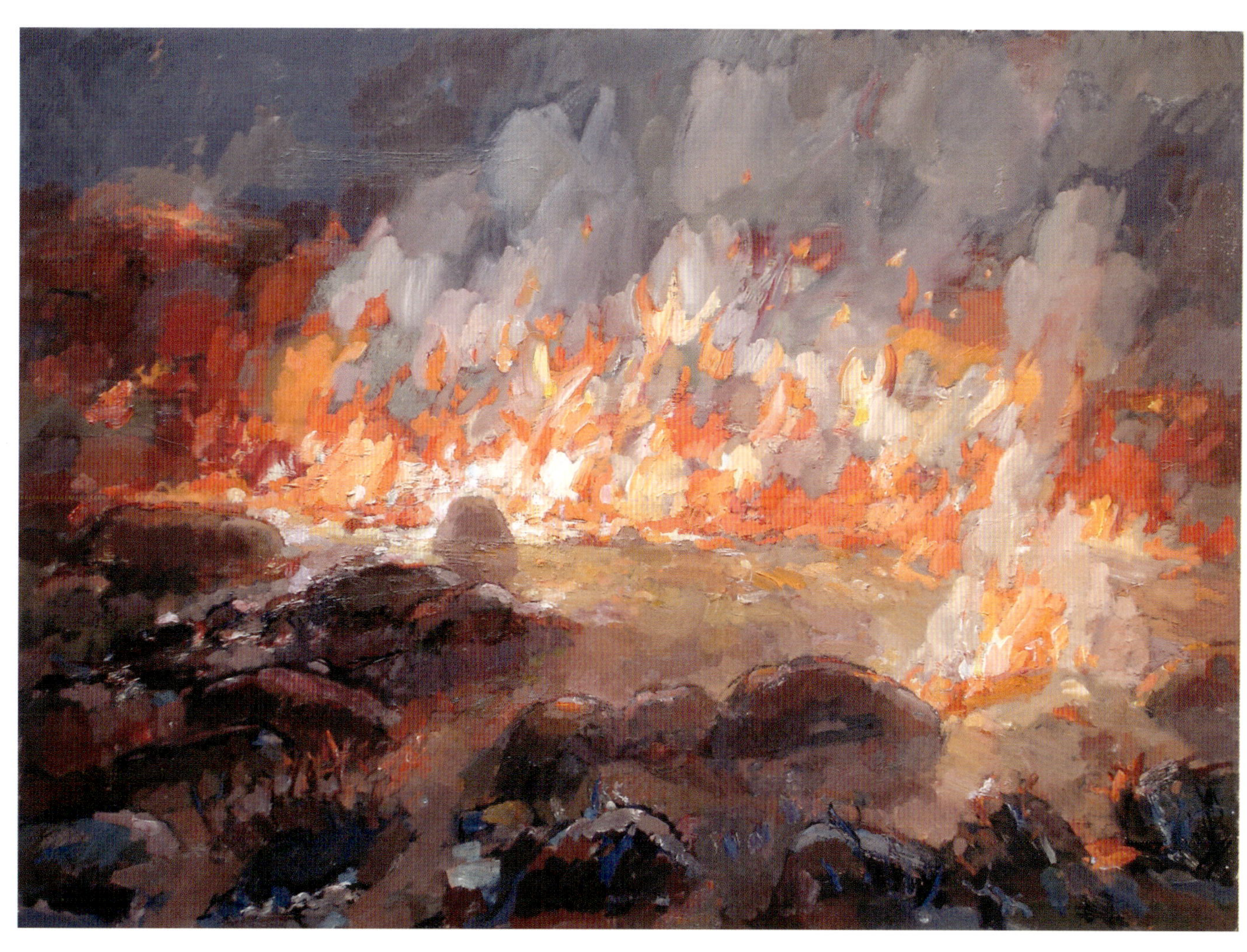

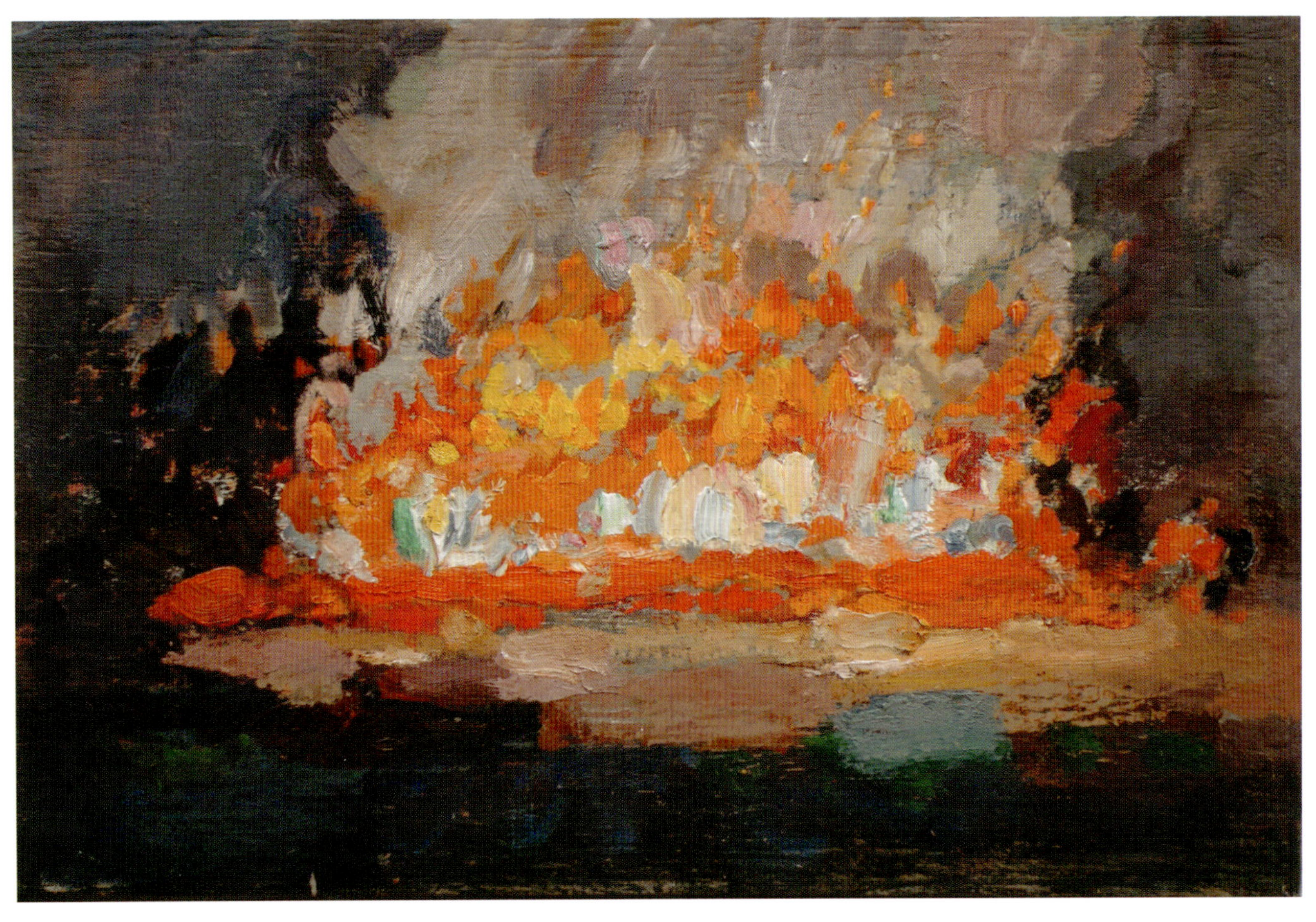

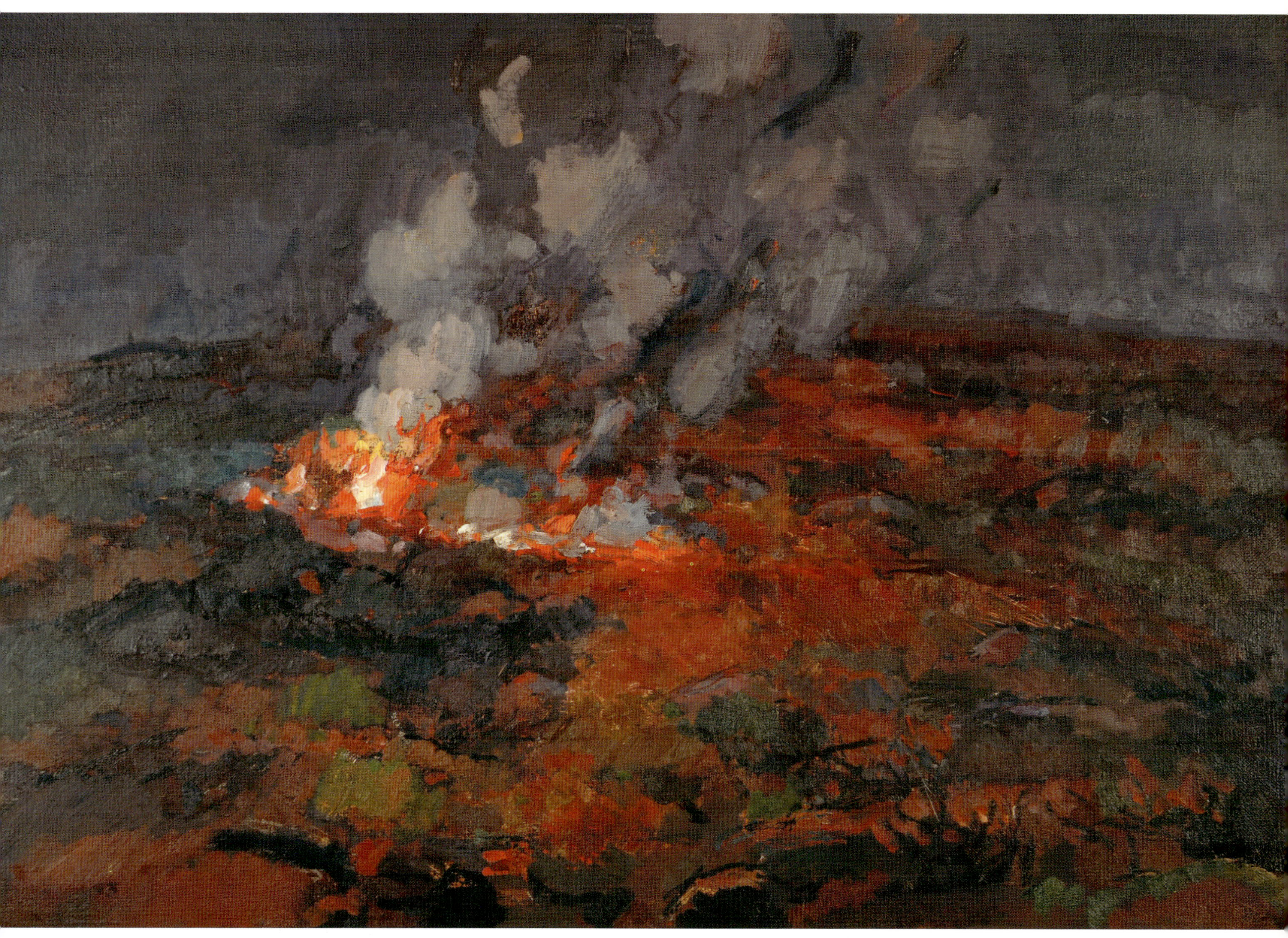

115
Frieze of Apples, Tommy Knight, 2007
Oil on canvas, 39.5x50.5cms

Frieze of Apples, Tommy Knight (2007) Felcey comments: 'It's an extraordinary tree that Tommy Knight, it's so laden, like continuous bunches of grapes all over it. They do these cascades of fruit, these great arabesques. And the beautiful way the red of the apple goes into the branches and into the leaf. The leaves end up even redder. It's just about the idea of this whole carpet which is yet three-dimensional moving back to the sky. And about the rhythms, like Jackson Pollock.' The painting has one of those all-over surfaces much favoured by the Abstract Expressionists, though it was an idea originally pioneered by Cézanne. The movements Felcey has traced through the surface, those sinuosities, are indeed reminiscent of Cézanne. Notice where a patch of blue sky is coming through the leaf cover – almost like a butterfly shape of blue appearing. This is important to Felcey: 'When you're looking at a tree you suddenly see a bunch of leaves that is much closer, and then suddenly there's a piece of sky that jumps – that is closer than anything. That's what that's about.' A beautiful study of surface and depth.

116, left
Walnut Tree with Robin, 2007
Oil on canvas, 127.5x99.5cms

116, right
Young Walnut Tree, 2003
Oil on canvas, 90x60cms

117
Apple Branch, 2008
Oil on canvas, 30x53.5cms

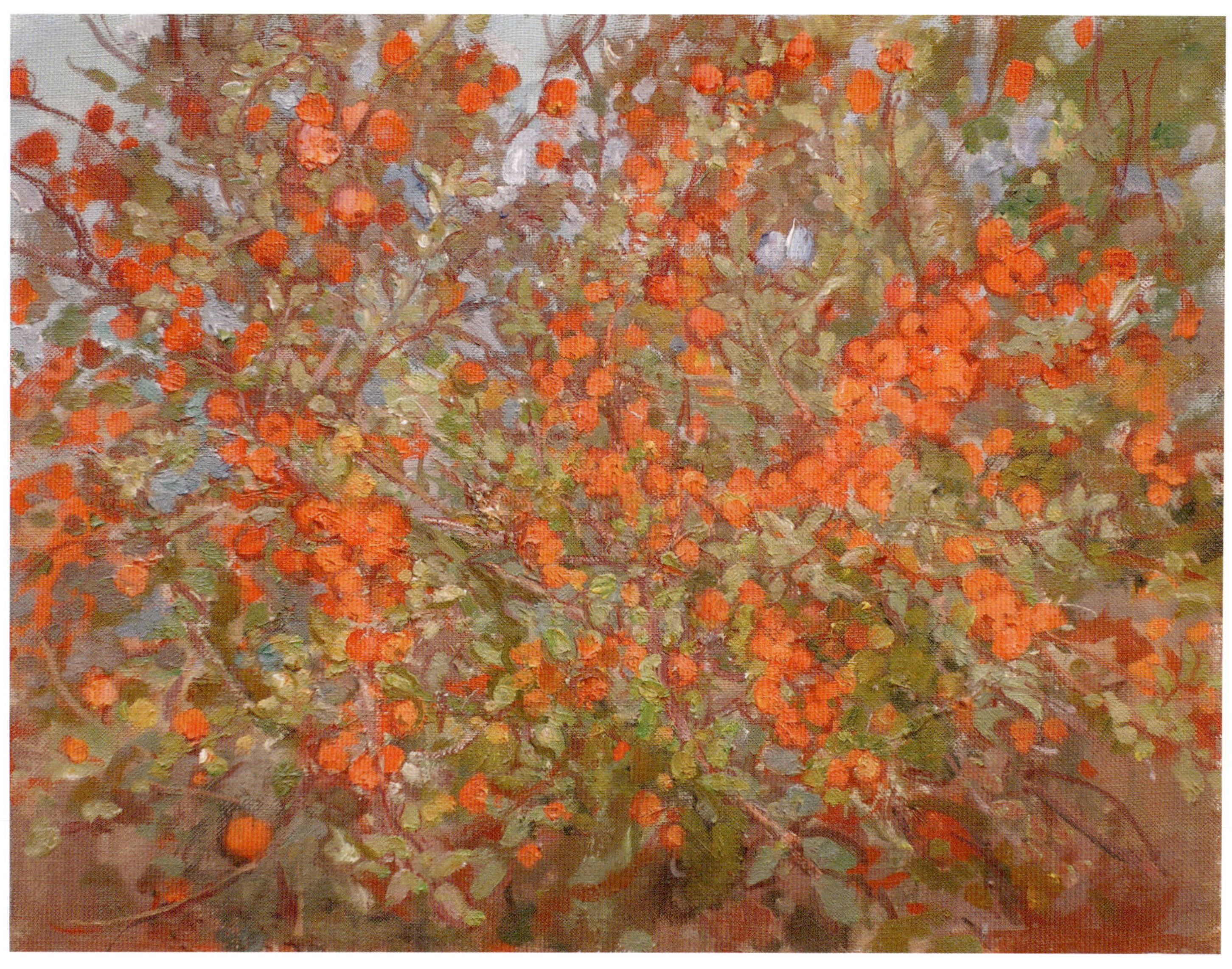

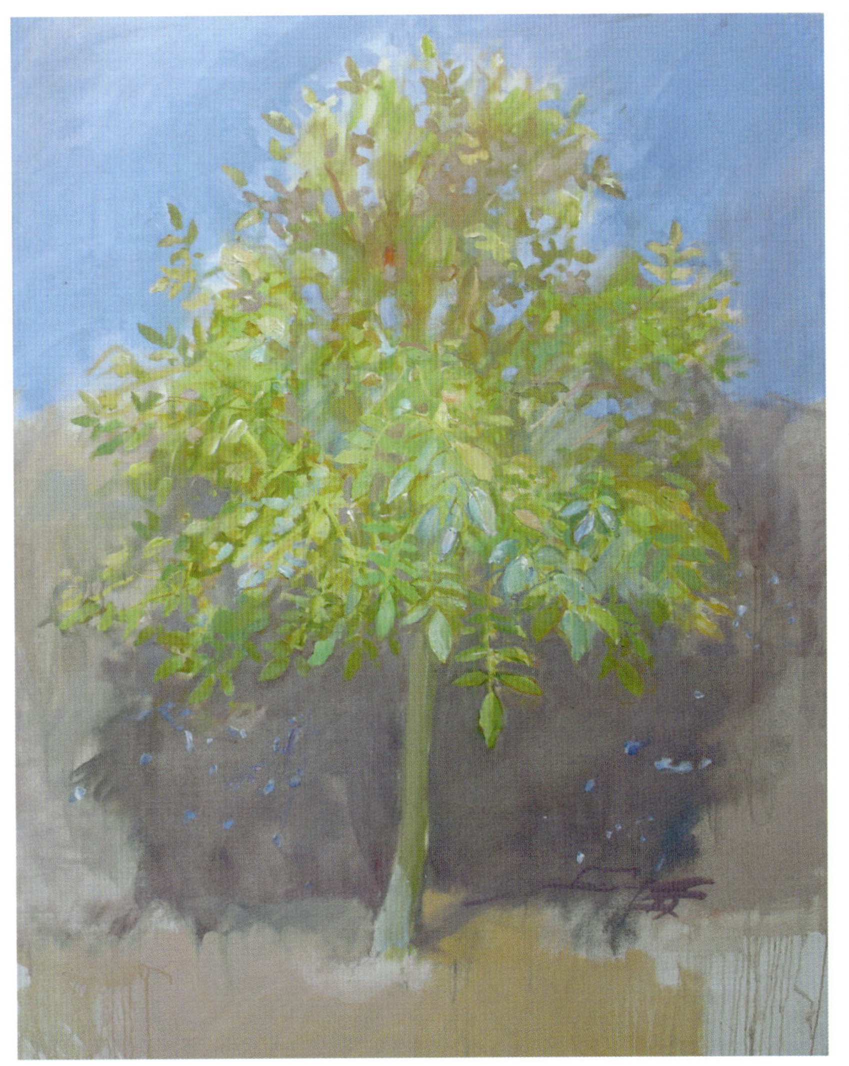

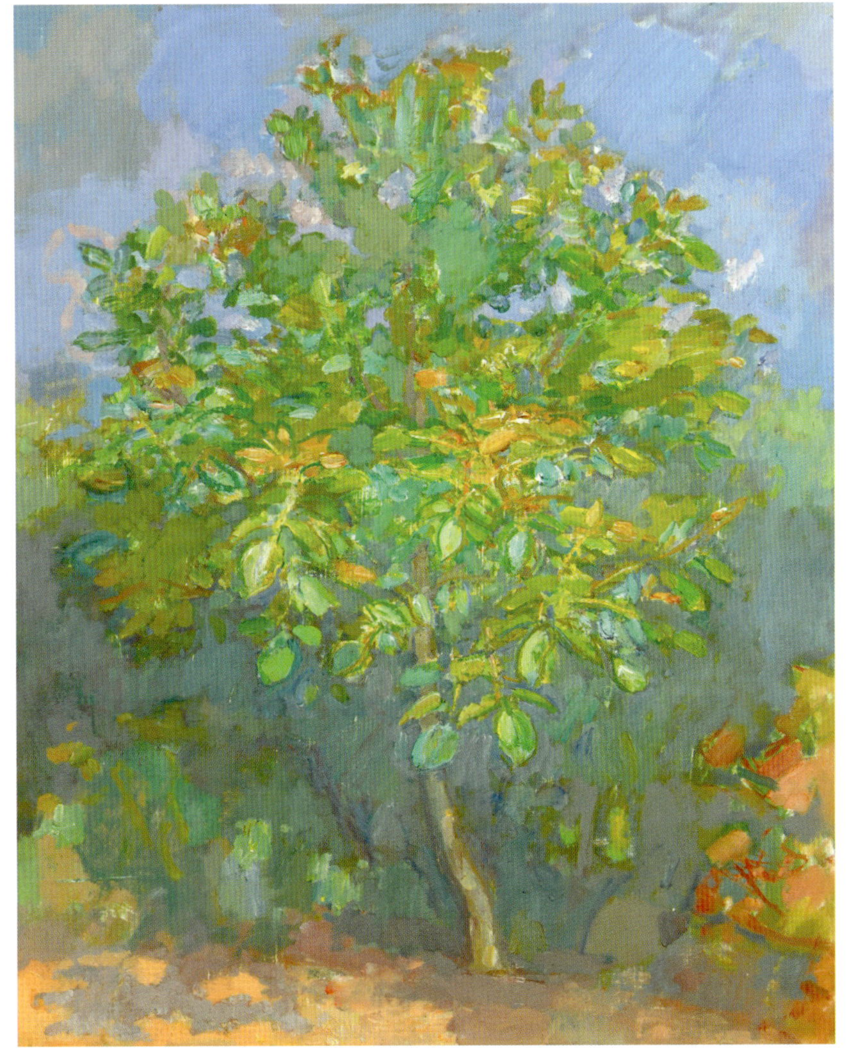

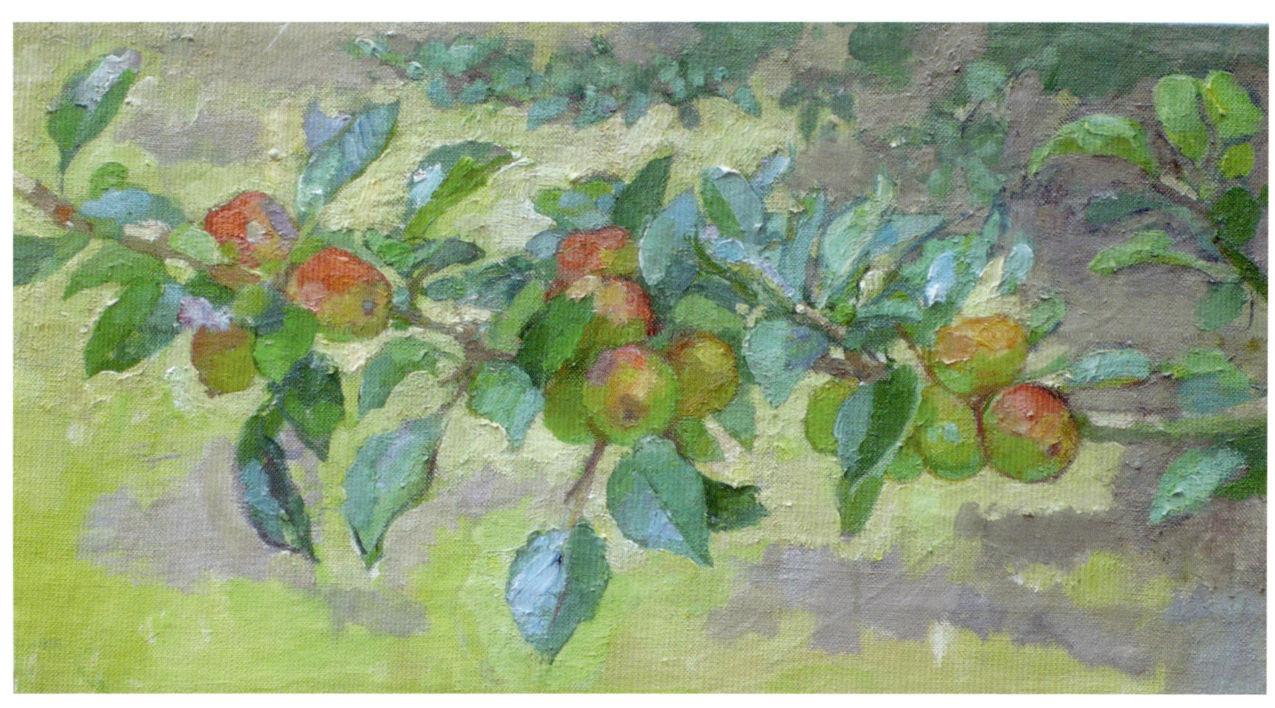

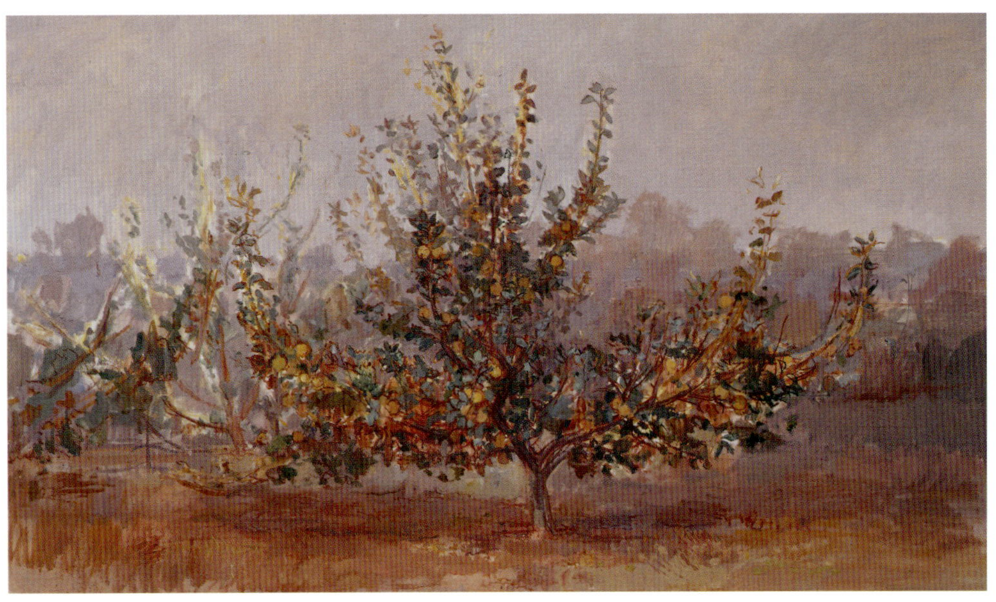

118
Russett, 1996
Oil on canvas, 90x150cms

119
Apple Tree, No. III, 1999
Japanese and Indian ink on paper, 63.5x88.3cms

There are three drawings of an apple tree in the garden – Apple Tree No I, Apple Tree No 2 and Apple Tree No 3 (all 1999). 'The first one was the charcoal. I spent a long time drawing that, then I really felt the scale of the mark, the charcoal, was too big for the thing I was trying to draw. So I drew it again in pencil, over a couple of months. A similar scale drawing but the marks seemed more appropriate. Then by the time I'd done both those drawings the apples had dropped off the tree, and I still didn't feel the drawing was done, so I made this third drawing from memory and from those two drawings, in Indian and Japanese inks, and worked much longer on that. I thought that was the definitive drawing of the three. I worked on all three through the autumn. That's a different kind of drawing where the drawing is the work, it's not going anywhere else, I'm not making a painting with it. It's not just about gathering information or about getting ideas.'

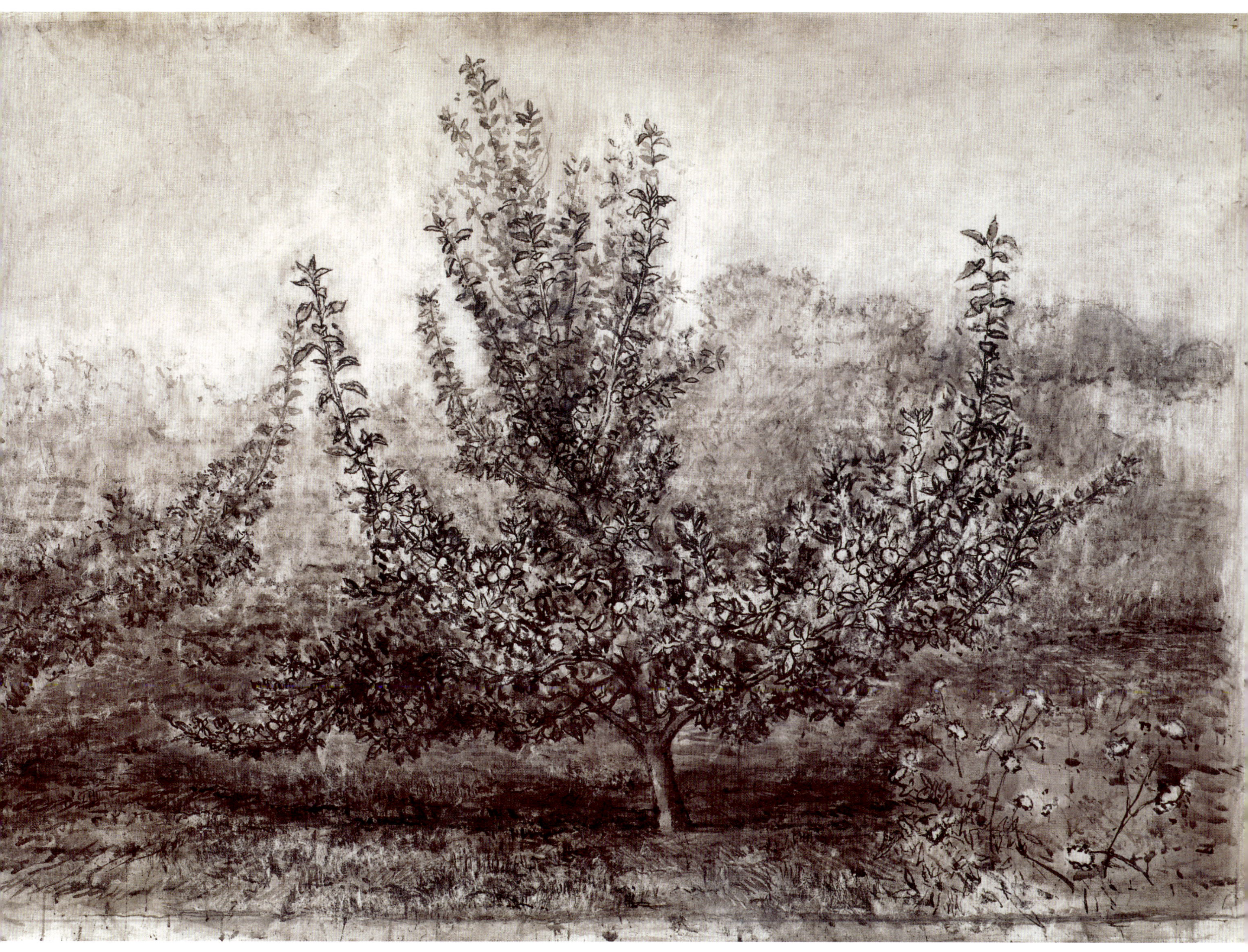

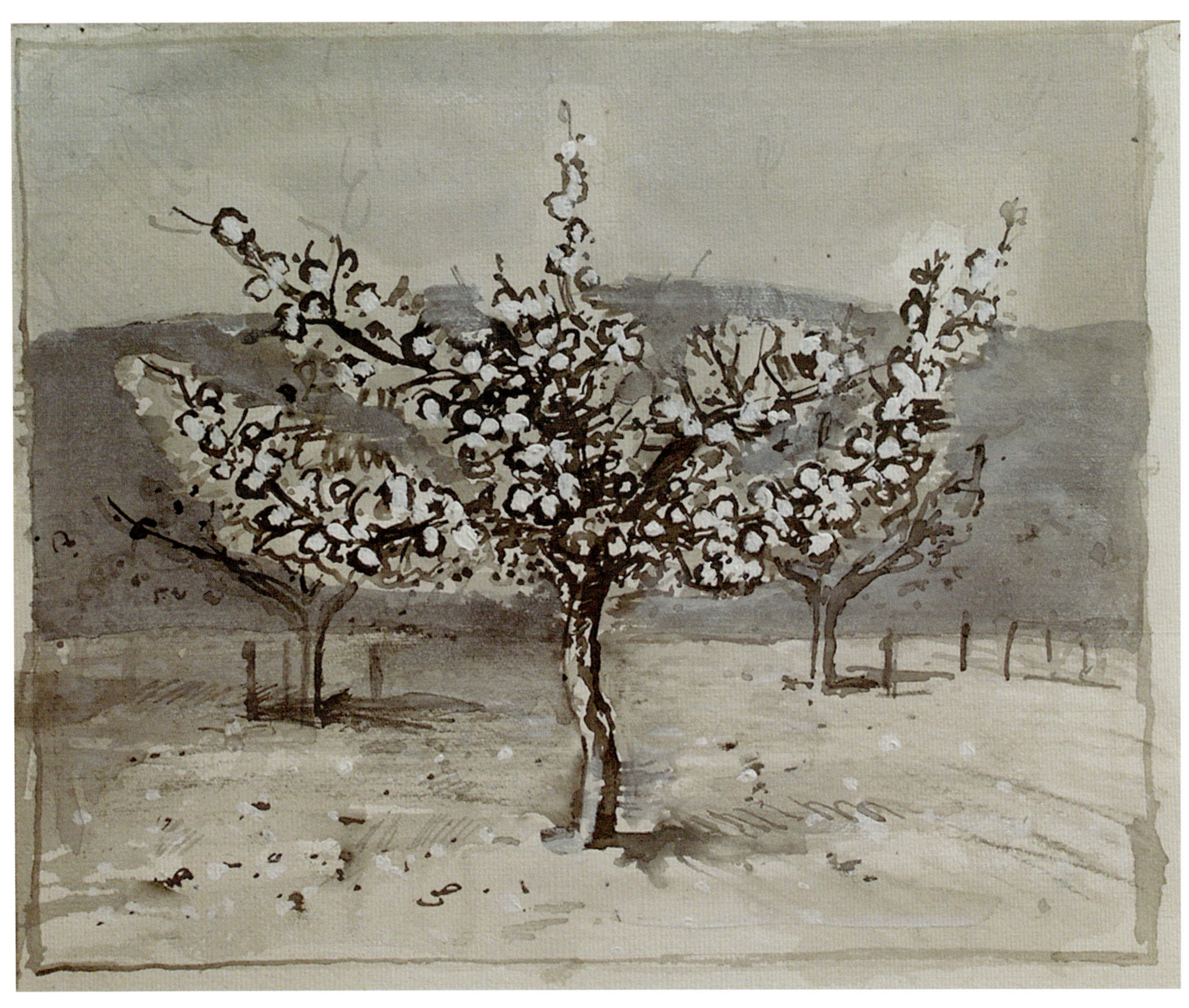

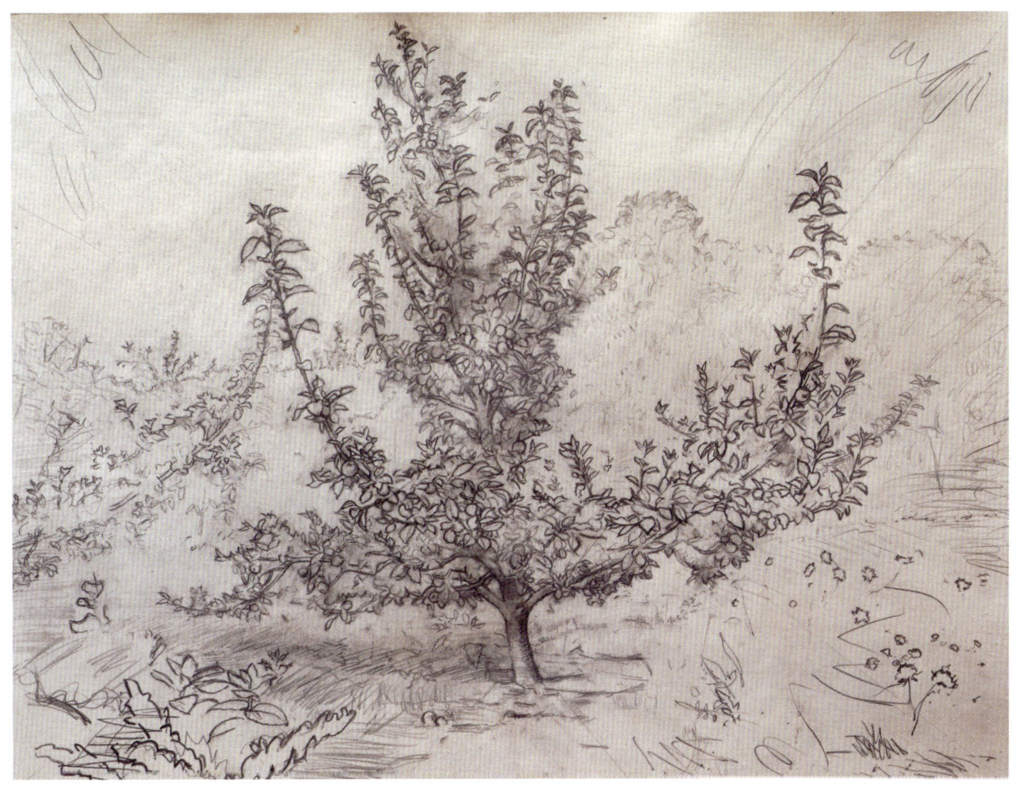

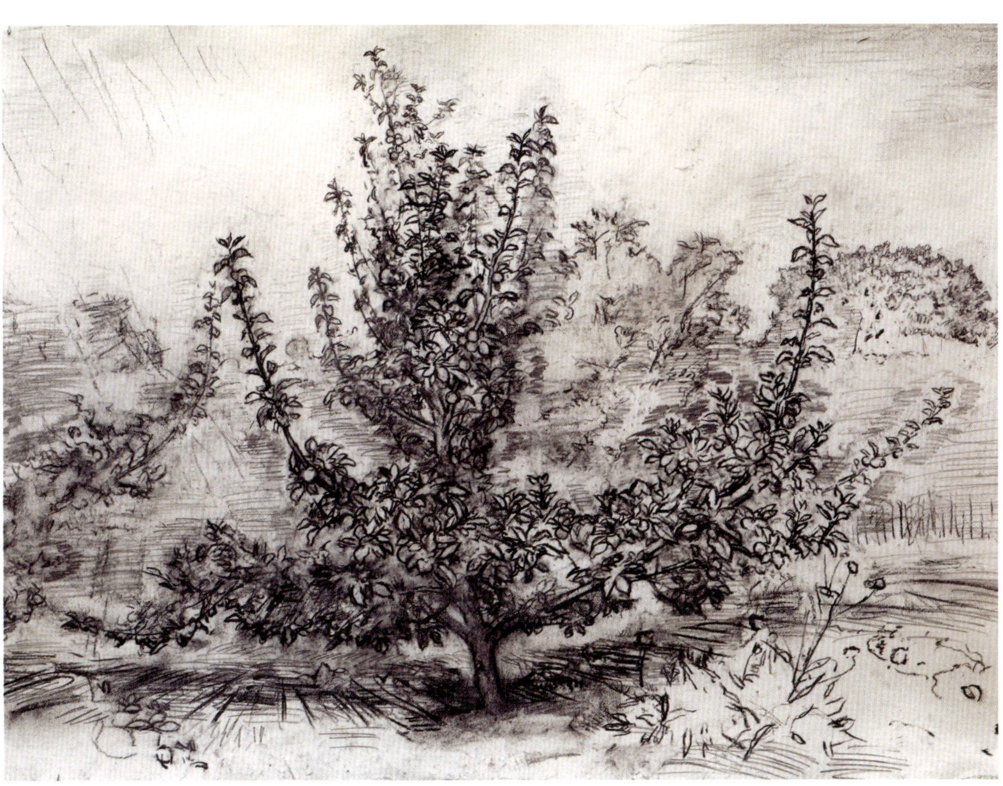

120
Apple Tree in Blossom, 2007
Mixed media on paper, 26x31.5cms

121, top
Apple Tree, No. II, 1999
Pencil on paper, 63.5x88.3cms

121, bottom
Apple Tree, No. I, 1999
Charcoal on paper, 90x70cms

122, top
Winter Apple, 2007
Charcoal and acrylic on paper, 54x70cms

122, bottom
Winter Apple, 2007
Mixed media on paper, 80x100cms

123
Apple Blossom (Winston), 1998
Pencil on paper, 68x62cms

124
Young Oak, Wistman's Wood, 1996
Etching, 24.5x30.2cms

125
Bramley Apple Tree, 2007
Mixed media on paper, 76x100cms

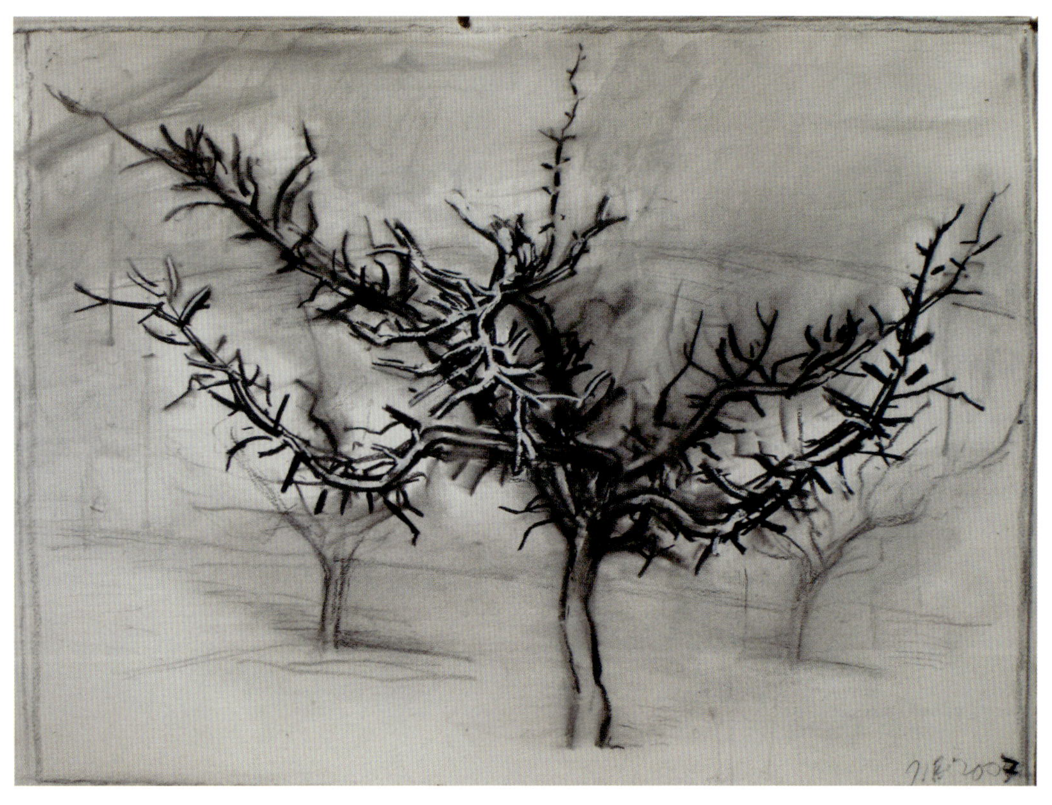

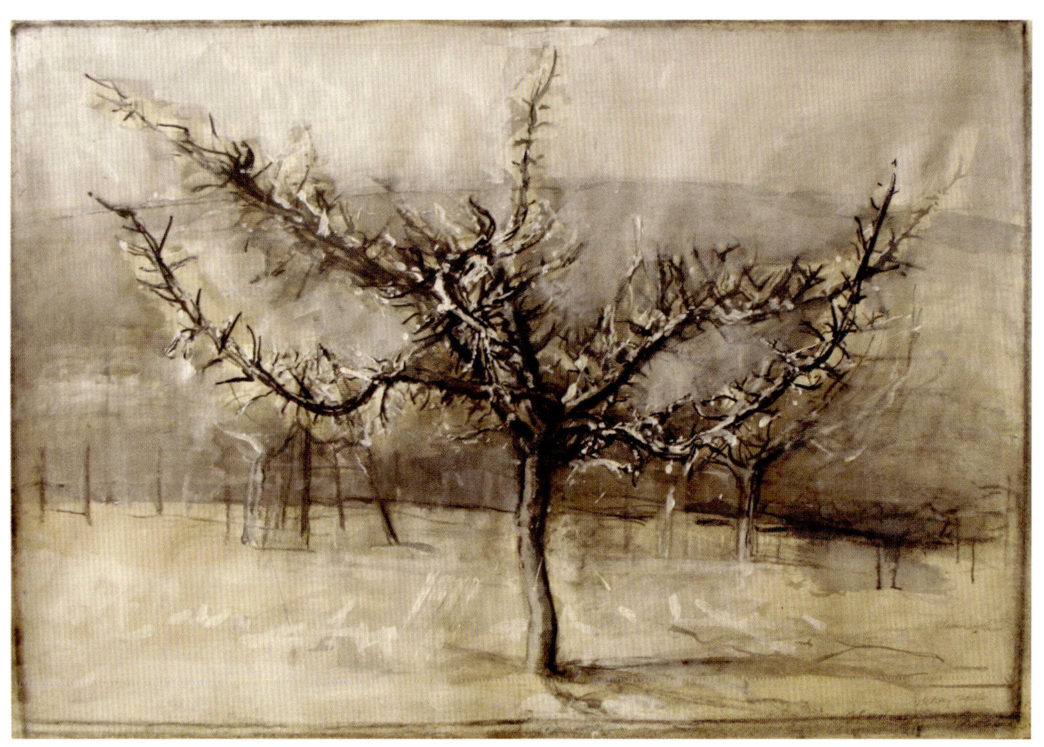

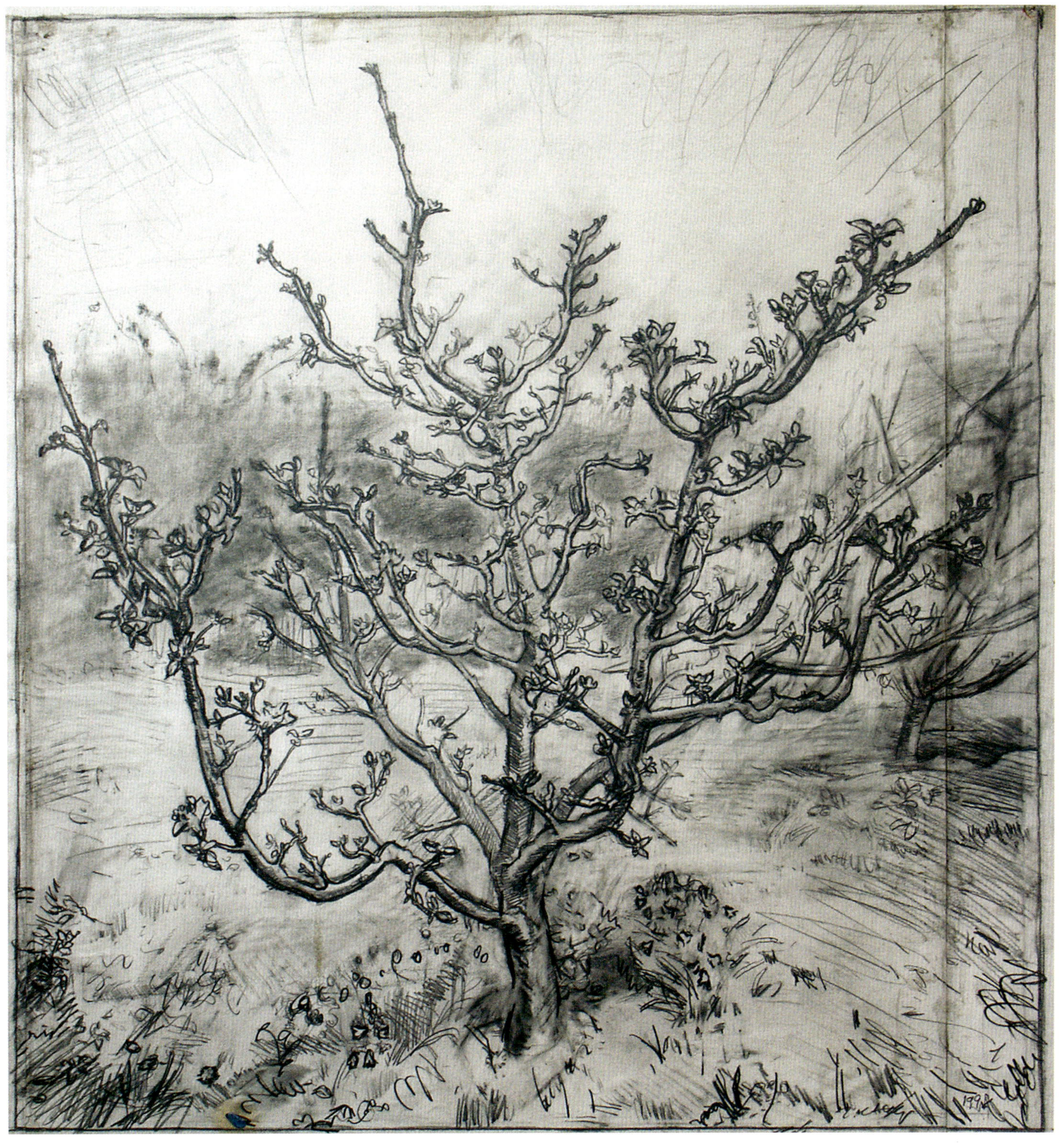

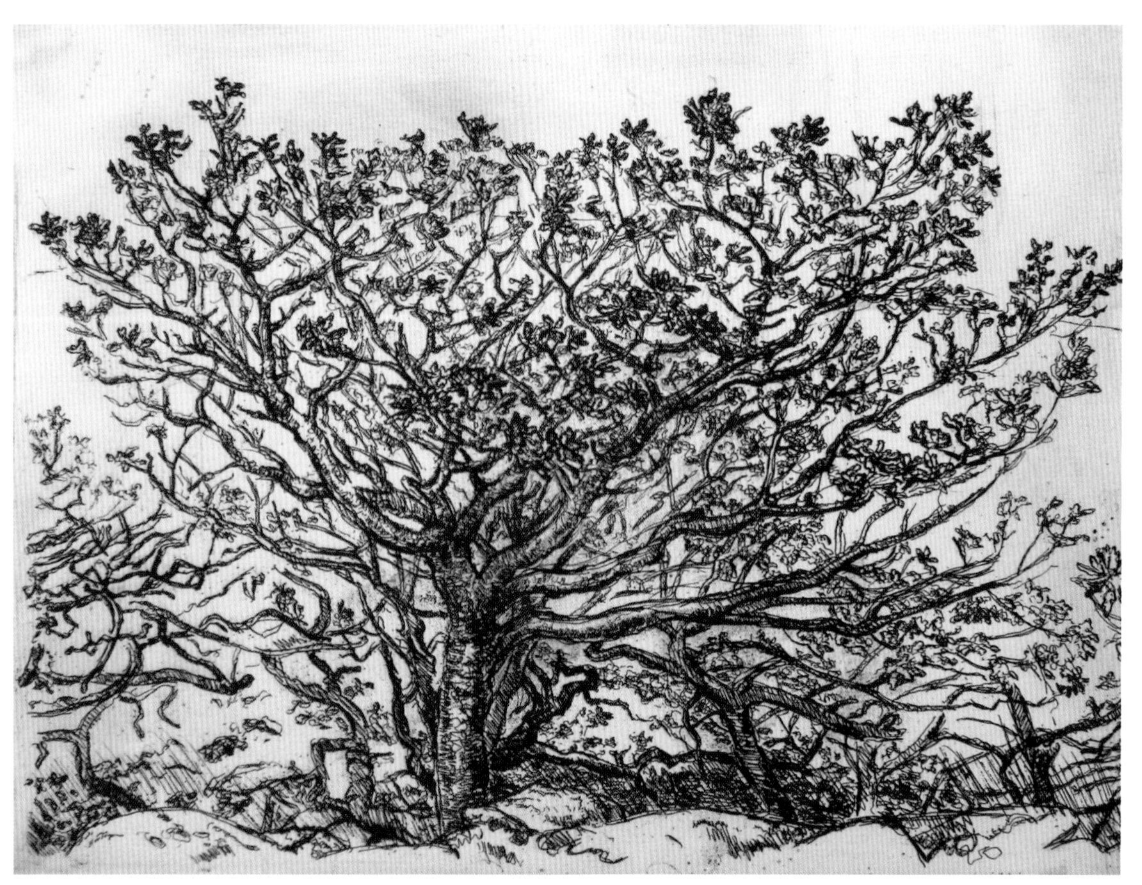

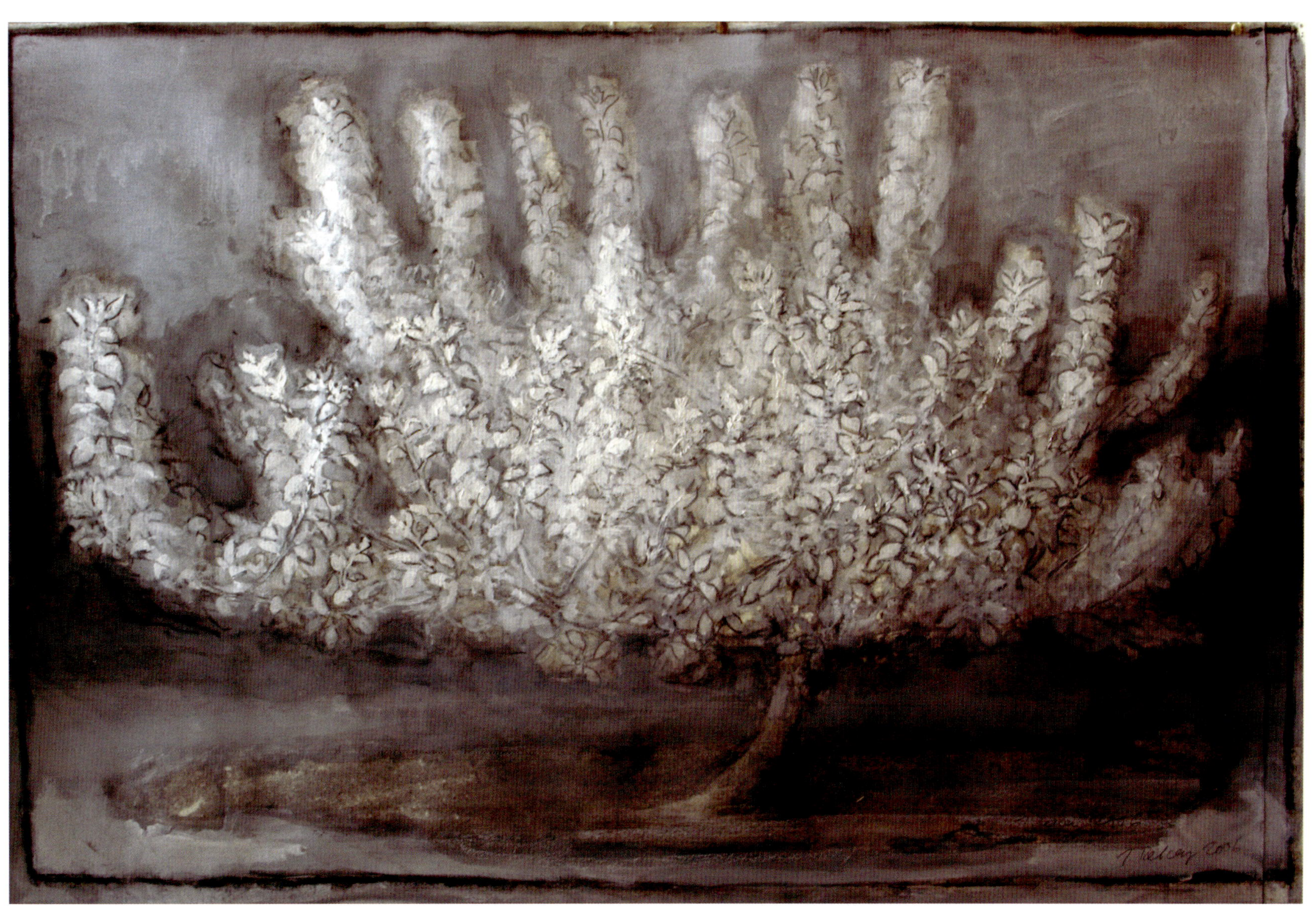

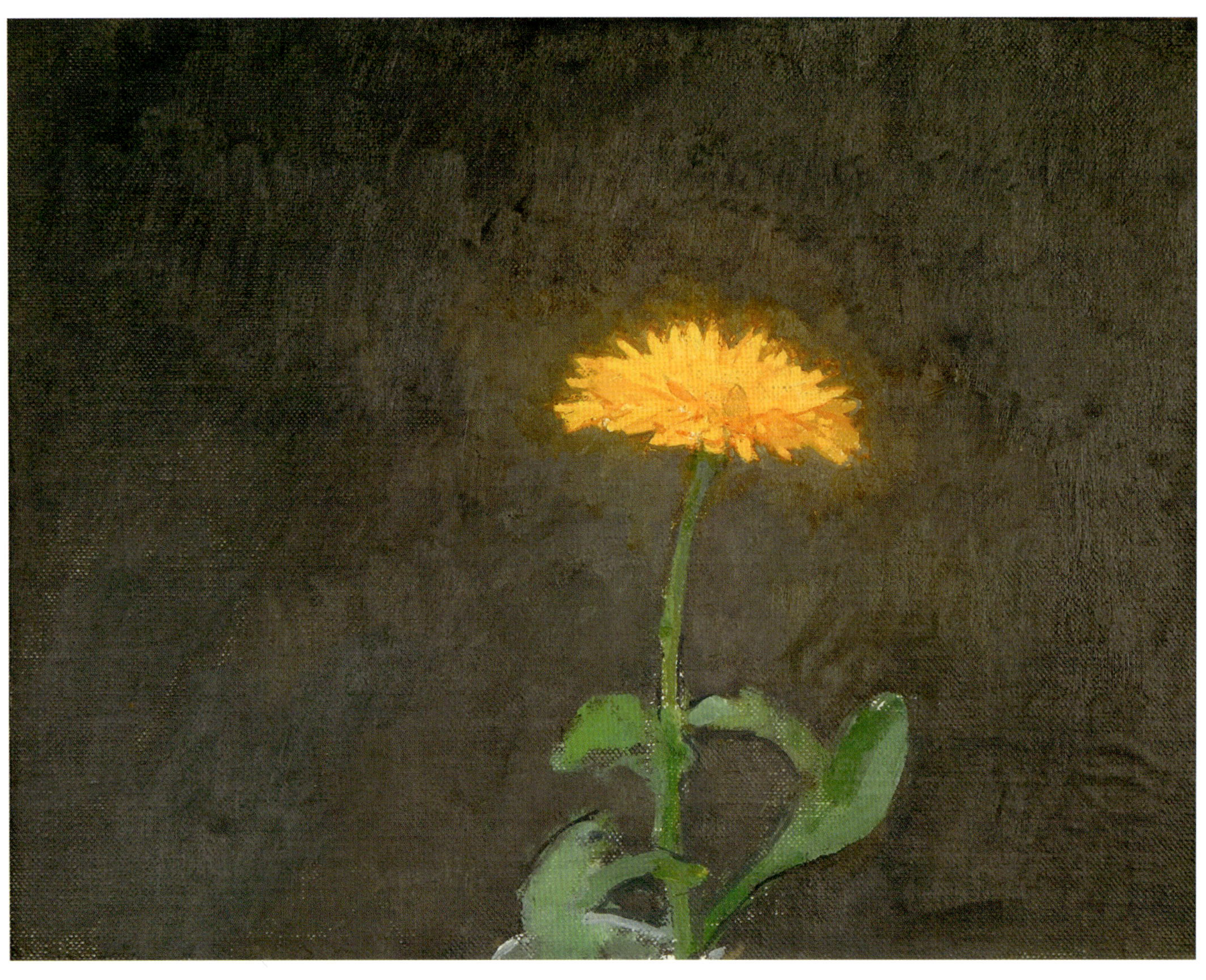

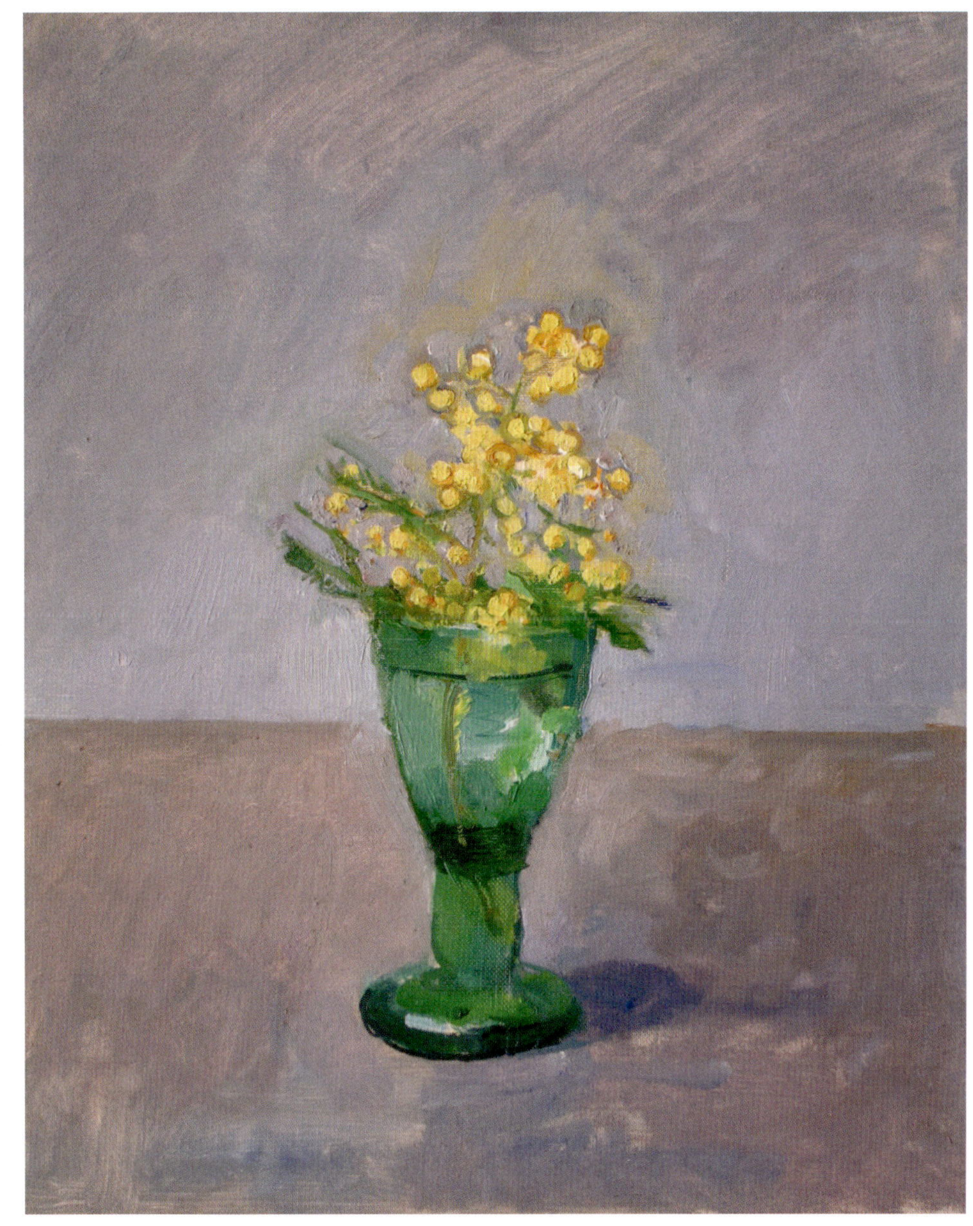

127
Mimosa, 2008
Oil on canvas, 50x40cms

Mimosa (2008) is presented in a recycled 7-Up bottle. 'It's a kind of brief celebratory picture, a bit like Mariglow (126),' says Felcey, 'they do positively glow across the blue-grey background. Pretty crude and direct, about authenticity and vibrancy – and very much to do with the line of the stem making that curve down. I like the way that it's setting off the diagonal – that really holds the vase. It was painted over a few days. I was just trying to be as direct and as naïve as possible, just trying to make it.'

126
Mariglow, 2002
Oil on board, 28.5x35.5cms

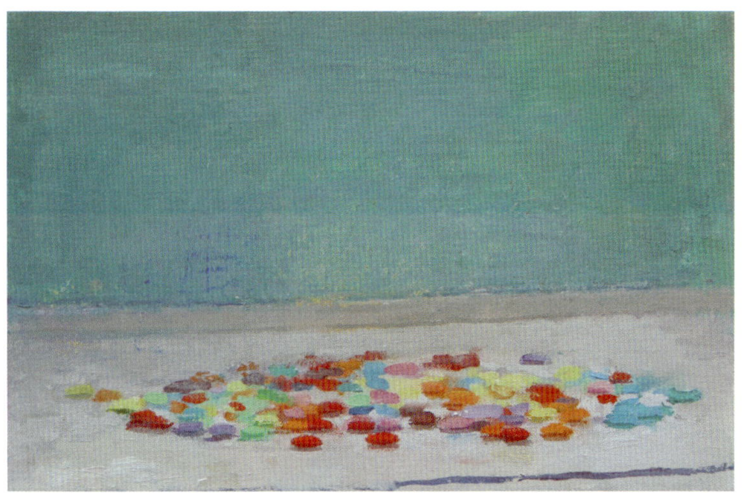

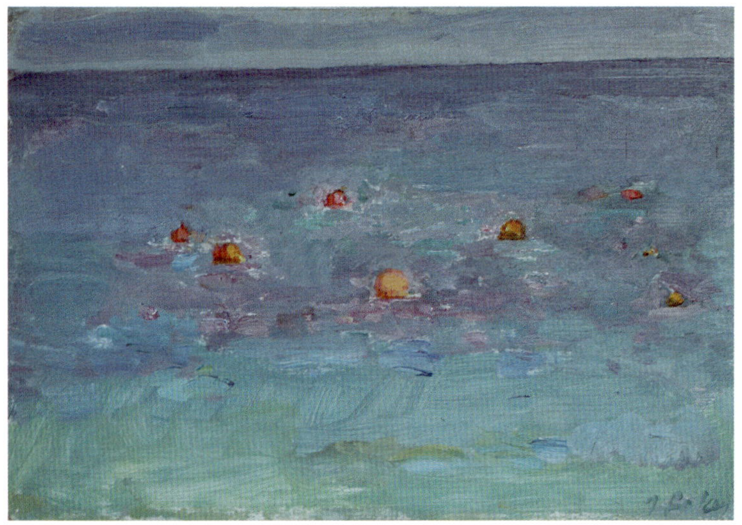

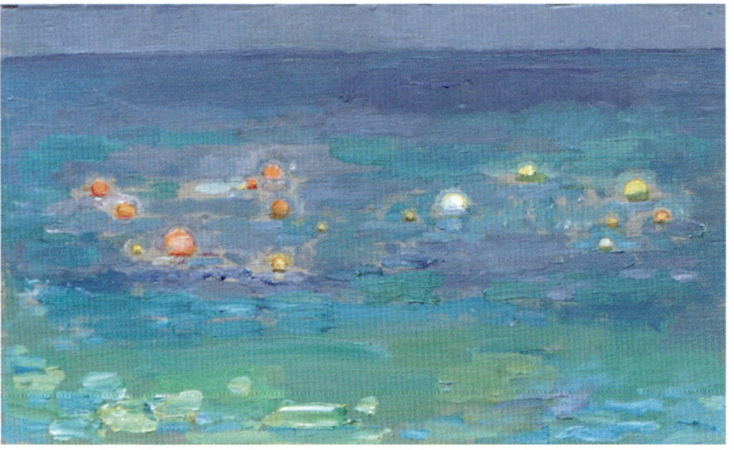

129

Smarties and Tangerine on a Round Table, 2007

Oil on canvas, 41.2x51.5cms

Smarties and Tangerine on a Round Table (2007). The smarties are floating, seeming to hover over the shiny polished table: a pool of colour in reflection, they resonate across it. 'I don't measure', says Felcey, 'but I was measuring visually when I was drawing this. The floor moves so the smarties did wobble a bit and then I saw these four orange ones coming together to make a flower shape. And I thought – how did I not see that? And then later on in the day it had gone – they'd moved off. They were all migrating across the table.' An interesting comparison here with Uglow. He would never have allowed that to happen: he'd have glued each smartie down. Felcey is after different effects. 'I quite like them bouncing a little bit, resonating. It increases the richness of the image. I suppose I thought of it as a thing like a comet – the tangerine and the comet's tail. These are the new coloured Smarties, not the old ones which I preferred. I loved those turquoise ones, but they did fade terrifically quickly.'

128, top

Smarties, 2003

Oil on board, 29x43cms

128, middle

Buoys at Sea, 2004

Oil on canvas, 20x30cms

128, bottom

Buoys at Sea, No. II, 2004

Oil on board, 17.5x24.7cms

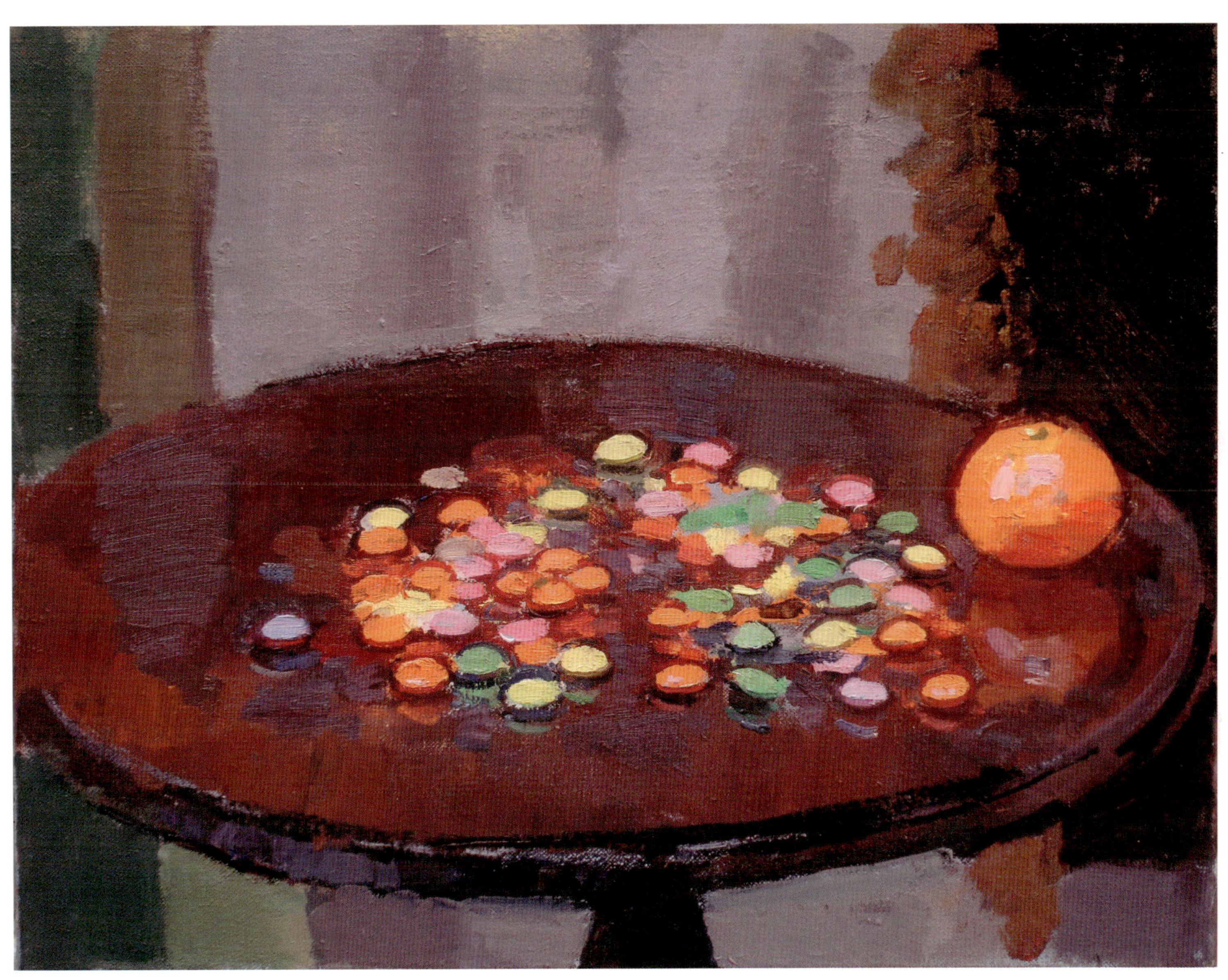

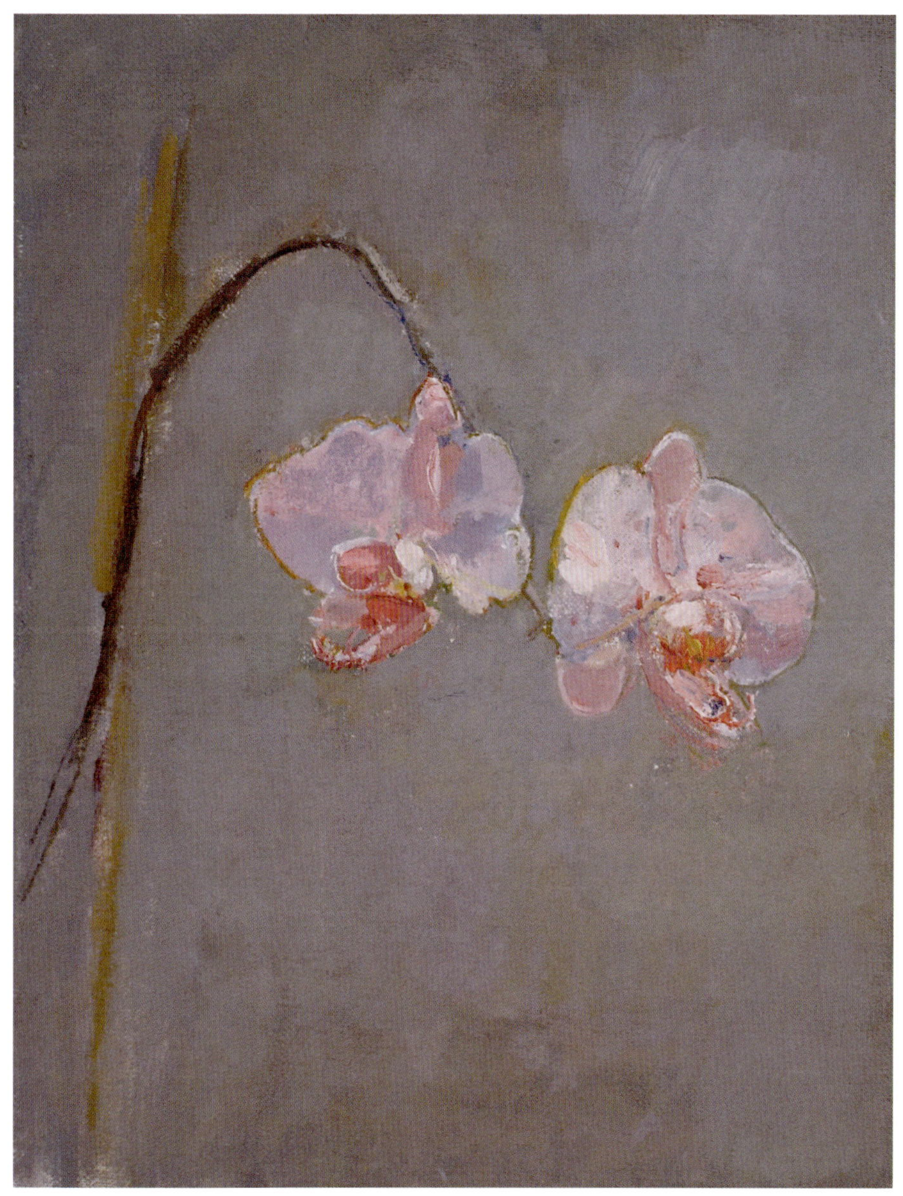

130
Moth Orchid, 2003
Oil on canvas, 38.5x29cms

131, top left
Three Apples and a Spoon, 2004
Oil on canvas, 12.5x30.8cms

131, top right
Pyramid of Apples, 2003
Oil on board, 34x36.6cms

131, lower left
Still Life with Bowl of Light, 2004
Oil on canvas, 33x53.8cms

131, lower right
Hanging Grapes, 2004
Oil on canvas, 31.5x25.5cms

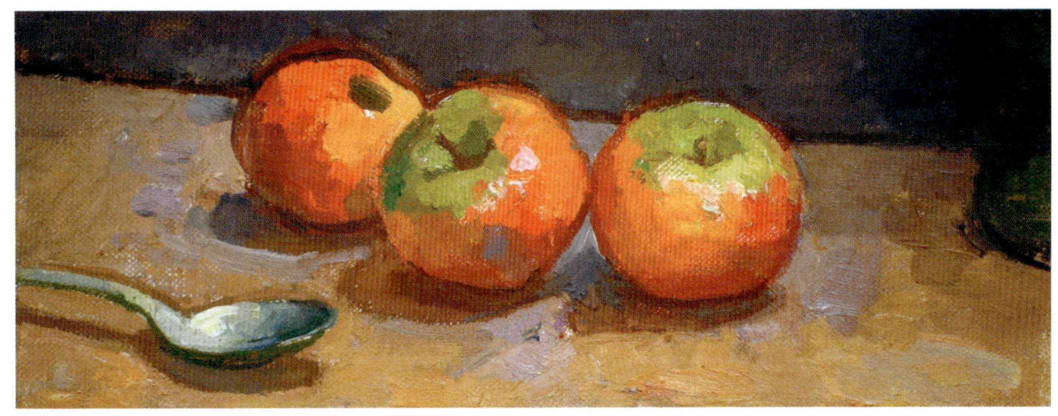

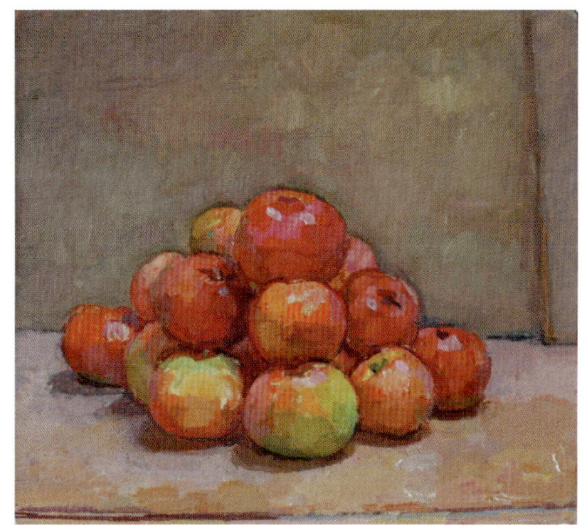

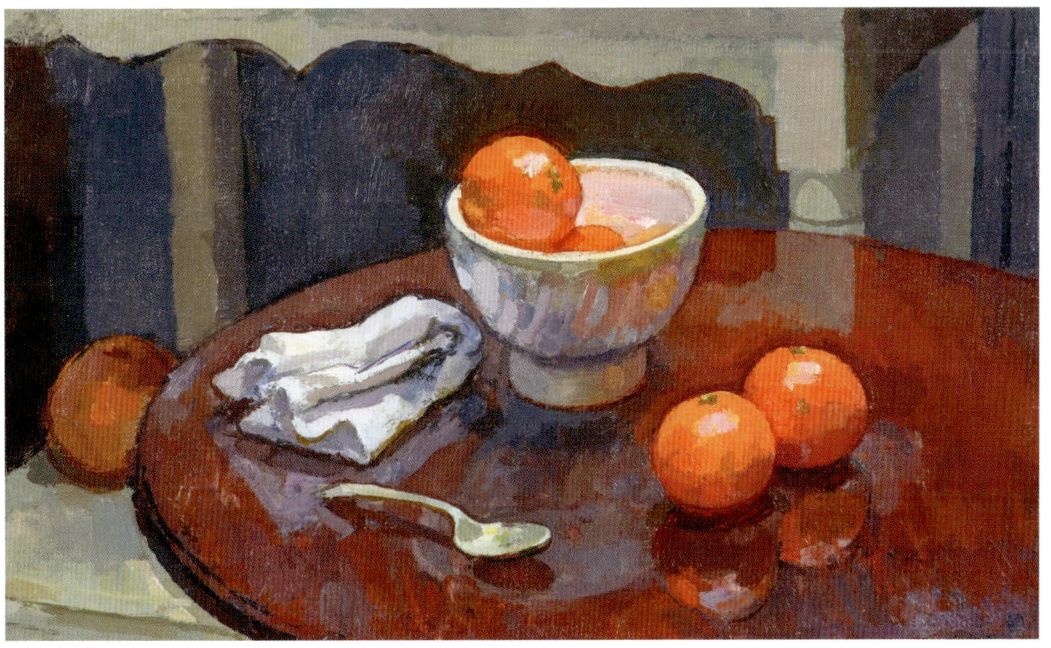

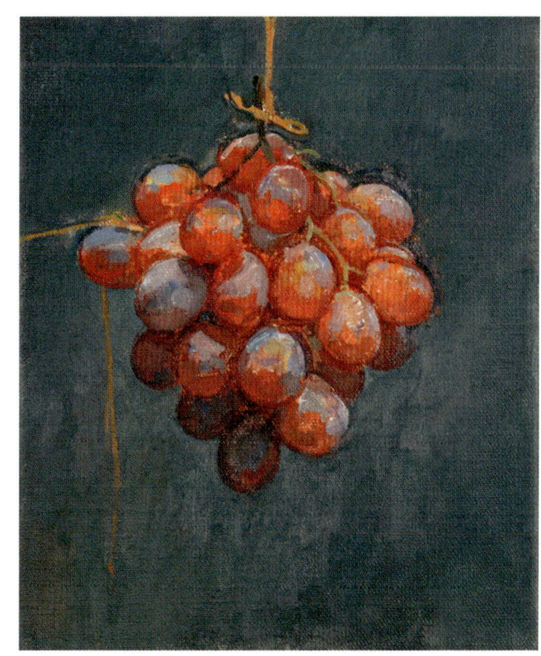

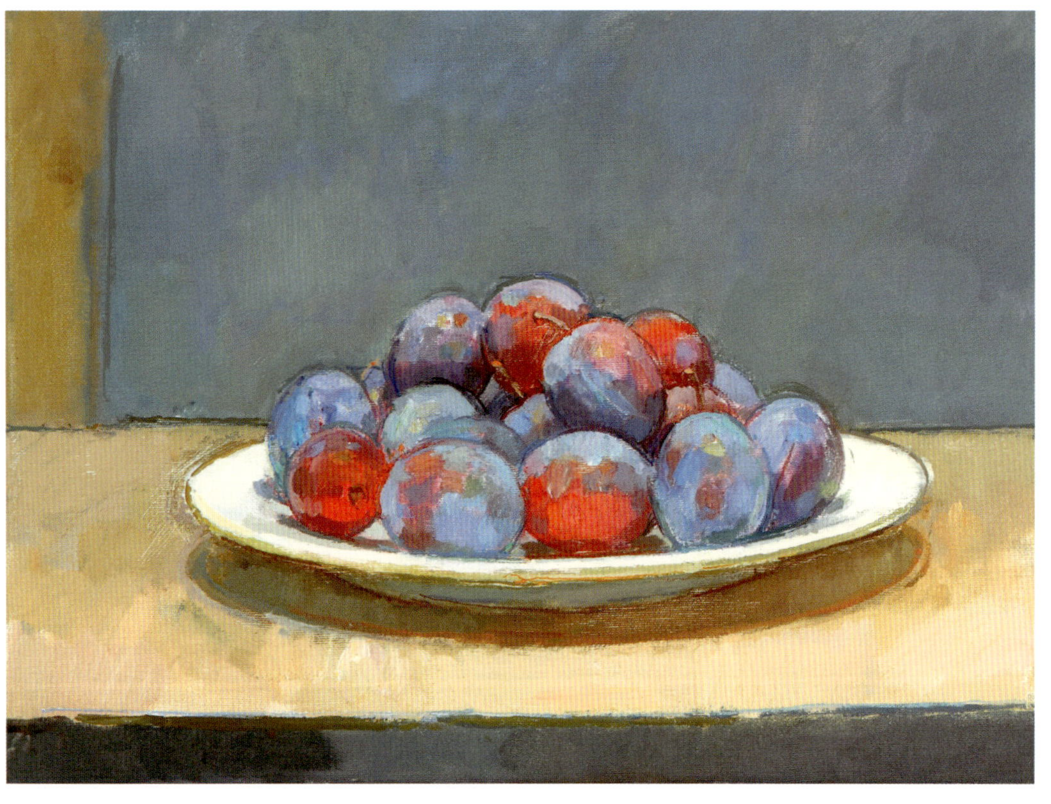

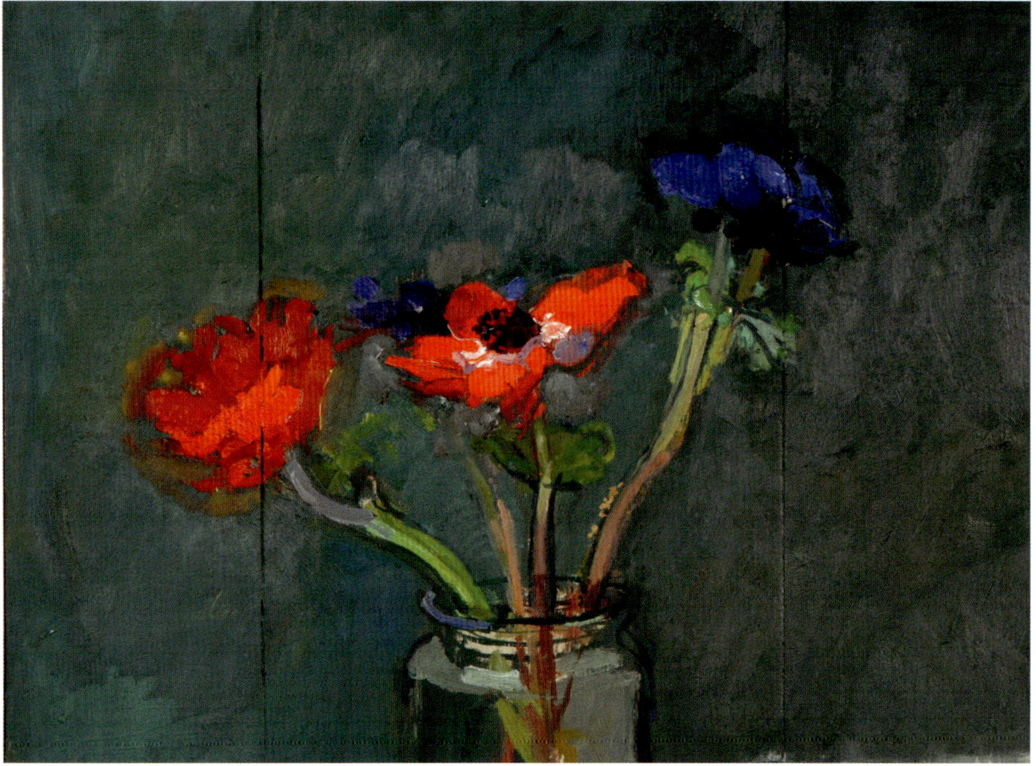

132, top
Plate of Plums, 2004
Oil on canvas, 50x40cms

132, bottom
Anemones, 2004
Oil on board, 30x40cms

133
Gyroscopic Still Life, 2007
Oil on canvas, 46x60cms

134, top
Meniscus, 2004
Oil on canvas, 30 x 48.5cms

134, bottom
Table and Pyramid, 2006
Oil on canvas, 60x100cms

135
Sea Bass, 2008
Oil on canvas, 46x60cms

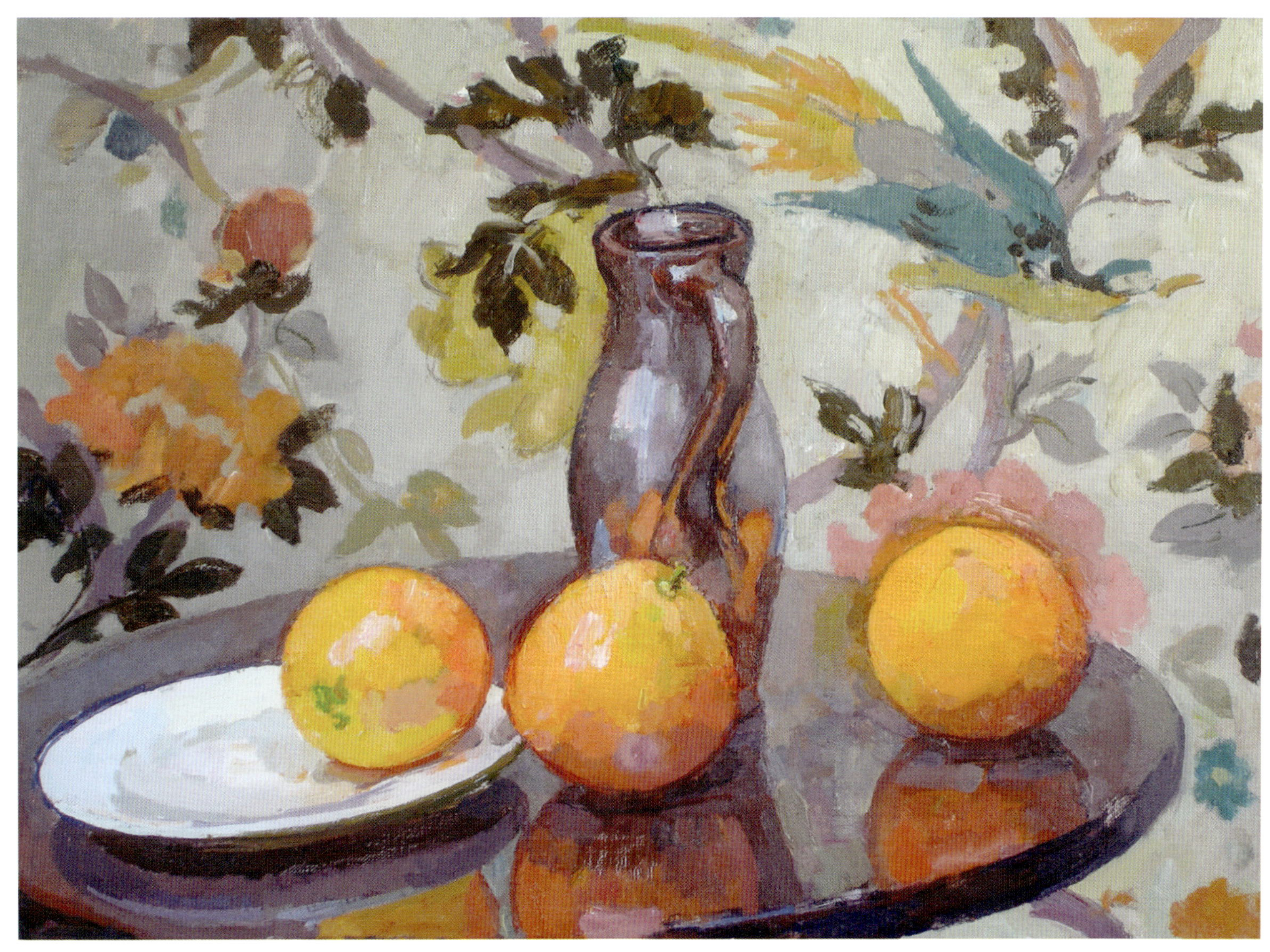

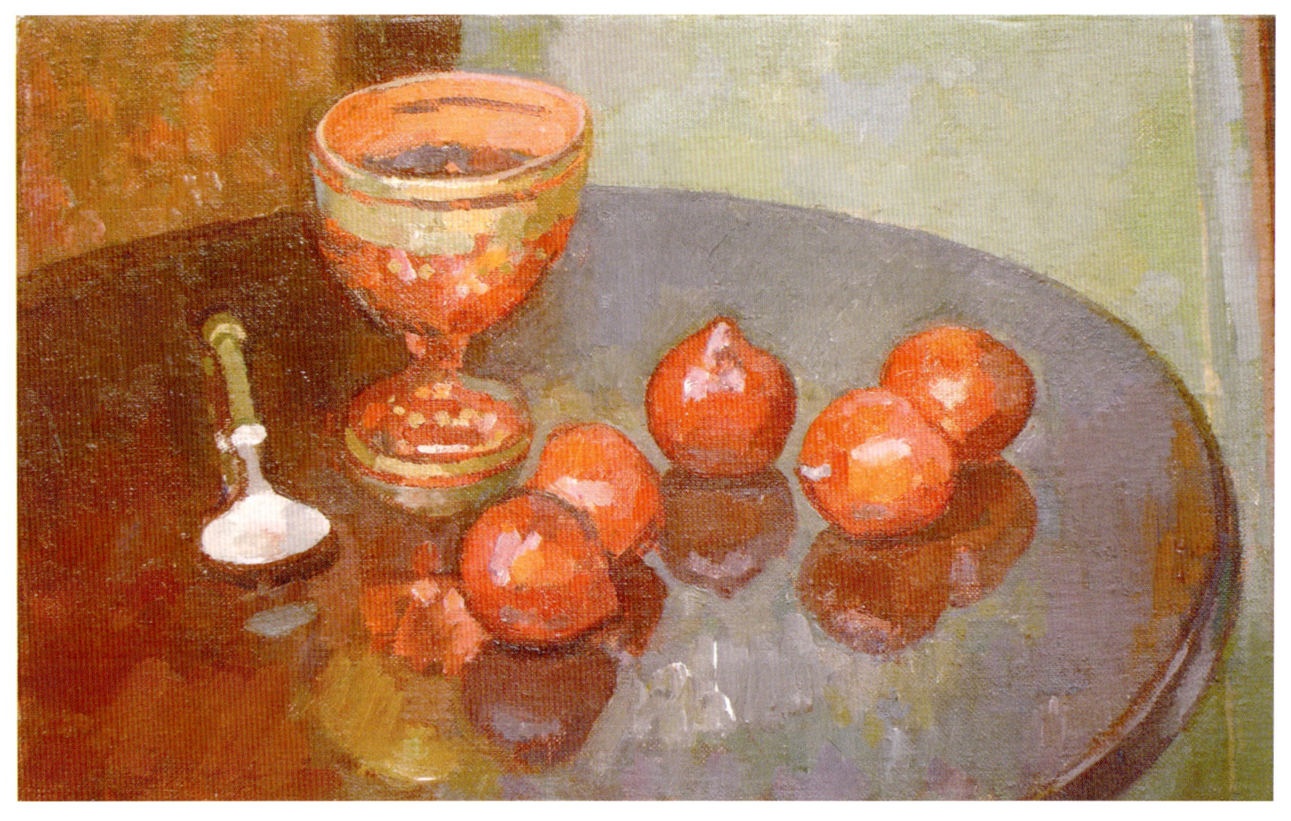

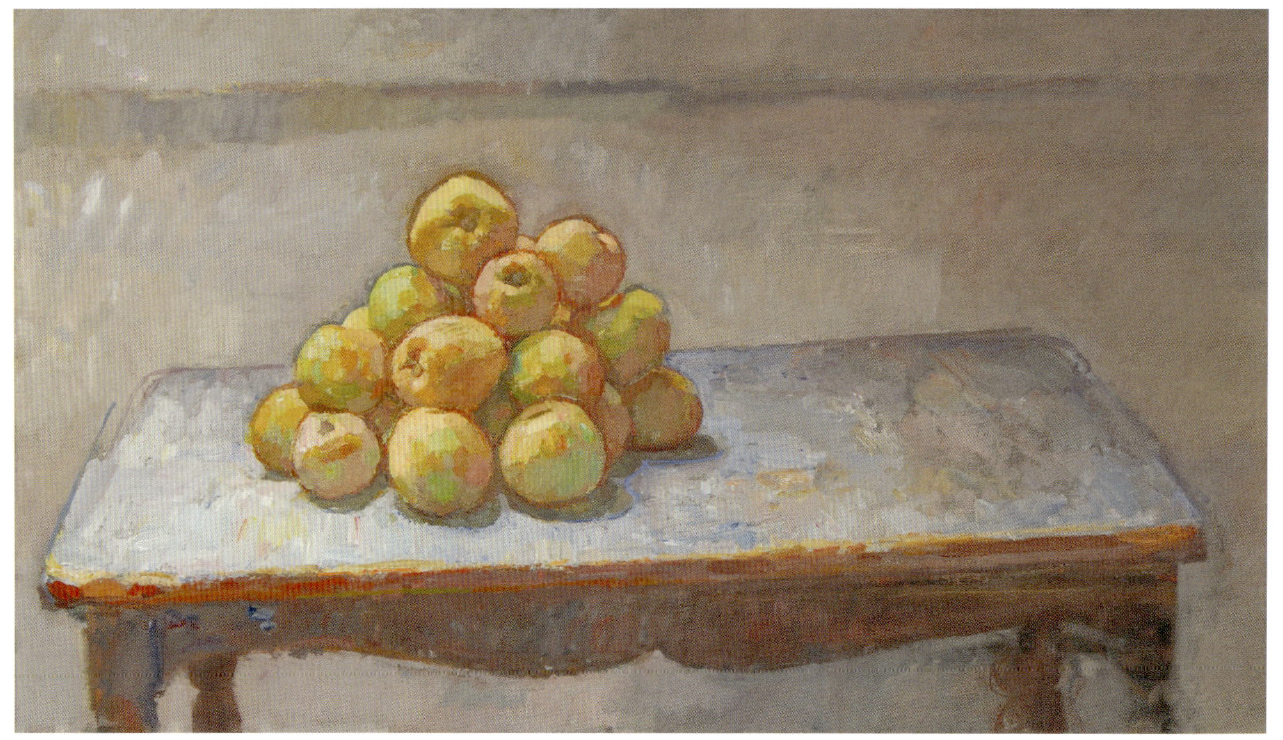

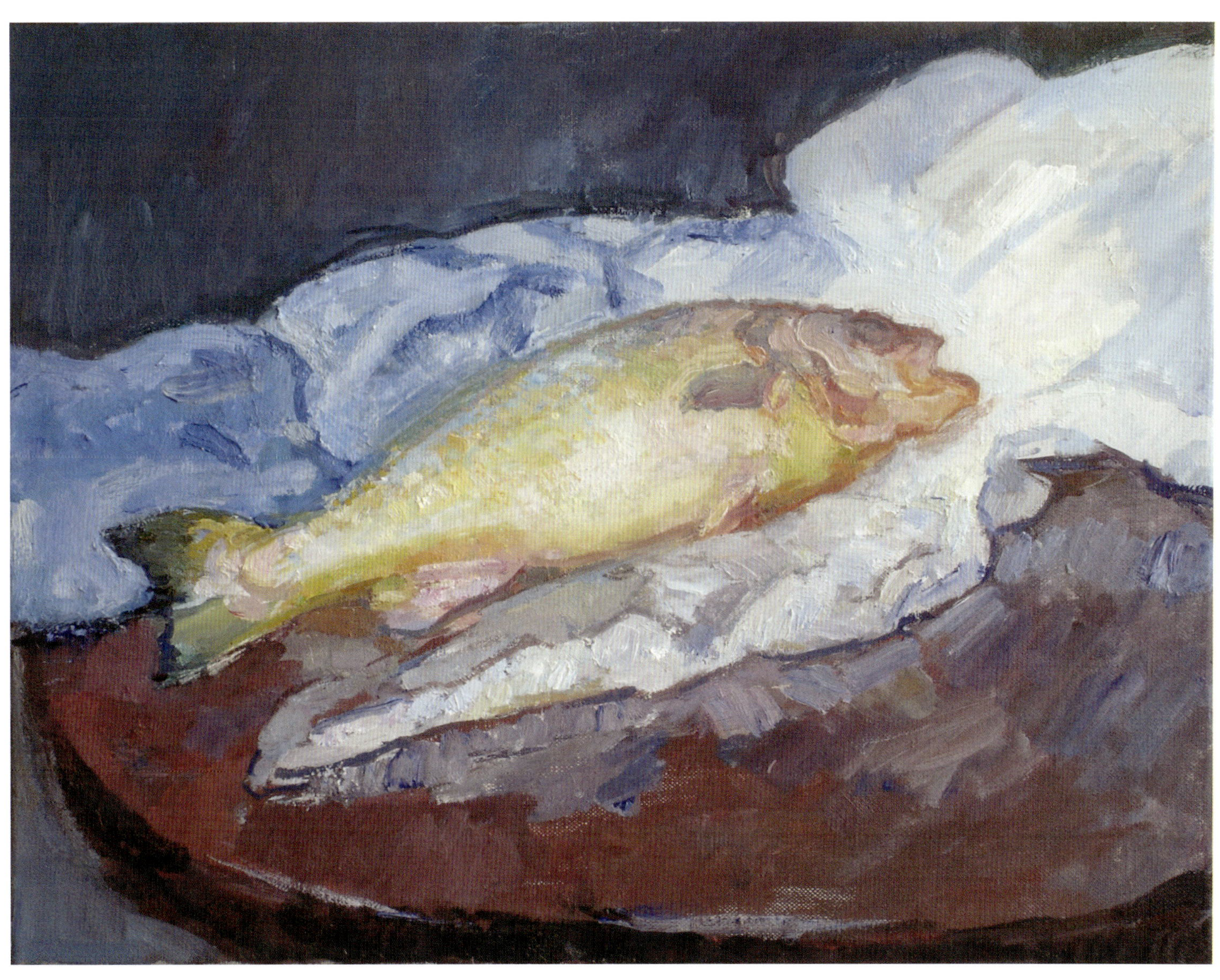

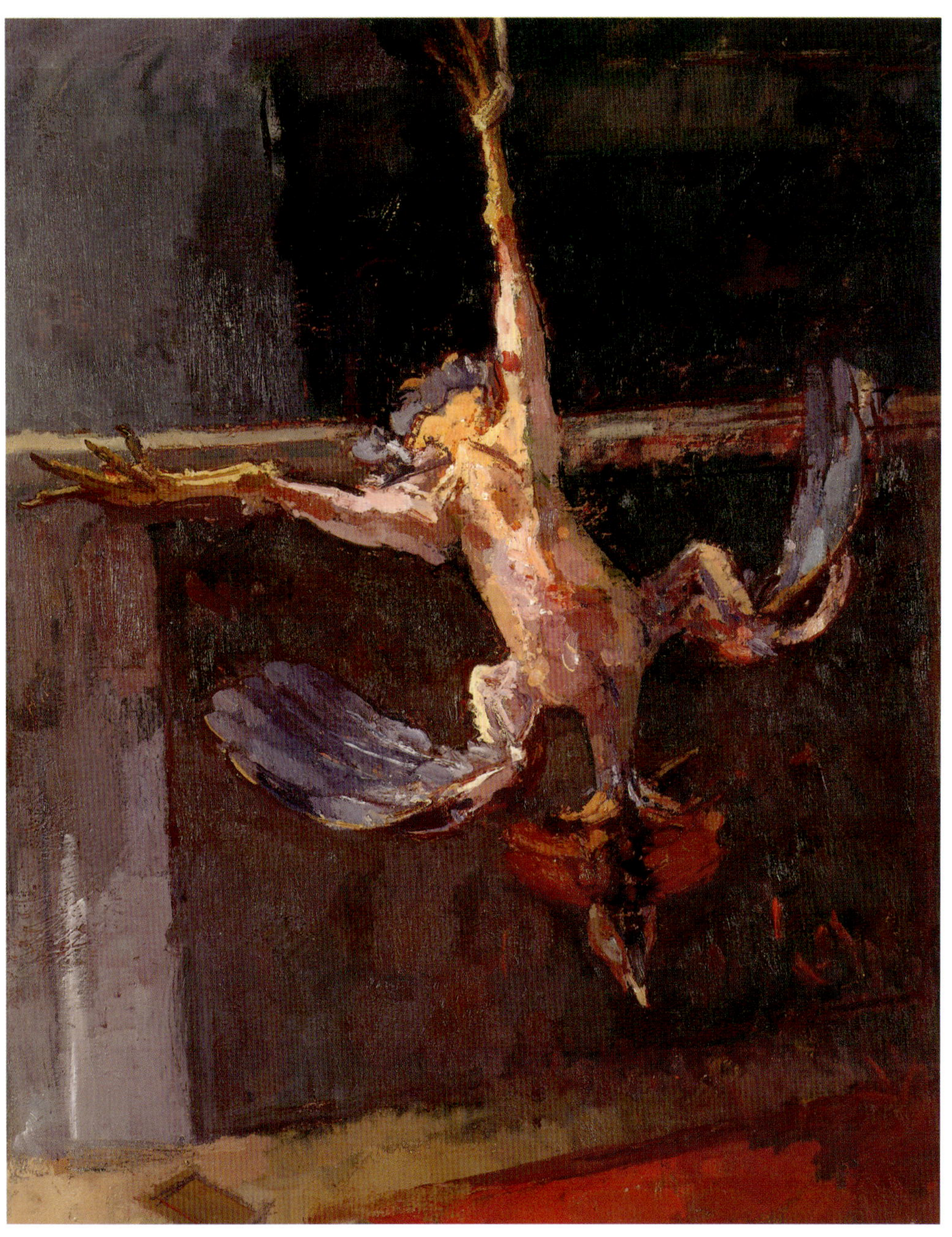

136
Hanging Fowl, 2000
Oil on canvas, 91.5x71cms

137, top
Sheep Skull, 2000
Oil on canvas, 25x31.8cms

137, bottom
Flayed Ram's Head, 2000
Oil on board, 29.3x37cms

138
The Bolivian Jacket, 2007-08
Oil on canvas, 118x83cms

139
Claire and Cat, 2009
Oil on canvas, 120x100cms

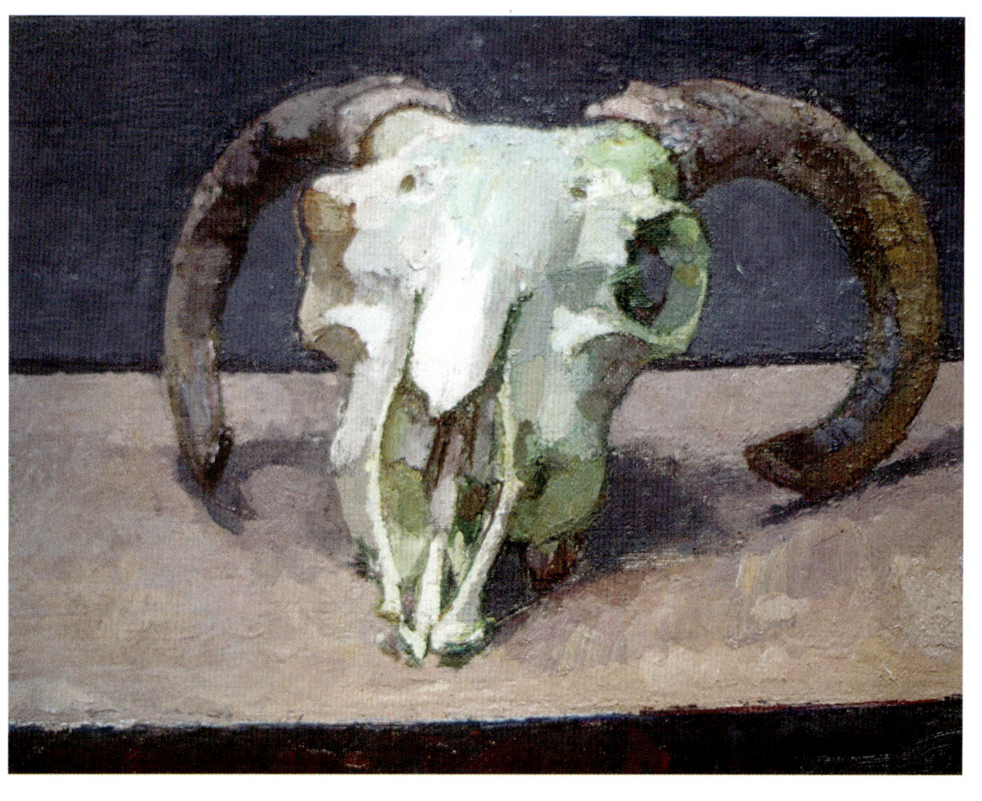

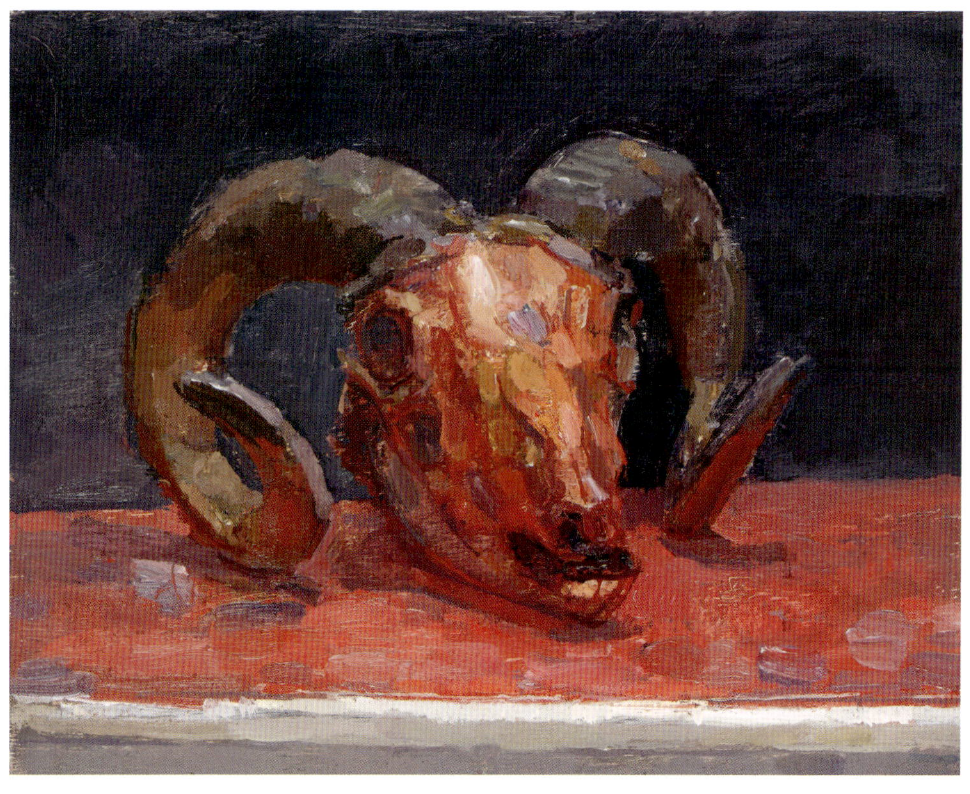

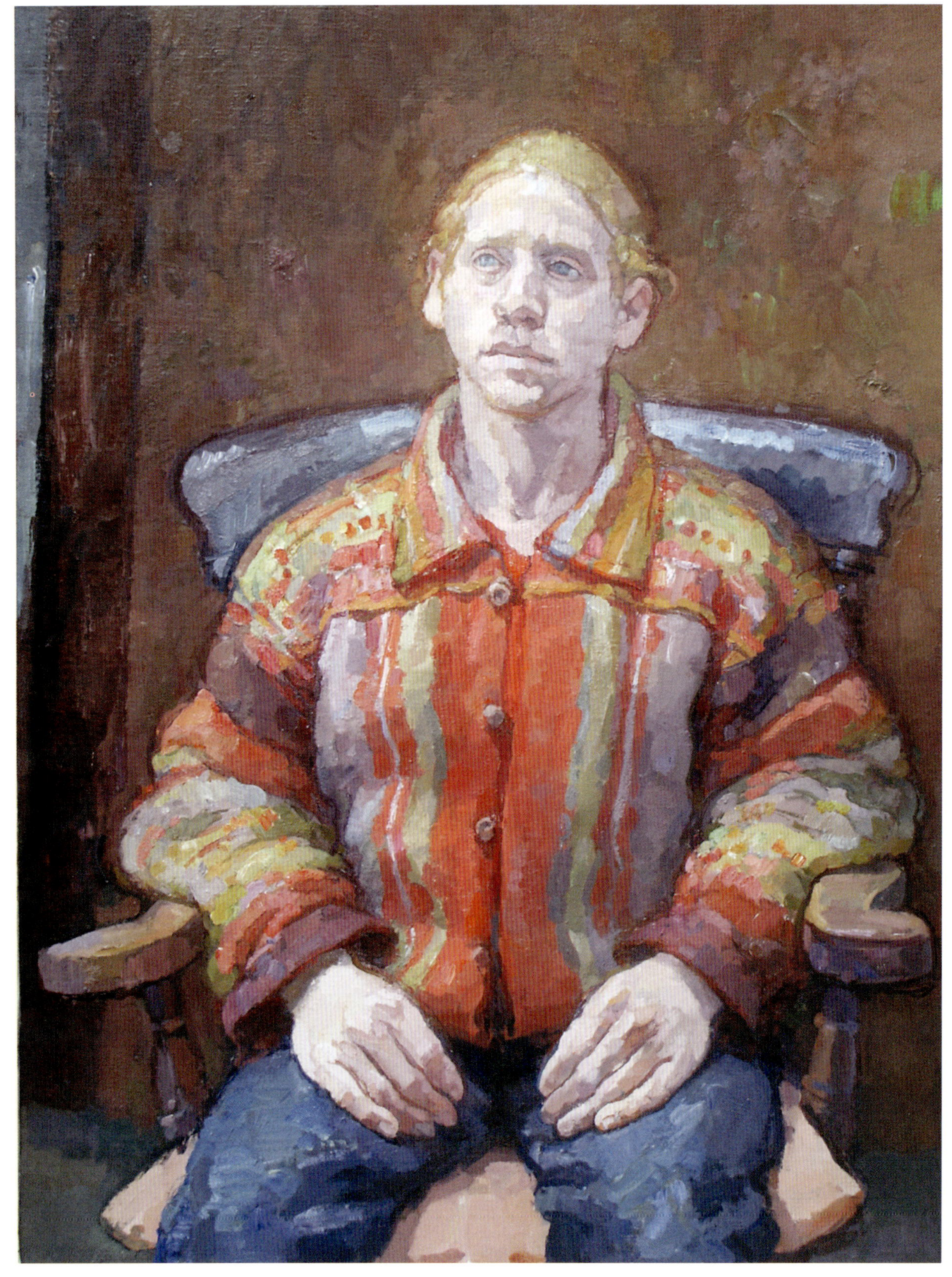

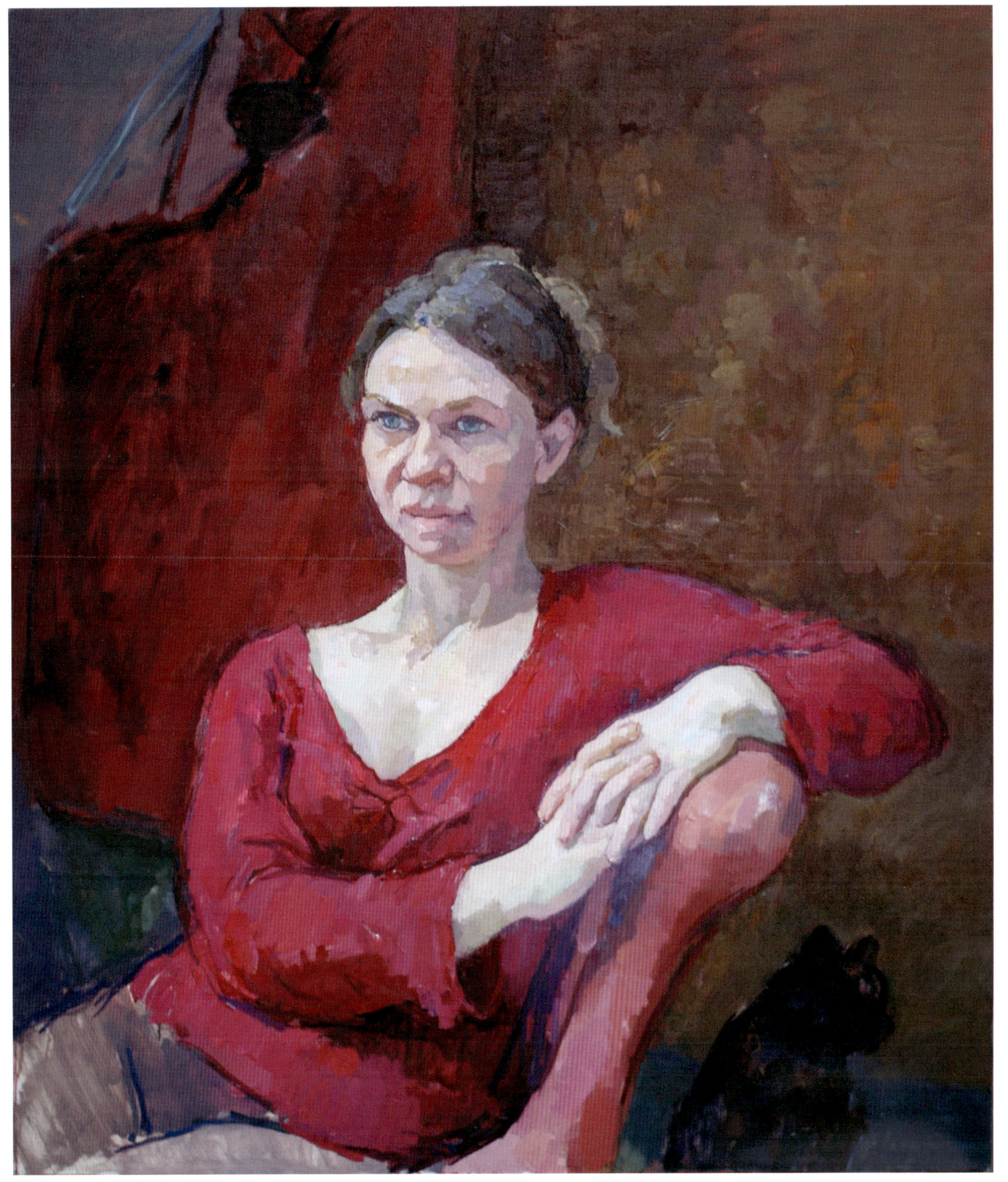

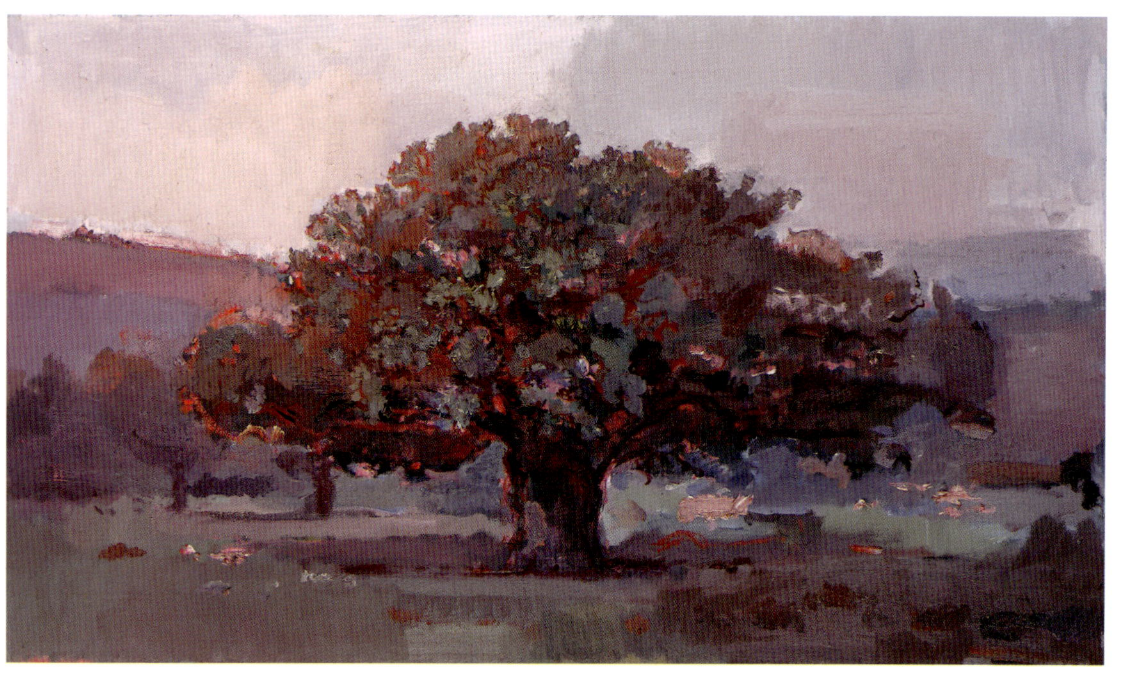

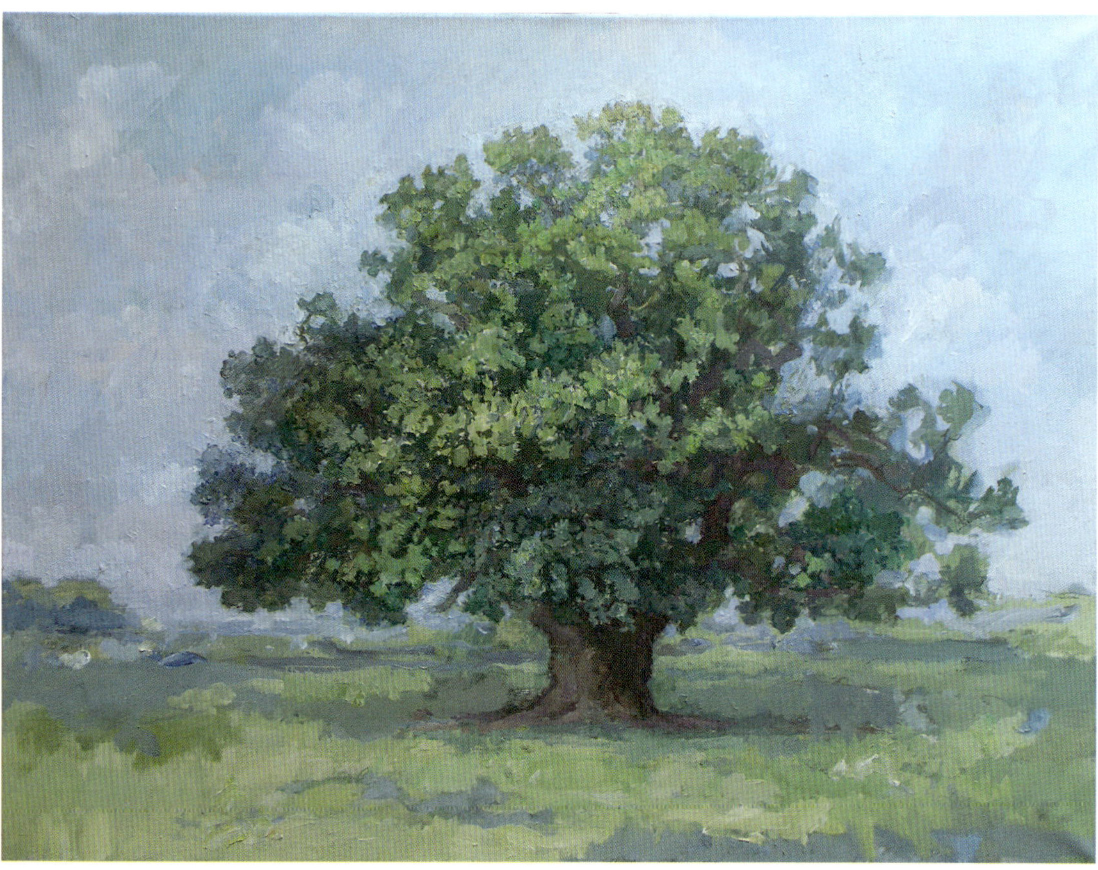

140, top
Field Oak Sunset, 1996
Oil on canvas, 61x101.2cms

140, bottom
Field Oak, 2009
Oil on canvas, 80x101.5cms

141
Oak Reflection, 2009
Oil on canvas, 120x100cms

142
Tamar Valley Orchard, 2014
Acrylic on canvas,
183x213cms

143
Sycamore, Wind, 2008
Inks and acrylic on paper,
53x39cms

144
Skull, 2015
Oil on canvas, 60x100cms

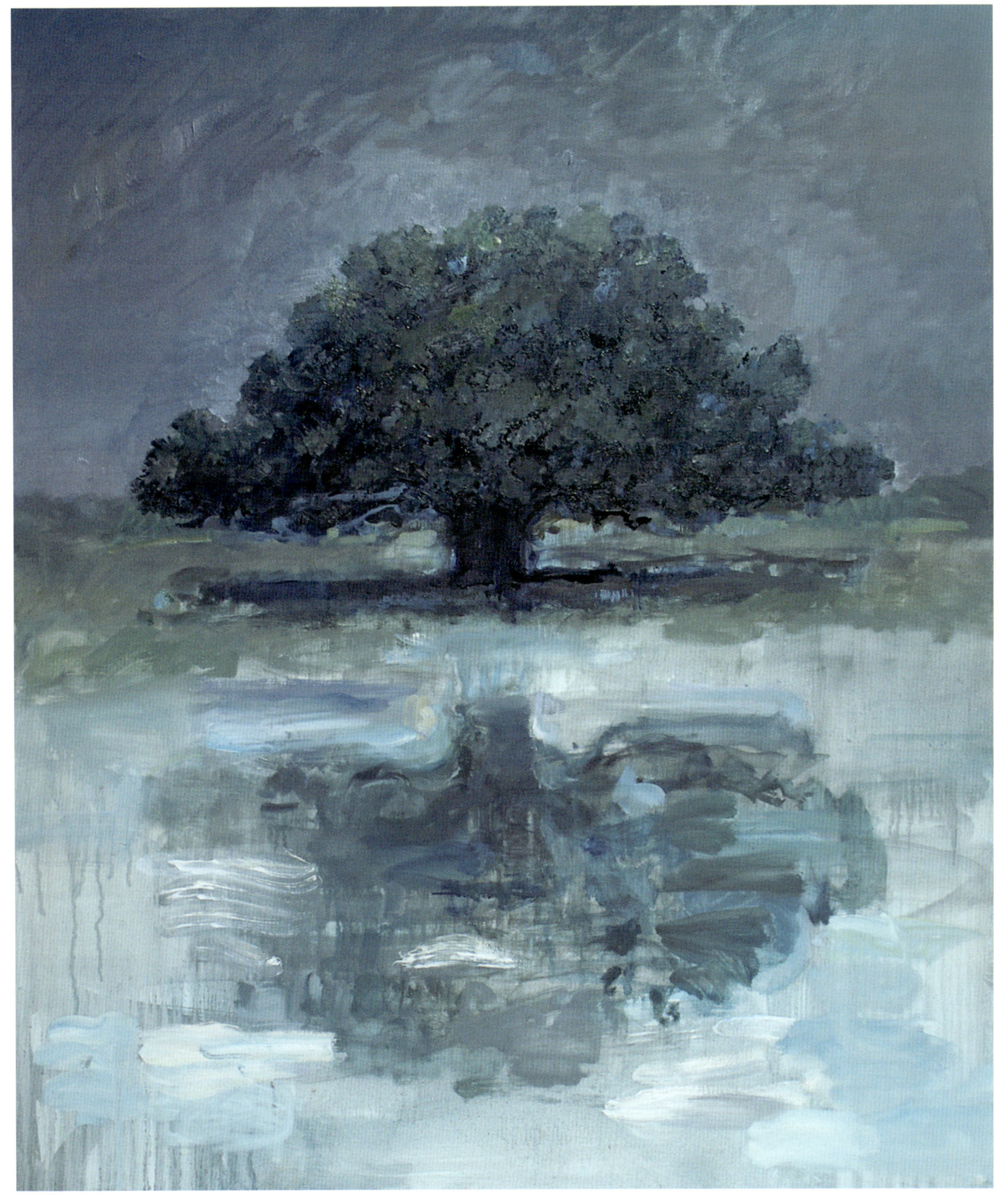

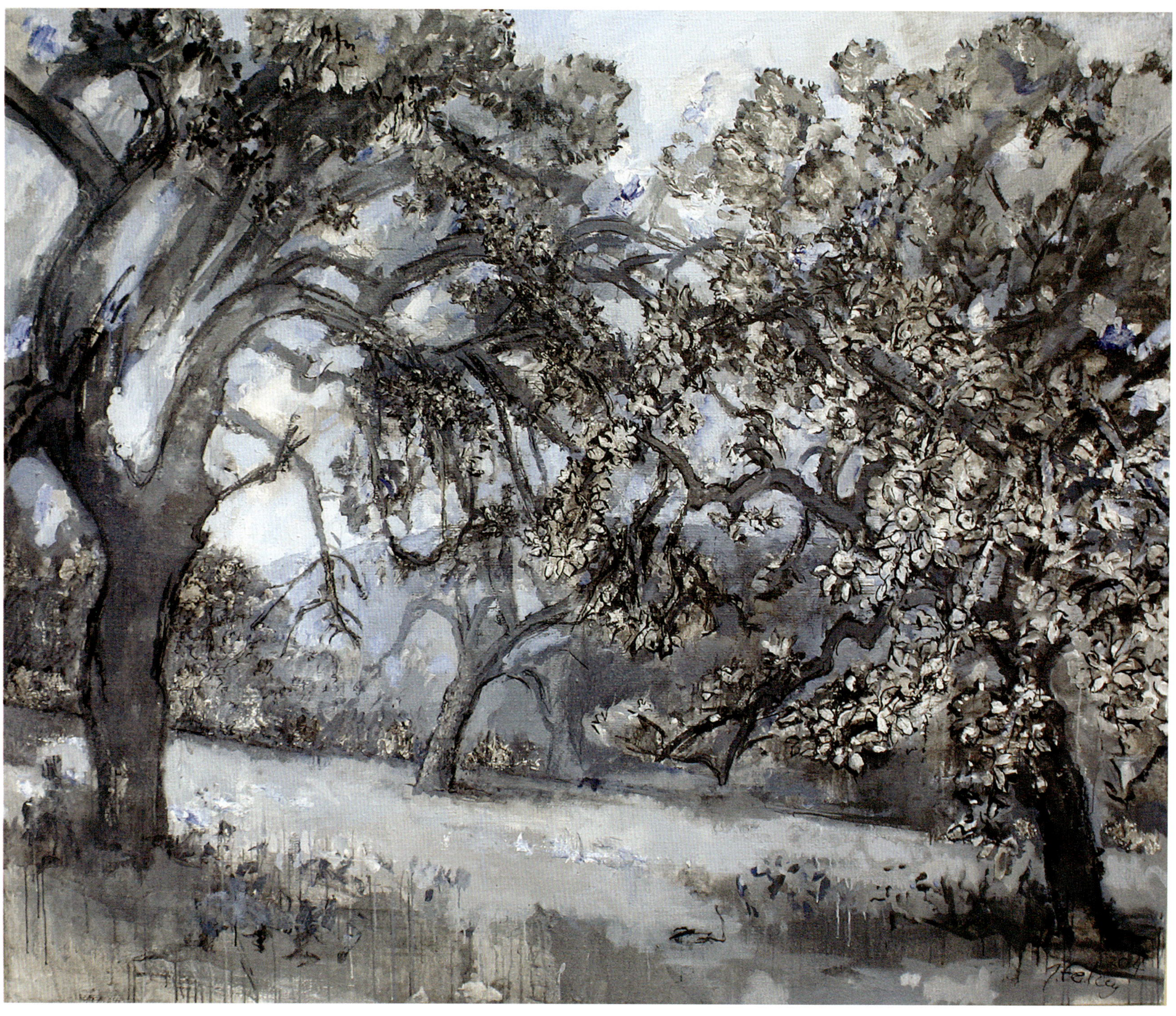

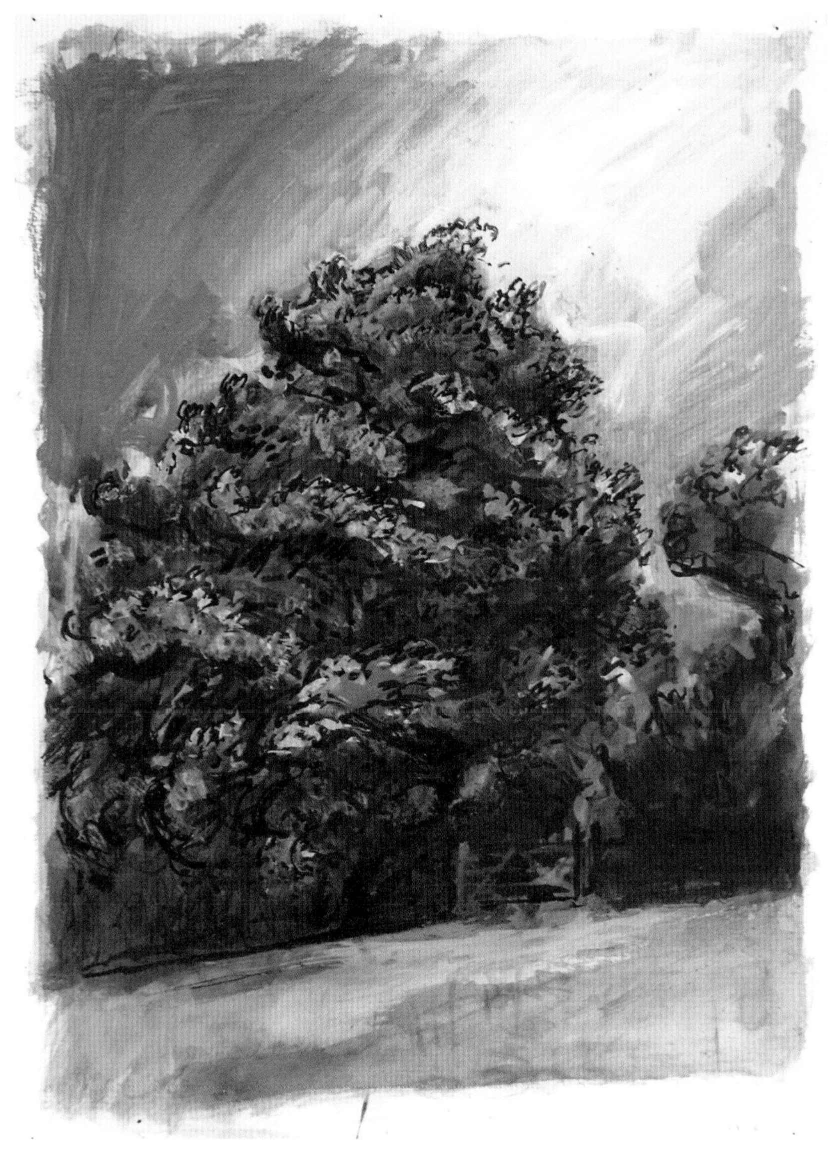

'Looking is a marvellous thing of which we know but little. Through it we are turned absolutely towards the outside, but when we are most of all so, things happen in us that have waited longingly to be observed; and while they reach completion in us their significance grows up in the object outside.'

Rainer Maria Rilke

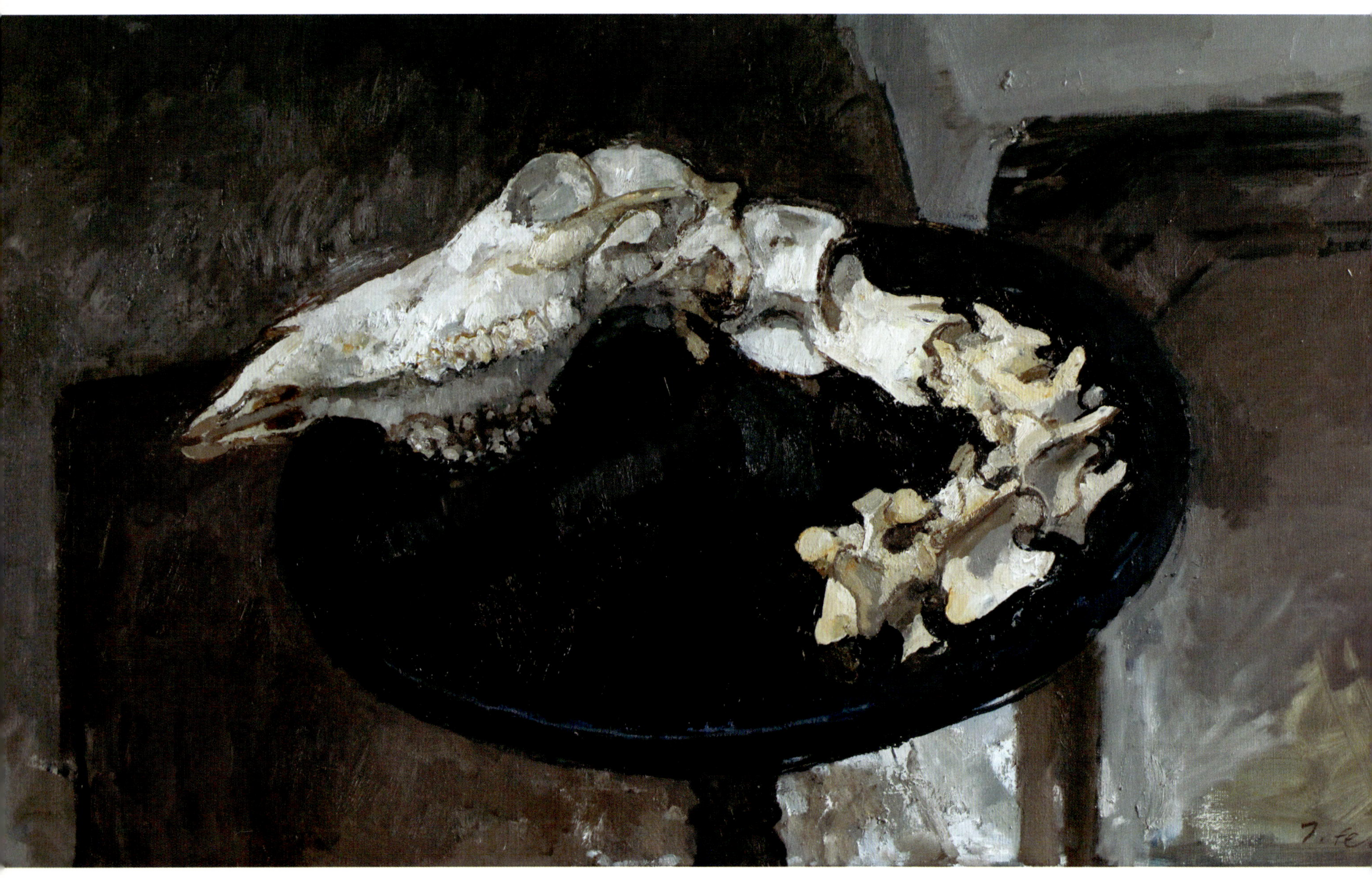